T

Modern Critical Views

Continued at back of book

Modern Critical Views

ALFRED, LORD TENNYSON

Modern Critical Views

ALFRED, LORD TENNYSON

Edited with an introduction by

Harold Bloom

Sterling Professor of the Humanities
Yale University

1985
CHELSEA HOUSE PUBLISHERS
New York

THE COVER:
The Tennyson cover represents the poet against the background of what might be called his landscape of repression. The deeply erotic nature of his poetry, caused by a daemonic element in his imagination, expressed itself consummately in the intensely charged aspect of his vistas.—H.B.

Cover illustration by Michael Garland

Copyright © 1985 by Chelsea House Publishers,
a division of Chelsea House Educational Communications, Inc.
  345 Whitney Avenue, New Haven, CT 06511
  95 Madison Avenue, New York, NY 10016
  5068B West Chester Pike, Edgemont, PA 19028

Printed and bound in the United States of America

10 9 8 7 6 5 4 3

Library of Congress Cataloging in Publication Data

Alfred Lord Tennyson.
  (Modern critical views)
  Bibliography: p.
  Includes index.
  1. Tennyson, Alfred Tennyson, Baron, 1809–1892—
Criticism and interpretation—Addresses, essays,
lectures.   I. Bloom, Harold.   II. Series.
PR5588.A44   1985   821'.8   85-6613
ISBN 0-87754-615-0

Contents

Editor's Note

This volume gathers together a representative selection of the best criticism devoted to Tennyson during the last half-century. It begins with the editor's general overview of Tennyson's place in Romantic tradition, written in 1966. The chronological sequence follows, starting with T. S. Eliot's essay of the early thirties, centering on *In Memoriam*, and indicating indirectly the profound and abiding influence of Tennyson upon Eliot. This is followed by the social historian G. M. Young's masterly essay on Tennyson's relation to his age, written at the end of the thirties.

The reading of "Tears, Idle Tears" by Cleanth Brooks is emblematic of the New Critics' attempt to save Tennyson as an ironist, during the Formalist forties (as they might be called). With the late Marshall McLuhan's endeavor to redeem the "picturesque" Tennyson, in 1951, a new defense of the poet began to shape itself. The remaining critical essays here, all from the seventies, show the culmination of this view, which has now become prevalent in literary, critical, and academic circles. Robert Langbaum's analysis of *In Memoriam* as a kind of unified drama is followed here by scrutinies of Tennyson's self-borrowings by Christopher Ricks and of *Idylls of the King* by John Rosenberg. The essay on "Tennyson's Melody" by John Hollander is an advanced study of the idea of music in Tennyson's work. The editor's antithetical reading of Tennyson proposes a more controversial mode of criticism, centering upon Tennyson's repressed ironies and daemonic evasions, particularly in regard to "Mariana," "Ulysses," "Tithonus," and the quest of Percivale in "The Holy Grail." A. Dwight Culler's essay on *Maud* is a powerful analysis of Tennyson's "*Hamlet*-in-little," and reminds us that monodrama is a mode in its own right. In its emphasis upon the return of the poet's apocalyptic stance, it brings us back full circle to the problematical relationship of Tennyson to the whole of the Romantic tradition in poetry. I have concluded the volume with Robert Bernard Martin's biographical account of the poet's final years.

Introduction

The Laureate of *Despair* and *The Ancient Sage* is of course one of the
memorable disasters of poetic tradition, surpassing the Wordsworth of the
Ecclesiastical Sonnets and even the Arnold of *Merope*. The whole being of
Tennyson was at no single time absorbed into the energy of sense, and for
this failure of experience the price was paid, alas even overpaid:

> And more—think well! Do-well will follow thought,
> And in the fatal sequence of this world
> An evil thought may soil thy children's blood;
> But curb the beast would cast thee in the mire,
> And leave the hot swamp of voluptuousness
> A cloud between the Nameless and thyself,
> And lay thine uphill shoulder to the wheel,
> And climb the Mount of Blessing, whence, if thou
> Look higher, then—perchance—thou mayest—beyond
> A hundred ever-rising mountain lines,
> And past the range of Night and Shadow—see
> The high-heaven dawn of more than mortal day
> Strike on the Mount of Vision!
>   So, farewell.

There are still Tennyson scholars who can read this, or say they can, but the indefensible badness of it all is plain enough. Sixty years or so before this, as a boy of fourteen, Tennyson possessed the verbal exuberance of an absolute poetic genius, and manifested it in the splendid speeches of the Devil in *The Devil and the Lady*, and in the remarkable movement of an exercise like the *Ode: O Bosky Brook*. The extremes of a poet's values, if they are manifested merely as a chronological continuum, do not much matter. Vision darkens, life triumphs, the poet becomes the man whose pharynx is bad. So went Wordsworth, the founder of modern poetry, and where a Moses was lost, other losses must follow. Yeats and Wallace Stevens appear today to be the first and only poets in the Romantic tradition who flowered anew both in middle and in old age, and yet it can be questioned if either will rival Tennyson and Browning after the fogs of fashion have been dispelled.

At the center of Tennyson the problem is not whether or why he hardened and kept hardening in poetic character, or just how his vision darkened perpetually into the abysses of much of the later verse, but why and how the sensibility of a major Romantic poet was subverted even in his earlier years. What the most sympathetic reader can still find wanting in the best of Tennyson is a power of imagination shown forth uncompromisingly in *The Fall of Hyperion* and *The Triumph of Life*, in *Resolution and Independence* and *The Mental Traveller*, and on the largest scale in *The Prelude* and *Jerusalem*. Romance, lyric, epic were raised to greatness again in the two generations just before Tennyson. In a lyrical monologue like *Andrea del Sarto*, a romance like "Childe Roland to the Dark Tower Came," and in the curious epic of *The Ring and the Book* a poet of Tennyson's own generation comes close to approximating the Romantic achievement. Tennyson was as legitimately the heir of Keats as Browning was of Shelley, and as much a betrayal of Keats's imaginative honesty and autonomy as Browning was of Shelley's. To make such a point is to reveal in oneself an unreconstructed Romantic bias, like that of Swinburne, or Yeats, or Shaw or Hardy, to bring in four Shelleyans who were contemporaries of the older Browning and Tennyson. There are achievements in Tennyson that are not Romantic, but they are small enough. The Tennyson who counts for most, seen in the longest and clearest perspective we now can begin to recover, is certainly a Romantic poet, and not a Victorian anti-Romantic resembling the Arnold of *Merope* or the straining Hopkins of *The Wreck of the Deutschland*. He is a major Romantic poet, but not perhaps one of the greatest, though there is an antithetical storm-cloud drifting through the center of his work that sometimes shows us what his proper greatness should have been. His affinities in his own time were to no other poet but to Ruskin, a great ruin of a Romantic critic, and his value to us now is rather like Ruskin's, since he shows forth as a most crucial instance of the dilemma of post-Romantic art.

Hallam, who remains Tennyson's best critic, found "five distinctive excellences" in his friend's poetic manner: (1) the control of a luxuriant imagination; (2) accuracy of adjustment in "moods of character," so that narration and feeling naturally corresponded with each other; (3) skill in emotionally fusing a vivid, "picturesque" portrayal of objects ("picturesque" being opposed here to Wordsworthian descriptiveness); (4) modulation of verbal harmony; (5) "mellow soberness of tone," addressed to the understanding heart rather than the mere understanding. Yeats, in his old age, spoke of "the scientific and moral discursiveness of In Memoriam," but I cannot recognize the poem from that description. What lives in the elegies for Hallam are precisely the excellences that Hallam picked out in his friend's earlier manner, and the various tracts of discursiveness one learns to step over quickly. Discursiveness became a Tennysonian vice, but it did not in itself inhibit the development of Tennyson's poetry. Tennyson, like Browning, but to a still worse extent, never achieved even a pragmatic faith in the autonomy of his own imagination. Such a faith was a ruling passion in Blake, Shelley, and Keats, and such a faith, though held with earnest misgivings, for a while allowed Wordsworth and Coleridge to yield themselves to their greatest achievements. Though the overt Victorian Romantics of the Pre-Raphaelite group struggled back to a version of this faith, it was not held again with similar intensity in Tennyson's age except by Pater, who fostered Yeats even as he gave the more disjunctive and ironical Stevens a fresh point of departure in America. To trace the conflict in Tennyson's earlier poetry between a Romantic imagination and an emergent societal censor is hardly to conduct a fresh investigation, and I will not attempt it here. Such conflicts, whether found in a Spenser or even in a D. H. Lawrence, seem recurrent in the history of poetry, and belong more to the study of consciousness than to the study of poetic tradition. The more rewarding problem for pondering is the young Tennyson's profounder distrust of his own creative powers. A god spoke in him, or a demon, and a revulsion accompanied the maturing of this voice. No really magical poem by Tennyson ever became quite the work he intended it to be, and this gap between his intention and his actual achievement saved him as a poet, though it could not save him altogether. Most considerable poems by Tennyson do not mean what they meant to mean, and while this is true of all poets whatsoever to some degree, Tennyson is the most extreme instance I know of the imagination going one way and the will going quite another. Blake thought that the Milton of Paradise Lost had to be rescued from himself, an opinion that most recent Miltonists find dubious, perhaps without fully understanding it. But Tennyson's best poems are a much more radical version of Blake's paradox; they address themselves simultaneously and overtly to both a conventional and a "diabolic" reading.

Partly this is due to the prevalence in Tennyson's poetic mind of the "damned vacillating state" of the early *Supposed Confessions*. No lyric by Tennyson is more central to his sensibility than *Mariana*, entirely a poem of the autonomous imagination running down into isolated and self-destructive expectation. Wordsworth, in his sublime Tale of Margaret, wrote the contrary to Tennyson's poem, for Margaret is destroyed by an imaginative hope that will not take account of the mundane. The hope is all too willing to be fed, and the prevalence of the imagination could hardly be more dangerous. Wordsworth does, here and in *Michael*, what Tennyson could only approximate in *Dora*; the poet creates a consciousness narrower and purer than his own, and measures his own malady of self-concern by its distance from that pure intensity. Mariana, unlike Margaret, is a poetess, and she sings a Dejection ode that Tennyson scarcely ventured to write in his own person. Her disease is Romantic self-consciousness, and no bridegroom can come to heal her. "She could not look on the sweet heaven," for much the same cause as the singer of Blake's *Mad Song* turns his back to the east and rejects the comforts of the sun. Wilful and unwilling, she is poised between two states of being, one in which the world has been taken up into the mind (the mind of a Picturesque rather than Descriptive poet) and the other in which the solipsistic mind rejects the world as an unreal intruder; hence the landscape of her poem, which as a poetic achievement could not be overpraised. The poplar, seen as a phallic symbol by some recent Tennyson critics, is rather an indication of the border realm between the two states in which Mariana lives. She can neither absorb its presence nor utterly reject it, and it serves therefore to show how precarious her mode of existence is. The poem's strongest impulse is to see the world as phantasmagoria, in which case Mariana's lament would be transvalued and appear as an ironic cry of triumph for the autonomy of her vision. But there are other impulses in the poem, and "He cometh not" remains a lament.

The Shelleyan origins of Tennyson's female solitary, in *Mariana* and other poems, has been demonstrated ably by Lionel Stevenson, who unfortunately reduces this emblematic figure in both Shelley and Tennyson to Jung's archetype of the *anima*. The reduction is unnecessary in any case, since *Epipsychidion* demonstrates how consciously and deliberately Shelley used his epipsyche figure. Tennyson's use of his cynosure-female is presumably not as conscious or as deliberate, though no theory of the two Tennysons, and no prosaic psychoanalytic reduction, need be ventured in consequence. Tennyson's poetry is too many-sided for anyone to suggest plausibly that it was written by uneasy collaboration between a Shelley-Keats and a Victorian Christian humanist, and I intend no such notion in this essay. There is a profound sense of the limitations of poetry in both Keats and Shelley, but each learned how to convert this sense into an overt poetic strength. Tennyson wrote in an age of reform, both voluntary and involuntary, while the younger Romantics faced a time of apparent stasis, an exhaustion following an apocalyptic fervor. The temper of poetic imagination is peculiarly and favorably responsive to the thwarting of political hope, and Shelley and Keats and Byron gained immensely by their good fortune of having the era of Metternich and Castlereagh to contend against, little as they would appreciate so cynical a judgment. Like Beddoes and Darley, a half-generation before him, Tennyson found himself with a fiercely autonomous imagination confronting a time that neither challenged nor repelled such an imagination, yet also gave it no proper arena in which to function. Keats was of course not a political poet, indeed was far less one than Tennyson, but there still existed provocations for Keats's humanism and his naturalism to become combative. Browning found provocation enough in the Evangelicism of his parents, particularly his mother, but *Pauline* records too clearly how his Shelleyan sensibility failed guiltily before such a stimulus. Tennyson had no combative use to which an assertion of the imagination could be put, and no antidote therefore against any aesthetic corrosion that his moral doubts of imagination might bring about. The pride of imagination, and the distrust of it, had nowhere to go but within.

Sexual virginity for any poet, even a Jesuit, as Hopkins shows, is a kind of sickness unto action, a time of fear before the potential disorder of the strange. That Tennyson's Muse was (and always remained) Hallam has given Robert Graves occasion for innocent merriment, but need disturb no one any longer. The death of a beautiful young man strikes our social sense as a less appropriate theme for poetry than Poe's pervasive theme, but is of course much more traditional than Poe's preference in corpses. The sexual longings of a poet *qua poet* appear to have little relation to mere experience anyway, as for instance in the contrast between the sexually highly active Shelley, with his crucial antithetical theme of the inadequacy of nature to the imagination from *Alastor* on, and the probably virginal Keats of *Endymion*, with his profoundly primary sense of satisfaction in natural experience. Still, there is a line of poetry that goes from the complexly sensual aspirations of Spenser through the bitter sexual frustrations of Milton and Blake (particularly relevant to his Notebook poems and *Visions of the Daughters of Albion*), then to the curious argument between Shelley and Keats in *Alastor* and *Endymion*, and on to the astonishingly delayed entries into sexual experience of Tennyson and of Yeats. The analytical sophistication in aesthetic realms that would allow a responsible sexual history of English poetry to be written is not available to us, and yet such a history must and should come. The hidden fulfillment of Wordsworth is the aesthetic puzzle of *The Prelude*, since the 1805 version is marred by the inclusion of the Julia and Vaudracour episode, and the 1850 version suffers from its exclusion. The *malaise* of Tennyson's early poetry is very like that of

The Wanderings of Oisin, and the existence of Shelley and Keats as ancestor-poets-in-common is insufficient to explain the likeness. The tragedy of sexual intercourse, according to the older Yeats, was the perpetual virginity of the soul. The comedy of sexual intercourse is presumably the initial virginity of the body, but in poetry poised before experience the comedy tends to be negated, or rather displaced into the phantasmagoria of a Mariana, whose poem would be destroyed by the slightest touch of a comic spirit.

I am not, I would hope, alone in my puzzlement as to why Tennyson has not had the prestige of the hieratic in our time, while the more limited but precisely similar Mallarmé has. Tennyson's poems of the *Mariana* kind, centered on a self-embowered consciousness, are not less artful or persuasive than Mallarmé's, and are rather more universal in their implications. The English Decadence has, as its true monument, not Swinburne, admirable poet as he certainly was, but the more masterful Tennyson, whose "metaphysics of night" go beyond Mallarmé's in their elaborately indeliberate subtleties. Hallam's is necessarily a theory of pure poetry (as H. M. McLuhan shows) and while Tennyson could not allow himself to share the theory overtly, he inspired it by his early practice, and fell back on it implicitly to save his poetry time and time again. In a way that *In Memoriam* does not apprehend, the dead Hallam remained Tennyson's guardian angel.

Mariana is too pure a poem to test any argument by, so that an overview of its neighbors in early Tennyson seems likely to be helpful. *Recollections of the Arabian Nights* is a clearly Shelleyan poem, more confident indeed in its Shelleyan faith of imagination than anything else of Tennyson's. It echoes *Kubla Khan* also, but not the third part of that poem in which Coleridge to some degree withdraws from the full implications of his own vision. Like the Poet-hero of *Alastor*, Tennyson voyages through nature in search of a center transcending nature, and he finds it in a pleasure-dome like that of *Kubla Khan* or *The Palace of Art* or *The Revolt of Islam*:

> The fourscore windows all alight
> As with the quintessence of flame,
> A million tapers flaring bright
> From twisted silvers look'd to shame
> The hollow-vaulted dark, and stream'd
> Upon the mooned domes aloof
> In inmost Bagdat, till there seem'd
> Hundreds of crescents on the roof
>   Of night new-risen...

This is the young Tennyson's *Byzantium*, and perhaps it lingered in the mind of the old Yeats, though more likely both poets were recalling, however involuntarily, visions seen by Coleridge and by Shelley. Reasonable sophisticates will smile at my connecting Tennyson's playful *Recollections* to Yeats's supreme lyric, but there is a great deal legitimately to claim (or reclaim) for *Recollections of the Arabian Nights*. It was Hallam's favorite among the 1830 *Poems*, and his choice was a justified one, for the lyric is a complete and perfected miniature of Tennyson's poetic mind, and is even an *In Memoriam* in little. A very great, a consummate poet is at work in the full strength of his sensibility, and can be felt with especial power from the fifth line of this stanza on:

> Far off, and where the lemon grove
> In closest coverture upsprung,
> The living airs of middle night
> Died round the bulbul as he sung;
> Not he: but something which possess'd
> The darkness of the world, delight,
> Life, anguish, death, immortal love,
> Ceasing not, mingled, unrepress'd,
> > Apart from place, withholding time,
> > But flattering the golden prime
> > Of good Haroun Alraschid.

This stanza is at the poem's center of vision, and properly recalls the song of Keats's nightingale, also sung to a poet in darkness, and like this chant an overcoming of the limitations of space and time. The companion-poem to *Recollections* is the impressive *Ode to Memory*, and it is palpable that both lyrics are love poems addressed to Hallam. Palpable to us and not presumably to Tennyson and Hallam, I suppose I ought to add, but then the *Ode to Memory* ends:

> My friend, with you to live alone,
> Were how much better than to own
> A crown, a sceptre, and a throne!
>
> O strengthen me, enlighten me!
> I faint in this obscurity,
> Thou dewy dawn of memory.

The *Recollections* opens with an inspiriting breeze that takes the poet back to what Hart Crane in *Passage* beautifully called "an improved infancy." In that unitary joy, Tennyson emulates the Poet-hero of *Alastor* and sets forth on his quest for the good Haroun Alraschid, who is already the supernatural Hallam of *In Memoriam*, a poet-king dwelling at the center of vision, a type of god-man still to come. To reach this absolute being, the poet-voyager sails, with "a majesty of slow motion in every cadence," as Hallam observed, until he enters "another night in night," an "imbower'd" world of "imprisoning sweets." The voyage suggests not only the quest of *Alastor*, but also the journey to the Bower of Bliss in Book II of *The Faerie Queene*. Tennyson, as many critics by now have noted, is the most discreetly powerful erotic poet in the language, and this early lyric is a masterpiece of subdued erotic suggestiveness. The penultimate stanza, with its confectioner's delight of a Persian girl, is merely an erotic evasion, but the final stanza, directly celebrating Hallam, is sustained by a lyric rapture remarkable even in the younger Tennyson.

In section CIII of *In Memoriam*, Tennyson finds an after-morn of content because of another voyage-vision in which Hallam is again at the center, the Muse presiding over a realized quest. But the playfulness of *Recollections of the Arabian Nights* is now gone, that poem's greatest admirer being dead. Perhaps remembering how much Hallam had loved the poem, Tennyson returns to its design at one of the climaxes in his book of elegies, in which his grief is assuaged by the compensatory imagination, and Hallam is resurrected as a Titan capable of reviving Tennyson's lesser Muses. In itself, section CIII has rightly been judged to be one of Tennyson's great lyrics, but one can wonder how many of the poet's readers have seen how very little the poem has to do with the supposed faith of *In Memoriam*. Bradley, the definitive commentator on the elegies for Hallam, interpreted the dream of section CIII with his usual good sense, but declined to see its clearly Promethean pattern of consolation. In Numbers 13:32–33, the spies of Moses report on the Anakim, "which come of the giants," and the report appals the murmuring Israelites. Like the Titans, the Anakim testify to a time when there were giants in the earth, when men walked with gods as equals. In the titanic section CIII Tennyson dreams "a vision of the sea" during his last sleep in the house of his childhood, and in the vision he leaves behind him not only childhood, but all that precedes a rising Prometheanism as well. The poet's lesser Muses, his Daughters of Beulah as Blake patronizingly would have named them, sing "of what is wise and good / And graceful" to a veiled statue of Hallam, the unknown god who must lead them to a greater music. A dove summons Tennyson to an apocalyptic sea, an outward-flowing tide on which he will be reunited with "him I loved, and love / For ever." The weeping Muses sail with the poet:

> And still as vaster grew the shore
> And rolled the floods in grander space,
> The maidens gather'd strength and grace
> And presence, lordlier than before;
>
> And I myself, who set apart
> And watch'd them, wax'd in every limb;
> I felt the thews of Anakim,
> The pulses of a Titan's heart.

Watching the ministering spirits of his own creativity, Tennyson suddenly shares their participation in a daemonic possession, an influx of power as the poet rises in the body to be one again with the giants in the earth. With this transformation his Muses sing not of what is, but ought to be: the death of war, the great race that is to come, and a new cosmos—the shaping of a star. The New Man, the first of the crowning race, Tennyson's Albion "appearing ere the times were ripe," and so dying an early and unnatural death, is necessarily Hallam, whose epiphany "thrice as large as man" is the saving culmination of section CIII, and indeed of all the elegies. The ship of the reunited lovers, both now Titans and accompanied by the nervous Muses, fearful lest their function be gone, sails at last toward a land of crimson cloud, a realm where vapor, sea, and earth come together, a world out of space and time and free of all merely human moralities.

One never ceases to be puzzled that *In Memoriam*, an outrageously personal poem of Romantic apotheosis, a poem indeed of vastly eccentric mythmaking, should have been accepted as a work of consolation and moral resolution in the tradition of Christian humanism. *In Memoriam*, viewed as one poem, is rather a welter of confusions, but its main movement is clear enough, and establishes the work as having considerably less relation to a Christian elegy than even *Adonais* has. Whatever Tennyson thought he was doing, the daemon of imaginative autonomy got hold of the poem's continuity, and made the poem an argument for a personal love about as restrained and societal as Heathcliff's passion, or Blake's in *Visions of the Daughters of Albion* or Shelley's in *Epipsychidion*. The vision of Hallam in sections CXXVI to CXXX for instance is a more extreme version of the transfiguration of Keats in the final stanzas of *Adonais*, and is a victory for everything in Tennyson that could accept neither God nor nature as adequate to the imaginative demands of a permanently bereaved lover who was also a professional poet.

No poet in English seems to me as extreme and fortuitous as Tennyson in his sudden moments of recognition of his own powers, bursts of radiance against a commonplace conceptual background that cannot accommodate such radiance. The deeply imaginative reader learns instinctively to listen to the song and not the singer, for Lawrence's adage is perfectly relevant to Tennyson. More relevant still was the prophetic warning of Hallam, in one sentence of his review that one wishes Tennyson had brooded upon daily, and so perhaps saved for poetry more fully than he did one of the major Romantic sensibilities:

> That delicate sense of fitness which grows with the growth of artist feelings, and strengthens with their strength, until it acquires a celerity and weight of decision hardly inferior to the correspondent judgments of conscience, is

weakened by every indulgence of heterogeneous aspirations, however pure they may be, however lofty, however suitable to human nature.

Had Tennyson heeded this, he might have ended like the sinful soul of his own *The Palace of Art*, howling aloud "I am on fire within." One cannot be sure it would not have been the fitting end his imagination required.

T. S. ELIOT

"In Memoriam"

Tennyson is a great poet, for reasons that are perfectly clear. He has three qualities which are seldom found together except in the greatest poets: abundance, variety, and complete competence. We therefore cannot appreciate his work unless we read a good deal of it. We may not admire his aims: but whatever he sets out to do, he succeeds in doing, with a mastery which gives us the sense of confidence that is one of the major pleasures of poetry. His variety of metrical accomplishment is astonishing. Without making the mistake of trying to write Latin verse in English, he knew everything about Latin versification that an English poet could use; and he said of himself that he thought he knew the quantity of the sounds of every English word except perhaps *scissors*. He had the finest ear of any English poet since Milton. He was the master of Swinburne; and the versification of Swinburne, himself a classical scholar, is often crude and sometimes cheap, in comparison with Tennyson's. Tennyson extended very widely the range of active metrical forms in English: in *Maud* alone the variety is prodigious. But innovation in metric is not to be measured solely by the width of the deviation from accepted practice. It is a matter of the historical situation: at some moments a more violent change may be necessary than at others. The problem differs at every period. At some times, a violent revolution may be neither possible nor desirable; at such times, a change which may appear very slight, is the change which the important poet will make. The innovation of Pope, after Dryden, may not seem very great; but it is the mark of the master to be able to make small changes which will be highly significant, as at another time to

From *Essays Ancient and Modern*, Copyright © 1950 by Harcourt Brace Jovanovich; copyright renewed 1978 by Esme Valerie Eliot.

make radical changes, through which poetry will curve back again to its norm.

There is an early poem, only published in the official biography, which already exhibits Tennyson as a master. According to a note, Tennyson later expressed regret that he had removed the poem from his Juvenilia; it is a fragmentary *Hesperides*, in which only the 'The Song of the Three Sisters' is complete. The poem illustrates Tennyson's classical learning and his mastery of metre. The first stanza of 'The Song of the Three Sisters' is as follows:

> The Golden Apple, the Golden Apple, the hallow'd fruit,
> Guard it well, guard it warily,
> Singing airily,
> Standing about the charmèd root.
> Round about all is mute,
> As the snowfield on the mountain peaks,
> As the sandfield at the mountain-foot.
> Crocodiles in briny creeks
> Sleep and stir not; all is mute.
> If ye sing not, if ye make false measure,
> We shall lose eternal pleasure,
> Worth eternal want of rest.
> Laugh not loudly: watch the treasure
> Of the wisdom of the West.
> In a corner wisdom whispers. Five and three
> (Let it not be preach'd abroad) make an awful mystery:
> For the blossom unto threefold music bloweth;
> Evermore it is born anew,
> And the sap to threefold music floweth,
> From the root,
> Drawn in the dark,
> Up to the fruit,
> Creeping under the fragrant bark,
> Liquid gold, honeysweet through and through.
> Keen-eyed Sisters, singing airily,
> Looking warily
> Every way,
> Guard the apple night and day,
> Lest one from the East come and take it away.

A young man who can write like that has not much to learn about metric; and the young man who wrote these lines somewhere between 1828 and 1830 was doing something new. There is something not derived from any of his predecessors. In some of Tennyson's early verse the influence of Keats is visible—in songs and in blank verse; and less successfully, there is the influence of Wordsworth, as in *Dora*. But in the lines I have just quoted, and in the two Mariana poems, 'The Sea-Fairies', 'The Lotos-Eaters', 'The Lady of Shalott', and elsewhere, there is something wholly new.

> All day within the dreamy house,
>   The doors upon their hinges creak'd;
> The blue fly sung in the pane; the mouse
>   Behind the mouldering wainscot shriek'd,
> Or from the crevice peer'd about.

The blue fly sung in the pane (the line would be ruined if you substituted *sang* for *sung*) is enough to tell us that something important has happened.

The reading of long poems is not nowadays much practised: in the age of Tennyson it appears to have been easier. For a good many long poems were not only written but widely circulated; and the level was high: even the second-rate long poems of that time, like *The Light of Asia*, are better worth reading than most long modern novels. But Tennyson's long poems are not long poems in quite the same sense as those of his contemporaries. They are very different in kind from *Sordello* or *The Ring and the Book*, to name the greatest by the greatest of his contemporary poets. *Maud* and *In Memoriam* are each a series of poems, given form by the greatest lyrical resourcefulness that a poet has ever shown. The *Idylls of the King* have merits and defects similar to those of *The Princess*. An *idyll* is a 'short poem descriptive of some picturesque scene or incident'; in choosing the name Tennyson perhaps showed an appreciation of his limitations. For his poems are always descriptive, and always picturesque; they are never really narrative. The *Idylls of the King* are no different in kind from some of his early poems; the *Morte d'Arthur* is in fact an early poem. *The Princess* is still an idyll, but an idyll that is too long. Tennyson's versification in this poem is as masterly as elsewhere: it is a poem which we must read, but which we excuse ourselves from reading twice. And it is worthwhile recognizing the reason why we return again and again, and are always stirred by the lyrics which intersperse it, and which are among the greatest of all poetry of their kind, and yet avoid the poem itself. It is not, as we may think while reading, the outmoded attitude towards the relations of the sexes, the exasperating views on the subjects of matrimony, celibacy, and female education, that make us recoil from *The Princess*. We can swallow the most antipathetic doctrines if we are given an exciting narrative. But for narrative Tennyson had no gift at all. For a static poem, and a moving poem, on the same subject, you have only to compare his 'Ulysses' with the condensed and intensely exciting narrative of that hero in the XXVIth Canto of Dante's *Inferno*. Dante is telling a story. Tennyson is only stating an elegiac mood. The very greatest poets set before you real men talking, carry you on in real events moving. Tennyson could not tell a story at all. It is not that in *The Princess* he tries to tell a story and failed: it is rather that an idyll protracted to such length becomes unreadable. So *The Princess* is a dull poem; one of the poems of which we may say, that they are beautiful but dull.

But in *Maud* and in *In Memoriam*, Tennyson is doing what every conscious artist does, turning his limitations to good purpose. Of the content of *Maud*, I cannot think so highly as does Mr. Humbert Wolfe, in his interesting essay on Tennyson which is largely defence of the supremacy of that poem. For me, *Maud* consists of a few very beautiful lyrics, such as 'O let the solid ground', 'Birds in the high Hall-garden', and 'Go not, happy day', around which the semblance of a dramatic situation has been constructed with the greatest metrical virtuosity. The whole situation is unreal; the ravings of the lover on the edge of insanity sound false, and fail, as do the bellicose bellowings, to make one's flesh creep with sincerity. It would be foolish to suggest that Tennyson ought to have gone through some experience similar to that described: for a poet with dramatic gifts, a situation quite remote from his personal experience may release the strongest emotion. And I do not believe for a moment that Tennyson was a man of mild feelings or weak passions. There is no evidence in his poetry that he knew the experience of violent passion for a woman; but there is plenty of evidence of emotional intensity and violence—but of emotion so deeply suppressed, even from himself, as to tend rather towards the blackest melancholia than towards dramatic action. And it is emotion which, so far as my reading of the poems can discover, attained no ultimate clear purgation. I should reproach Tennyson not for mildness, or tepidity, but rather for lack of serenity.

> Of love that never found his earthly close,
> What sequel?

The fury of *Maud* is shrill rather than deep, though one feels in every passage what exquisite adaptation of metre to the mood Tennyson is attempting to express. I think that the effect of feeble violence, which the poem as a whole produces, is the result of a fundamental error of form. A poet can express his feelings as fully through a dramatic, as through a lyrical form; but *Maud* is neither one thing nor the other: just as *The Princess* is more than an idyll, and less than a narrative. In *Maud*, Tennyson neither identifies himself with the lover, nor identifies the lover with himself: consequently, the real feelings of Tennyson, profound and tumultuous as they are, never arrive at expression.

It is, in my opinion, in *In Memoriam*, that Tennyson finds full expression. Its technical merit alone is enough to ensure its perpetuity. While Tennyson's technical competence is everywhere masterly and satisfying, *In Memoriam* is the most unapproachable of all his poems. Here are one hundred and thirty-two passages, each of several quatrains in the same

form, and never monotony or repetition. And the poem has to be comprehended as a whole. We may not memorize a few passages, we cannot find a
'fair sample'; we have to comprehend the whole of a poem which is
essentially the length that it is. We may choose to remember:

> Dark house, by which once more I stand
>   Here in the long unlovely street,
>   Doors, where my heart was used to beat
> So quickly, waiting for a hand,
>
> A hand that can be clasp'd no more—
>   Behold me, for I cannot sleep,
>   And like a guilty thing I creep
> At earliest morning to the door.
>
> He is not here; but far away
>   The noise of life begins again,
>   And ghastly thro' the drizzling rain
> On the bald street breaks the blank day.

This is great poetry, economical of words, a universal emotion in what could
only be an English town: and it gives me the shudder that I fail to get from
anything in *Maud*. But such a passage, by itself, is not *In Memoriam*: *In
Memoriam* is the whole poem. It is unique: it is a long poem made by putting
together lyrics, which have only the unity and continuity of a diary, the
concentrated diary of a man confessing himself. It is a diary of which we
have to read every word.

Apparently Tennyson's contemporaries, once they had accepted *In
Memoriam*, regarded it as a message of hope and reassurance to their rather
fading Christian faith. It happens now and then that a poet by some strange
accident expresses the mood of his generation, at the same time that he is
expressing a mood of his own which is quite remote from that of his
generation. This is not a question of insincerity: there is an amalgam of
yielding and opposition below the level of consciousness. Tennyson himself,
on the conscious level of the man who talks to reporters and poses for
photographers, to judge from remarks made in conversation and recorded in
his son's Memoir, consistently asserted a convinced, if somewhat sketchy,
Christian belief. And he was a friend of Frederick Denison Maurice—
nothing seems odder about that age than the respect which its eminent
people felt for each other. Nevertheless, I get a very different impression from
In Memoriam from that which Tennyson's contemporaries seem to have got.
It is of a very much more interesting and tragic Tennyson. His biographers
have not failed to remark that he had a good deal of the temperament of the
mystic—certainly not at all the mind of the theologian. He was desperately
anxious to hold the faith of the believer, without being very clear about

what he wanted to believe: he was capable of illumination which he was incapable of understanding. The 'Strong Son of God, immortal Love', with an invocation of whom the poem opens, has only a hazy connection with the Logos, or the Incarnate God. Tennyson is distressed by the idea of a mechanical universe; he is naturally, in lamenting his friend, teased by the hope of immortality and reunion beyond death. Yet the renewal craved for seems at best but a continuance, or a substitute for the joys of friendship upon earth. His desire for immortality never is quite the desire for Eternal Life; his concern is for the loss of man rather than for the gain of God.

> ... shall he,
>
> Man, her last work, who seem'd so fair,
>   Such splendid purpose in his eyes,
>   Who roll'd the psalm to wintry skies,
> Who built him fanes of fruitless prayer,
>
> Who trusted God was love indeed
>   And love Creation's final law—
>   Tho' Nature, red in tooth and claw
> With ravine, shriek'd against his creed—
>
> Who loved, who suffer'd countless ills,
>   Who battled for the True, the Just,
>   Be blown about the desert dust,
> Or seal'd within the iron hills?

That strange abstraction, 'Nature', becomes a real god or goddess, perhaps more real, at moments, to Tennyson than God ('Are God and Nature then at strife?'). The hope of immortality is confused (typically of the period) with the hope of the gradual and steady improvement of this world. Much has been said of Tennyson's interest in contemporary science, and of the impression of Darwin. *In Memoriam*, in any case, antedates *The Origin of Species* by several years, and the belief in social progress by democracy antedates it by many more; and I suspect that the faith of Tennyson's age in human progress would have been quite as strong even had the discoveries of Darwin been postponed by fifty years. And after all, there is no logical connection: the belief in progress being current already, the discoveries of Darwin were harnessed to it:

> No longer half-akin to brute,
>   For all we thought and loved and did,
>   And hoped, and suffer'd, is but seed
> Of what in them is flower and fruit;

> Whereof the man, that with me trod
>   This planet, was a noble type
>   Appearing ere the times were ripe,
> That friend of mine who lives in God,
>
> That God, which ever lives and loves,
>   One God, one law, one element
>   And one far-off divine event,
> To which the whole creation moves.

These lines show an interesting compromise between the religious attitude and, what is quite a different thing, the belief in human perfectibility; but the contrast was not so apparent to Tennyson's contemporaries. They may have been taken in by it, but I don't think that Tennyson himself was, quite: his feelings were more honest than his mind. There is evidence elsewhere—even in an early poem, 'Locksley Hall', for example—that Tennyson by no means regarded with complacency all the changes that were going on about him in the progress of industrialism and the rise of the mercantile and manufacturing and banking classes; and he may have contemplated the future of England, as his years drew out, with increasing gloom. Temperamentally, he was opposed to the doctrine that he was moved to accept and to praise.

Tennyson's feelings, I have said, were honest; but they were usually a good way below the surface. In Memoriam can, I think, justly be called a religious poem, but for another reason than that which made it seem religious to his contemporaries. It is not religious because of the quality of its faith, but because of the quality of its doubt. Its faith is a poor thing, but its doubt is a very intense experience. In Memoriam is a poem of despair, but of despair of a religious kind. And to qualify its despair with the adjective 'religious' is to elevate it above most of its derivatives. For The City of Dreadful Night, and the Shropshire Lad, and the poems of Thomas Hardy, are small work in comparison with In Memoriam: it is greater than they and comprehends them.

In ending we must go back to the beginning and remember that In Memoriam would not be a great poem, or Tennyson a great poet, without the technical accomplishment. Tennyson is the great master of metric as well as of melancholia; I do not think any poet in English has ever had a finer ear for vowel sound, as well as a subtler feeling for some moods of anguish:

> Dear as remember'd kisses after death,
> And sweet as those by hopeless fancy feign'd
> On lips that are for others; deep as love,
> Deep as first love, and wild with all regret.

And this technical gift of Tennyson's is no slight thing. Tennyson lived in a time which was already acutely time-conscious: a great many things seemed to be happening, railways were being built, discoveries were being made, the face of the world was changing. That was a time busy in keeping up to date. It had, for the most part, no hold on permanent things, on permanent truths about man and God and life and death. The surface of Tennyson stirred about with his time; and he had nothing to which to hold fast except his unique and unerring feeling for the sounds of words. But in this he had something that no one else had. Tennyson's surface, his technical accomplishment, is intimate with his depths: what we most quickly see about Tennyson is that which moves between the surface and the depths, that which is of slight importance. By looking innocently at the surface we are most likely to come to the depths, to the abyss of sorrow. Tennyson is not only a minor Virgil, he is also with Virgil as Dante saw him, a Virgil among the Shades, the saddest of all English poets, among the Great in Limbo, the most instinctive rebel against the society in which he was the most perfect conformist.

Tennyson seems to have reached the end of his spiritual development with In Memoriam; there followed no reconciliation, no resolution.

> And now no sacred staff shall break in blossom,
> No choral salutation lure to light
> A spirit sick with perfume and sweet night,

or rather with twilight, for Tennyson faced neither the darkness nor the light, in his later years. The genius, the technical power, persisted to the end, but the spirit had surrendered. A gloomier end than that of Baudelaire: Tennyson had no singulier avertissement. And having turned aside from the journey through the dark night, to become the surface flatterer of his own time, he has been rewarded with the despite of an age that succeeds his own in shallowness.

G. M. YOUNG

The Age of Tennyson

Some thirty years ago, walking in Sussex, I fell into conversation with an innkeeper, very proud of his neighbourhood and of the great men who had honoured it by being born, or coming to live, there. Then, as he ended the list, he suddenly added, 'But there: not one of them could have written *Enoch Arden*. What a beautiful piece that is!'

The volumes of *Poems* (1842) established Tennyson in the regard of the critical public as the first, after Wordsworth, of living poets; a regard qualified, however, with certain misgivings as to his intellectual grasp, his power to bring under poetic control the turbulent manifold of contemporary life, misgivings which *The Princess* in 1847 certainly did not remove. *In Memoriam* was influential in extending his renown, but within a limited range: many of its earliest readers disliked it, many did not understand it, and those who admired it most were not always the best judges of its poetry. *Maud* in 1855 was a decided set-back: it puzzled, it irritated, it shocked. But with the first four *Idylls of the King* in 1859 the Laureate won the great educated public, and with *Enoch Arden* five years later, the people. Not in his own country only, for as his German biographer has written, 'with *Enoch Arden* Tennyson took the heart of the German people by storm': a fact well illustrating a truth of which we have constantly to remind ourselves, that our Victorian Age is only the local phase of a cultural period common to all Western Europe and North America. Indeed we need not limit our view to the West, because I am fairly sure that if the last canto of *Evgeny Onegin* in Professor Elton's translation fell anonymously into the hands of

From *Proceedings of the British Academy*, vol. 25 (1939). Copyright © 1939 by G. M. Young. Oxford University Press, 1939.

one of our younger reviewers, he would unhesitatingly characterize Tatiana's refusal to desert her elderly husband for the man whom she still loves, as a typical example of Victorian smugness, unless, indeed, complacency was the word that week in vogue.

For the rest of his life Tennyson was The Poet: and to the people poetry was the sort of thing that Tennyson wrote. There was, I well remember, a sixpenny encyclopaedia of great service to young schoolboys on the eve of examinations, which contained, with other useful matter, a list of the Hundred Greatest Men: 'to know their deeds is to know the history of civilization'; it began of course with Homer, and ended, not less of course, with Tennyson. Lord Morley once, wishing to affirm some idea of social stratification, divided the people of England into those who had a Tennyson at home and those who had not. When I cast my memory back to the bookshops in our more elegant suburbs, or at a seaside resort, the first picture I see is rows and shelves and boxes full of Tennyson; and just as John Stuart Mill used to fret himself with the thought that some day all melodious combinations of sound would be exhausted, and music come to an end, so I used to wonder, what more, when Tennyson had written

> Calm and deep peace on this high wold,
>   And on these dews that drench the furze,
>   And all the silvery gossamers
> That twinkle into green and gold:
>
> Calm and still light on yon great plain
>   That sweeps with all its autumn bowers,
>   And crowded farms and lessening towers,
> To mingle with the bounding main:

what more, I say, there was for poetry to do. And, let me add, this was not an inculcated sentiment: no one had told me to admire him: the star of Browning, the star of Meredith were blazing above a landscape all silver with the moonlight of Pater. I must conclude that Tennyson gave me what he gave to the earlier generation which placed him beside Virgil. I cannot conjure up again the enchantment, but I can indicate, I think, the field it covered, and the theme on which I wish to write is not the poetry of Tennyson by itself or the thought of Tennyson by itself, but the adjustment of both to the world in which he lived, an adjustment so perfect that, as Saintsbury once said, 'no age of poetry can be called the age of one man with such critical accuracy as the later Nineteenth Century is, with us, the Age of Tennyson'.

Take up the faded green Moxon volume with its list of Mr. Tennyson's other works, *Poems*, 16th edition, *The Princess*, 12th edition, *In Memoriam*, 15th edition, and imagine yourself to be one of its 60,000 purchasers: or better still, perhaps, sitting in the village schoolroom to hear it read by the vicar or the squire. What do you find? An abundance, a vast profusion of poetic learning, of ornate phrasing and verbal music—which you will recognize and admire, because it is the familiar accent of Tennyson, though in detail much of it may be above your head—applied to a tale of common life lived on the heroic level. Reading it again, I recalled the story of the French duchess who paid her social and charitable visits in the same attire, an old shawl and a diamond brooch, because, as she said, her rich friends only saw the diamonds and her poor friends only saw the shawl. Listen to the Laureate deploying all his magnificence of sound and imagery to bring before us the tropical island and the shipwrecked sailor waiting for a sail:

> No sail from day to day, but every day
> The sunrise broken into scarlet shafts
> Among the palms and ferns and precipices;
> The blaze upon the waters to the east;
> The blaze upon his island overhead;
> The blaze upon the waters to the west;
> Then the great stars that globed themselves in Heaven,
> The hollower-bellowing ocean, and again
> The scarlet shafts of sunrise—but no sail.

But listen also to what, if you are holding hands in the back row of the schoolroom, will touch you more nearly, the poet's tale of Enoch's ambition.

> Enoch set
> A purpose evermore before his eyes,
> To hoard all savings to the uttermost,
> To purchase his own boat, and make a home
> For Annie...
> And all men look'd upon him favourably:
> And ere he touch'd his one-and-twentieth May
> He purchased his own boat, and made a home
> For Annie, neat and nestlike, halfway up
> The narrow street that clamber'd toward the mill.

When his child is born, then

> In him woke,
> With his first babe's first cry, the noble wish
> To save all earnings to the uttermost,
> And give his child a better bringing-up
> Than his had been, or hers.

Accident and competition set him back. So he decides to stock a little shop for Annie, and ship himself on a China barque; meaning to trade and so

> ... returning rich,
> Become the master of a larger craft,
> With fuller profits lead an easier life,
> Have all his pretty young ones educated,
> And pass his days in peace among his own.

He will in fact become a small employer; in 1867 Liberal speakers will challenge Bob Lowe to justify a law which excludes from the franchise our worthy neighbour Mr. Arden: while for the daughter there is evidently reserved the destiny of the young lady in the ballad:

> And now she is the lawyer's wife
> And dearly he does love her:
> And she lives in a happy condition of life,
> And well in the station above her.

To the simple-hearted reader or listener, in fact, Tennyson has done what the critic of 1842 demanded of him. He has brought the living world of shops and ships and going to sea and going to school, under poetic control. It is all there, and it is all poetry. We may object that it is not all there: that this living world is a highly selective composition, this poetry very largely a practised mannerism. I am not concerned to refute either objection, but I will ask you to consider for a little, not the ethical or artistic presumptions— if there be any such—by which poetry ought to be judged, but those which contemporaries actually applied.

'In metaphysical enquiries egoism is the truest modesty', and what little I understand of poetry regarded as an activity of the mind I learnt from a trifling incident in my own youth. The subject set for the Newdigate in my second or third year was King Charles at Oxford. I had no intention of competing, which was perhaps a pity, because the only copy which was submitted contained, I was afterwards told, the passage:

> The Queen from France with admirable tact
> Supplied the money which the Army lacked;
> Grateful the King accepts the proffered boon,
> And gives it to his troops who spend it soon.

But while I was thinking, in an idle and quite disinterested mood, how the theme could be treated, the notion—not the image—of Oxford, with its towers and lawns and trees lying like an island in the sea of civil strife, occurred to me, and with the notion came a line. I wrote it down, and the next line came at once, completing the couplet. In all, I wrote a simile ten lines long, as fast as if I was writing from dictation, and, as I wrote each word, not knowing in the least what the next would be. Then the spring failed as suddenly as it had started.

Guided by this experience of my own I have always supposed poetic experience to be a kind of compulsion which has its locus on the boundary between the apprehension of a theme and its rendering in metrical form; and there is this much truth, I believe, in Matthew Arnold's perilous doctrine of the Great Line, that such lines mark, as it were, the moments when the boundary disappears in a sudden intensity of poetic insight, so that apprehension and expression become a single act. Such moments are rare, and in the great bulk of every poet's work the two aspects, call them thought and form, are at least critically distinguishable. And corresponding to these two aspects of poetic activity there are, I think, two aspects of reception in the hearer or reader. He wishes to have certain things set before him because they interest him; and every age has its own set of interests. The later eighteenth century, for example, did not want to hear the things that Blake had to say, and so it hardly noticed that Blake was there. The early nineteenth century did most eagerly want something like *Childe Harold*, and having got it, went on to accept from Byron much which a less avid taste would have rejected. But the reader also desires to have these things set before him in a way which is poetically gratifying, and here also his pleasure and satisfaction are very largely conditioned for him by the aesthetic ambient of his time. All which things taken together produce what I have called adjustment; and, if I may ask you to admit one distinction more, within the aesthetic appeal and response itself two elements may be observed. In every work of art there is something which addresses the nerves, a thrill, beside those other things which reach the spirit. It is in virtue of this thrill, very often, that a writer makes his entry and secures his public—Swinburne is as good an example as one can recall—and I believe the curious anger, or detestation, so much beyond any reasonable ground of distaste, with which each age for a time regards the literature of the last, has its cause in this: that it perceives the appeal, but cannot answer it. Nothing is more exasperating to the nerves or the temper than a thrill which has begun to be a bore. You remember Mr. Pepys at *Midsummer Night's Dream*: 'Insipid: ridiculous: I shall never see it again!'

I am thinking now of those years between 1840 and 1860 when Tennyson was rising to the throne of poetry, and I ask what was the element in his art which was most stimulating to the nerves, and most satisfying to the taste of his contemporaries, and why. I call upon the memories of that young enthusiast, and without hesitation I answer; in the first instance his descriptive power. I need not tell again a tale which has been told so often, and, to relieve your anxieties at once, I may say I do not intend to mention Lady Winchelsea. But I must pause for a moment on a greater name, a more persistent influence. For about a century the repute and vogue of Thomson varied singularly little. 'From 1750 to 1850', one of his biographers wrote:

Thomson was in England the poet, par excellence, not of the eclectic and literary few, but of the large and increasing cultivated middle class. 'Thomson's "Seasons" looks best (I maintain it) a little torn and dogeared.'

He is quoting Lamb.

When Coleridge found a dogeared copy of *The Seasons* in an inn, and remarked 'That is fame', Thomson's popularity seemed quite as assured as Milton's. As late as 1855 Robert Bell remarked that it seemed even on the increase. The date may be taken to mark the turning point in his fame, for since about 1850 he has been unmistakably eclipsed on his own ground, in the favour of the class to which he was once dear, by Tennyson.

For a generation or so before the birth of Tennyson English senses had been brought to a degree of fineness they had never possessed before. The practice of the poets counted for much, of Cowper and those others to whom in this context we need not deny their good old name of the Lake Poets. The new interest in landscape painting, the addiction to sketching in pencil or water-colour, are, as Hazlitt pointed out, influences not to be overlooked in studying the evolution of our literary tastes. I would add the habit of travel, especially of domestic travel imposed by the closure of the Continent and facilitated by the labours of Telford and Macadam. Finally, I would include an influence which I believe to be well worth the attention of some student of the literature of science: I mean the growing devotion to natural history in all its branches, the minute observation of form and colour in leaf and rock and feather and flower. High among those who formed the English aesthetic of the nineteenth century must always be placed the names of White and Gilpin and Bewick: after them of Lyell, and the contributors to the *Cabinet Encyclopaedia*.

This increasing fineness of observation demanded an increasing delicacy and exactitude of record, just as, in another sphere, the metrical practice of the great Romantic poets had created a demand for a richer and more various verbal music than had contented the Augustan ear. But as we go forward into the nineteenth century, this devotion to nature seems to become almost a nervous craving: possibly at the deepest level a biological necessity. The public of which I am speaking, Tennyson's public, was becoming, in spirit, suburban: a country-bred stock, entangled in a way of life which it had not learnt to control, was instinctively fighting for breath. And for sixty years its poet was there, flashing on it in phrases of faultless precision, pictures of the world from which it was exiled and in which it yearned to keep at least an imaginary footing.

The ground flame of the crocus breaks the mould.

That is Tennyson at twenty. It might be Tennyson at eighty.

Nothing in Tennyson's art is more admirable than the economy and certainty of his touch when he is on this ground:

> On either side the river lie
> Long fields of barley and of rye
> That clothe the wold *and meet the sky.*

No wonder the *Quarterly,* whether Croker or his editor, stigmatized that phrase, because, as everyone born in the eighteenth century would know, between the top of the wold and the bottom of the sky there is in fact a considerable gap. I quote it as one of the earliest and most convincing examples of Tennyson's mastery of the illusionist style, where words have the value of things seen, and the observation seems to go at once into poetry without any pause for reflection, or mental arrangement of the particulars. Think of the spring in *Balin and Balan*:

> ...the spring, that down
> From underneath a plume of lady-fern,
> Sang, and the sand danced at the bottom of it.

It does not matter whether you have ever seen that or not. If you have not, you know now exactly what it looks like. If you have, the words will keep it in your memory far more vividly than any recollection of your own. Here, as Miss Sitwell has said of Smart, 'the natural object is seen with such clarity that for the moment nothing else exists', and in Smart's recently published manuscript *Jubilate Agno* there is a sentence which I must quote because it seems to me exactly to describe the nature of the accomplishment which, after two generations of experiment, Tennyson brought to perfection.

> My talent is to give an impression upon words by punching, that when the reader casts his eye upon them, he takes up the image from the mould which I have made.

Tennyson's imagery was studied by men of science, and never once I think did they find his observation scientifically at fault. That melancholy achievement was reserved for me. No one who lives in downland and has ever seen a waning moon rising in a windy sky, can fail to respond to the magical aptitude of the lines

> And high in heaven the streaming cloud,
> And on the downs a rising fire.

That fire is a stage illumination: that moon a property moon. I have it on the authority of the Astronomer Royal, and—

> Solem quis dicere falsum
> Audeat?

that on 10 October 1842, the day of Cecilia Tennyson's wedding here commemorated, the moon did not rise after supper. It rose before lunch.

I think it is true to say that Tennyson's accomplishment in this branch of his art served to constrict for a time the range of our poetry, and to narrow our critical judgement. After all, images of external nature are not the only things a poet has to provide: and in the later part of the century you may sometimes encounter a naïve habit of criticism, based on the popular notion, as I said, that poetry was what Tennyson wrote, which assessed the poets by the number of nature-touches, as they were known in the trade, to be found in their respective works. But I need not remind you that it has often been the fate of great poets—and a proof of their greatness: the fate of Chaucer and Virgil—to impede the progress of poesy by their very mastery, by the domination they exercised over their contemporaries and immediate successors.

I have placed this gift of Tennyson's in the forefront of his equipment, because it is here that we are most conscious—whether we can still feel it or not—of what I have called the thrill. The profusion of his natural imagery, domestic or exotic, is—or was once—as intoxicating as the liquid richness of his verse, and its ravishing surprises. We are not called upon to be intoxicated, but to understand those who were, and to follow them as they see their poet, the poet of 'Mariana' and 'The Lotos-Eaters', grow in stature as a philosophic and religious teacher. Here again, to begin with what is outward, his mastery of another mode, not less grateful to an age immersed in anxious moral speculation, is equally conspicuous, not to say obtrusive. I mean the gnomic, hortatory utterance, the ethical *sententia*. Few lines of Tennyson, for example, were more admired or more often quoted than these:

> Let knowledge grow from more to more,
> But more of reverence in us dwell;
> That mind and soul, according well,
> May make one music as before,
>
> But vaster.

Perhaps to our less robust and exuberant ethical sense, they are, if anything, too quotable, too suggestive of the birthday book, the calendar, or the chairman of the governors at a prize-giving. They seem, like so much of Tennyson's verse, to be designed for public performance. Indeed I knew a man who, until I convinced him otherwise, had gone through life believing that

> Heated hot with burning fears
> And dipt in baths of hissing tears,

> And battered with the shocks of doom
> To shape and use:

was the second verse of *Scots wha hae*. We must acknowledge that we have lost the taste for moral declamation, just as the nineteenth century lost the taste for social elegance. But it may come back. In any case I am not defending or assailing Tennyson's manner. I am speaking historically; I am trying to account for what I have called his adjustment. But may I in passing observe that the greatest body of reflective and ethical poetry in European literature actually was designed for public performance? I mean the choruses of the Athenian stage: and it is here, I have often thought, especially among the choruses of Sophocles, that we shall find the nearest analogy to such pieces as 'Of old sat Freedom on the heights', many of the lyrics which make up *In Memoriam*, or this, which the Attic Muse herself might not have disdained or disavowed:

> And when no mortal motion jars
>   The blackness round the tombing sod,
> Thro' silence and the trembling stars
>   Comes Faith from tracts no feet have trod,
>   And Virtue, like a household god
>
> Promising empire; such as those
>   Once heard at dead of night to greet
> Troy's wandering prince, so that he rose
>   With sacrifice, while all the fleet
>   Had rest by stony hills of Crete.

And this gnomic manner was not less pleasing to the ear of a romantic age, when it dissolved, as it often does, into a riddling, oracular style like this:

> Pass not beneath this gateway, but abide
> Without, among the cattle of the field.
> For, an ye heard a music, like enow
> They are building still, seeing the city is built
> To music, therefore never built at all,
> And therefore built for ever.

Now are those lines a genuine poetic experience, or merely the application of poetic learning to a promising theme? Is Tennyson expressing himself or exploiting himself? That is the doubt, already audible in the seventies, which grew and culminated in the great revulsion from the Laureate and all his ways which is characteristic of the end of the last century and the beginning of this. There is no need to deny that much of

Tennyson's poetry is enveloped in an Alexandrian overgrowth of literary erudition, a kind of Great Exhibitionism not unalluring to an age which loved profusion, as much as it admired invention. He has passages which Callimachus could have approved: others which Ovid might have envied: and Mario Praz has actually called *Enoch Arden* a Hellenistic romance. I do not feel that judgement to be true, but if anyone chose to call the *Idylls*, where one can hardly say whether the figures are ancients dressed like moderns, or moderns like ancients, a Hellenistic epic, I am not sure I should greatly differ: and the decorous eroticism which hangs over much—not all— of that performance seems to me to have been finally and adequately characterized by the American schoolboy who observed: 'There is some pretty hot necking in Lord Tennyson, only they never quite make it.'

But in the 'Northern Farmer', 'The Churchwarden', and 'The Village Wife, or the Entail', we are far from Alexandria, we are among the oak-woods of Acharnae: and you may think that the spectacle of Tennyson unbending in dialect, and then resuming his poise as Bard to write 'The Wreck' or 'The Children's Hospital' indicates some weakness in the poetic fibre of the man, or the poetic judgement of his age. If you do, I think you would be right: and I wish to consider rather more closely what that weakness was.

I need not remark that the Christian religion and the elements of propriety were not introduced into the United Kingdom by Prince Albert of Saxe-Coburg-Gotha. At the beginning of the century, at least by 1805, the Germans had noticed and named as a national characteristic, or Engländerei, that nervousness and reticence in the sphere of passion which is popularly supposed to be a Victorian characteristic, and which in passing I may recall, had compelled Scott in 1824 to mar the catastrophe of *St. Ronan's Well*. Those who believe in the economic interpretation of everything, including poetry, may find it easier than I do to account for the readiness with which the England of Chaucer and Fielding submitted itself and its literature to this new asceticism. Never I suppose was there a time when people were so willing to be shocked, or when the habit of being shocked was so widespread and so commendable that a man could assert his superior refinement best by being shocked at something which no one else had noticed, like the critic of *Enoch Arden*, for example, who censured Tennyson for failing to observe that bigamy was not a misfortune but a criminal offence. Now it may be admitted that bigamy is rarer in the upper than in the lower walks of society: and what I think was in the back of the critic's mind was the notion that by taking Annie to himself, without proof of Enoch's death, Philip was descending from the station of a thoroughly respectable man.

I have always thought that the conception of respectability was in its place and time of the greatest moral service to us. To be respectable is to emerge from the anonymous amorphous mass: to be a personality: to live by a standard, actually, perhaps, the standard of the class just above that into which you had been born and in which your fellows were content to live. If we stopped there, we might think of respectability as the characteristic virtue of competitive individualism practised under the eye of an approving gentry. But we cannot stop there, because the respectable man is not only bettering himself, he is bettering his family. Through the family the most powerful of human instincts is harnessed to the secular task of improving the race. So viewed, social progress is a microcosmic section of the evolution of the world under the guidance of that Providence whose purpose, in the great words of Malthus, is ever to bring a mind out of the cold, but a section which has become conscious of itself and therefore capable of a directed effort. As Pitt Rivers said to a concourse of archaeologists shortly after the appearance of Darwin's *Descent of Man*, 'the thought of our humble origin'— from what I have heard of Pitt Rivers I think he must have said your humble origin—'may be an incentive to industry and respectability'.

In other words respectability means the continual production and reproduction of distinguished varieties, and to laughter, as George Meredith taught us, the distinguished variety is peculiarly sensitive. In this way we may account for that vicious dichotomy, deep-seated in the Victorian mind, between the idea of comedy, and the idea of beauty, which is so observable, for example, in Dickens: beyond question one of the greatest of all comic writers—and yet, how unlovely is much of his satire, how tasteless his sentiment. Seeing that comedy, that wit and humour, are among the most powerful and penetrating instruments which the mind has to work with, we must, I think, acknowledge that this notion of the fenced, secluded area where laughter must not be heard, weakened and hampered the whole intelligence of the age: and in none of its great writers is the mischief more apparent than in Tennyson. Matthew Arnold said he lacked intellectual power. He said much the same of Shelley: and I am not sure that his intense, exclusive, humanism qualified him to judge the intellectual calibre of a poet, whose chief interests, apart from poetry, were scientific: I cannot recall any passage in Arnold's writing which suggests that he had ever given a thought to the ichthyosaurus. At all events, contemporaries, not less fitted than he to judge, did not observe the want, partly because they were under the same limitations themselves, but more because they found in Tennyson the most complete statement of the great philosophic issue of the age: if not an answer to its problems, at least an indication of the lines along which the answer was to be sought. What he did lack, and they did not require, was precisely that restraining touch of comedy to save him from becoming, as he can be at times, vapidly pontifical and almost embarrassingly silly.

This issue, the central problem round which the minds of thoughtful men were coming to revolve, can be very simply stated. What was the standing of personality, the finite human personality, in a world which every year was revealing itself more clearly as a process of perpetual flux?

> The hills are shadows and they flow
> From form to form, and nothing stands;
> They melt like mist, the solid lands,
> Like clouds they shape themselves and go.

We may perhaps forget, among our own more pressing concerns, how formidable an attack on human dignity and personal values, the ground of all Western philosophy and religion, was implicit in the new conceptions of geological and biological time. When once you have mastered the thesis that inconceivable ages have gone to make the race, and that after inconceivable ages to come the whole conscious episode may have been nothing more than a brief iridescence on a cooling cinder, what solid ground of conduct is left to you? And Tennyson had mastered the thesis; from his undergraduate days, when Darwin was on the high seas in the *Beagle*, he had meditated on the mystery of development and the succession of types.

Thus when he appeared as a philosophic poet with *In Memoriam* he was not only equipped for the great debate which was soon to open; he had anticipated it, had formulated at least a conceivable conclusion; and one based on personal experience: on the mystical, or almost mystical assurance, recorded at the close of *The Holy Grail*.

> Let visions of the night or of the day
> Come, as they will; and many a time they come,
> Until this earth he walks on seems not earth,
> This light that strikes his eyeball is not light,
> This air that smites his forehead is not air
> But vision—yea, his very hand and foot—
> In moments when he feels he cannot die,
> And knows himself no vision to himself,
> Nor the high God a vision, nor that One
> Who rose again.

That is no borrowed language, no such working up of many possibilities into one plausibility as Victorian theology was so largely engaged in. It is Tennyson's own voice: you hear it again in 'The Ancient Sage'.

> The first gray streak of earliest summer-dawn,
> The last long stripe of waning crimson gloom,
> As if the late and early were but one—
> A height, a broken grange, a grove, a flower
> Had murmurs 'Lost and gone and lost and gone!'
> A breath, a whisper—some divine farewell—

Desolate sweetness—far and far away—
What had he loved, what had he lost, the boy?
I know not and I speak of what has been.
      And more, my son! for more than once when I
Sat all alone, revolving in myself
The word that is the symbol of myself,
The mortal limit of the self was loosed,
And past into the Nameless, as a cloud
Melts into Heaven. I touch'd my limbs, the limbs
Were strange not mine—and yet no shade of doubt
But utter clearness, and thro' loss of Self
The gain of such large life as match'd with ours
Were Sun to spark—unshadowable in words,
Themselves but shadows of a shadow-world.

It is Tennyson's own voice, telling of what he has known, and as such his age received it. *Perhibet testimonium de his, et scripsit haec: et scimus quia verum est testimonium ejus.*

But what in this vision of the world is the place of Christianity? Or, to put the question as Tennyson and his contemporaries felt it, when the traditional forms of faith have been subjected to the analysis of criticism and science, what will remain? The inerrancy of Scripture had gone, carrying with it both the cosmogony on which the scheme of redemption was founded, and the assurance of immortality. Was there anything left which might serve as a spiritual directive of progress? Now, from Tennyson's early grief over the loss of Hallam, there had emerged a belief in what I may call a hierarchy of types, each realizing possibilities only latent at a lower level, and indicating fresh possibilities to be realized at a higher. And here was a creed, or a supposition, reconcilable at once with the monistic or pantheistic trend which science was imposing on our thought, and on the other hand with historic Christianity, and the sublime claims which Christianity makes for personality, and on it. Granted that an initial act of faith is required, because, so far as we can see, progress may be morally downward as well as upward: granted also that the implied metaphysic will be in detail shadowy—a philosophy of Somehow, wavering between a hopeful doubt and a doubtful hope—yet it was open to any Christian to accept the hypothesis, in the assurance that the highest in this human hierarchy is a man, and that man Incarnate God. Thus the argument is rounded off, because, so conceived, personality is not an incident in evolution, but its consummation. Here then was a body of conviction, won from doubt, and even despair, which gave to thousands, in the season of their distress, the guidance and assurance for which they asked.

There is one passage in Tennyson and, as far as I can recall, one only, where he rises to the full poetic height of this argument, to a complete poetic apprehension of his own idea. I mean the close of *In Memoriam*.

> And rise, O moon, from yonder down,
>   Till over down and over dale
>   All night the shining vapour sail
> And pass the silent-lighted town,
>
> The white-faced halls, the glancing rills,
>   And catch at every mountain head,
>   And o'er the friths that branch and spread
> Their sleeping silver through the hills;
>
> And touch with shade the bridal doors,
>   With tender gloom the roof, the wall;
>   And breaking let the splendour fall
> To spangle all the happy shores
>
> By which they rest, and ocean sounds,
>   And, star and system rolling past,
>   A soul shall draw from out the vast
> And strike his being into bounds.

> *Con quanto di quel salmo è poscia scripto.*

Here, or so it seems to me, Tennyson has done the utmost that can be asked of a poet, in one act embracing the whole range of his deepest personal thought, and rendering it in the loveliest and most natural imagery that poetry affords, the moonlit sea and the lovers sleeping by its shores.

CLEANTH BROOKS

The Motivation of Tennyson's Weeper

Tennyson is perhaps the last English poet one would think of associating with the subtleties of paradox and ambiguity. He is not the thoughtless poet, to be sure: he grapples—particularly in his later period—with the 'big' questions which were up for his day; and he struggles manfully with them. But the struggle, as Tennyson conducted it, was usually kept out of the grammar and symbolism of the poetry itself. Like his own protagonist in *In Memoriam*, Tennyson 'fought his doubts'—he does not typically build them into the structure of the poetry itself as enriching ambiguities.

Yet substantially true as this generalization is, Tennyson was not always successful in avoiding the ambiguous and the paradoxical; and indeed, in some of his poems his failure to avoid them becomes a saving grace. The lyric 'Tears, Idle Tears' is a very good instance. It is a poem which, from a strictly logical point of view, Tennyson may be thought to have blundered into. But, whether he blundered into it or not, the poem gains from the fact that it finds its unity in a principle of organization higher than that which seems to be operative in many of Tennyson's more 'thoughtful' poems.

Any account of the poem may very well begin with a consideration of the nature of the tears. Are they *idle* tears? Or are they not rather the most meaningful of tears? Does not the very fact that they are 'idle' (that is, tears occasioned by no immediate grief) become in itself a guarantee of the fact

From *The Well Wrought Urn.* Copyright © 1947, 1975 by Harcourt Brace Jovanovich Inc.

that they spring from a deeper, more universal cause?

It would seem so, and that the poet is thus beginning his poem with a paradox. For the third line of the poem indicates that there is no doubt in the speaker's mind about the origin of the tears in some divine despair. They 'rise in the heart'—for all that they have been first announced as 'idle'.

But the question of whether Tennyson is guilty of (or to be complimented upon) a use of paradox may well wait upon further discussion. At this point in our commentary, it is enough to observe that Tennyson has chosen to open his poem with some dramatic boldness—if not with the bold step of equating 'idle' with 'from the depth of some divine despair', then at least with a bold and violent reversal of the speaker's first characterization of his tears.

The tears 'rise in the heart' as the speaker looks upon a scene of beauty and tranquillity. Does looking on the 'happy Autumn-fields' bring to mind the days that are no more? The poet does not say so. The tears rise to the eyes in looking on the 'happy Autumn-fields' *and* thinking of the days that are no more. The poet himself does not stand responsible for any closer linkage between these actions, though, as a matter of fact, most of us will want to make a closer linkage here. For, if we change 'happy Autumn-fields', say, to 'happy April-fields', the two terms tend to draw apart. The fact that the fields are autumn-fields which, though happy, point back to something which is over—which is finished—*does* connect them with the past and therefore properly suggests to the observer thoughts about that past.

To sum up: The first stanza has a unity, but it is not a unity which finds its sanctions in the ordinary logic of language. Its sanctions are to be found in the dramatic context, and, to my mind, there alone. Indeed, the stanza suggests the play of the speaker's mind as the tears unexpectedly start, tears for which there is no apparent occasion, and as he searches for an explanation of them. He calls them 'idle', but, even as he says 'I know not what they mean', he realizes that they must spring from the depths of his being—is willing, with his very next words, to associate them with 'some divine despair'. Moreover, the real occasion of the tears, though the speaker himself comes to realize it only as he approaches the end of the stanza, is the thought about the past. It is psychologically and dramatically right, therefore, that the real occasion should be stated explicitly only with the last line of the stanza.

This first stanza, then, recapitulates the surprise and bewilderment in the speaker's own mind, and sets the problem which the succeeding stanzas are to analyze. The dramatic effect may be described as follows: the stanza seems, not a meditated observation, but a speech begun impulsively—a statement which the speaker has begun before he knows how he will end it.

In the second stanza we are not surprised to have the poet characterize the days that are no more as 'sad', but there is some shock in hearing him apply to them the adjective 'fresh'. Again, the speaker does not pause to explain: the word 'fresh' actually begins the stanza. Yet the adjective justifies itself.

The past is fresh as with a dawn freshness—as fresh as the first beam glittering on the sail of an incoming ship. The ship is evidently expected; it brings friends, friends 'up from the underworld'. On the surface, the comparison is innocent: the 'underworld' is merely the antipodes, the world which lies below the horizon—an underworld in the sense displayed in old-fashioned geographies with their sketches illustrating the effects of the curvature of the earth. The sails, which catch the light and glitter, will necessarily be the part first seen of any ship which is coming 'up' over the curve of the earth.

But the word 'underworld' will necessarily suggest the underworld of Greek mythology, the realm of the shades, the abode of the dead. The attempt to characterize the freshness of the days that are no more has, thus, developed, almost imperceptibly, into a further characterization of the days themselves as belonging, not to our daylight world, but to an 'underworld'. This suggestion is, of course, strengthened in the lines that follow in which the ship metaphor is reversed so as to give us a picture of sadness: evening, the last glint of sunset light on the sail of a ship

> That sinks with all we love below the verge.

The conjunction of the qualities of sadness and freshness is reinforced by the fact that the same basic symbol—the light on the sails of a ship hull down—has been employed to suggest both qualities. With the third stanza, the process is carried one stage further: the two qualities (with the variant of 'strange' for 'fresh') are explicitly linked together:

> Ah, sad and strange as in dark summer dawns...

And here the poet is not content to suggest the qualities of sadness and strangeness by means of two different, even if closely related, figures. In this third stanza the special kind of sadness and strangeness is suggested by one and the same figure.

It is a figure developed in some detail. It, too, involves a dawn scene, though ironically so, for the beginning of the new day is to be the beginning of the long night for the dying man. The dying eyes, the poem suggests, have been for some time awake—long enough to have had time to watch the

> ... casement slowly [grow] a glimmering square.

The dying man, soon to sleep the lasting sleep, is more fully awake than the 'half-awaken'd birds' whose earliest pipings come to his dying ears. We know why these pipings are sad; but why are they *strange*? Because to the person hearing a bird's song for the last time, it will seem that he has never before really heard one. The familiar sound will take on a quality of unreality—of strangeness.

If this poem were merely a gently melancholy reverie on the sweet sadness of the past, stanzas II and III would have no place in the poem. But the poem is no such reverie: the images from the past rise up with a strange clarity and sharpness that shock the speaker. Their sharpness and freshness account for the sudden tears and for the psychological problem with which the speaker wrestles in the poem. If the past would only remain melancholy but dimmed, sad but worn and familiar, we should have no problem and no poem. At least, we should not have *this* poem; we should certainly not have the intensity of the last stanza.

That intensity, if justified, must grow out of a sense of the apparent nearness and intimate presence of what is irrevocably beyond reach: the days that are no more must be more than the conventional 'dear, dead days beyond recall'. They must be beyond recall, yet alive—tantalizingly vivid and near. It is only thus that we can feel the speaker justified in calling them

> Dear as remember'd kisses after death,
> And sweet as those by hopeless fancy feign'd
> On lips that are for others.

It is only thus that we can accept the culminating paradox of

> O Death in Life, the days that are no more.

We have already observed, in the third stanza, how the speaker compares the strangeness and sadness of the past to the sadness of the birds' piping as it sounds to dying ears. There is a rather brilliant ironic contrast involved in the comparison. The speaker, a living man, in attempting to indicate how sad and strange to him are the days of the past, says that they are as sad and strange as is the natural activity of the awakening world to the man who is dying: the dead past seems to the living man as unfamiliar and fresh in its sadness as the living present seems to the dying man. There is more here, however, than a mere, ironic reversal of roles; in each case there is the sense of being irrevocably barred out from the known world.

This ironic contrast, too, accounts for the sense of desperation which runs through the concluding lines of the poem. The kisses feigned by 'hopeless fancy' are made the more precious because of the very hopelessness; but memory takes on the quality of fancy. It is equally hopeless—the kisses can as little be renewed as those 'feign'd/On lips that are for others' can be obtained. The realized past has become as fabulous as the unrealizable future. The days that are no more are as dear as the one, as sweet as the other, the speaker says; and it does not matter whether we compare them to the one or to the other or to both: it comes to the same thing.

But the days that are no more are not merely 'dear' and 'sweet'; they are 'deep' and 'wild'. Something has happened to the grammar here. How can the *days* be 'deep as love' or 'wild with all regret'? And what is the status of the exclamation 'O Death in Life'? Is it merely a tortured cry like 'O God! the days that are no more'? Or is it a loose appositive: 'the days that are no more are a kind of death in life'?

The questions are not asked in a censorious spirit, as if there were no justification for Tennyson's licence here. But it is important to see how much licence the poem requires, and the terms on which the reader decides to accord it justification. What one finds on closer examination is not muddlement but richness. But it is a richness achieved through principles of organization which many an admirer of the poet has difficulty in allowing to the 'obscure' modern poet.

For example, how can the days of the past be *deep*? Here, of course, the problem is not very difficult. The past is buried within one: the days that are no more constitute the deepest level of one's being, and the tears that arise from thinking on them may be said to come from the 'depth of some divine despair'. But how can the days be 'wild with all regret'? The extension demanded here is more ambitious. In matter of fact, it is the speaker, the man, who is made wild with regret by thinking on the days.

One can, of course, justify the adjective as a transferred epithet on the model of Vergil's *maestum timorem*; and perhaps this was Tennyson's own conscious justification (if, indeed, the need to justify it ever occurred to him). But one can make a better case than a mere appeal to the authority of an established literary convention. There is a sense in which the man and the remembered days are one and the same. A man is the sum of his memories. The adjective which applies to the man made wild with regret can apply to those memories which make him wild with regret. For, does the man charge the memories with his own passion, or is it the memories that give the emotion to him? If we pursue the matter far enough, we come to a point where the distinction lapses. Perhaps I should say, more accurately, adopting the metaphor of the poem itself, we *descend* to a depth where the distinction lapses. The days that are no more are *deep* and *wild*, buried but not dead—below the surface and unthought of, yet at the deepest core of being, secretly alive.

The past *should* be tame, fettered, brought to heel; it is not. It is capable of breaking forth and coming to the surface. The word 'wild' is bold, therefore, but justified. It reasserts the line of development which has been maintained throughout the earlier stanzas: 'fresh', 'strange', and now 'wild'—all adjectives which suggest passionate, irrational life. The word 'wild', thus, not only pulls into focus the earlier paradoxes, but is the final stage in the preparation for the culminating paradox, 'O Death in Life'.

The last stanza evokes an intense emotional response from the reader. The claim could hardly be made good by the stanza taken in isolation. The stanza leans heavily upon the foregoing stanzas and the final paradox draws heavily upon the great metaphors in stanzas II and III. This is as it should be. The justification for emphasizing the fact here is this: the poem, for all its illusion of impassioned speech—with the looseness and *apparent* confusion of unpremeditated speech—is very tightly organized. It represents an organic structure; and the intensity of the total effect is a reflection of the total structure.

The reader, I take it, will hardly be disposed to quarrel with the general statement of the theme of the poem as it is given in the foregoing account; and he will probably find himself in accord with this general estimate of the poem's value. But the reader may well feel that the amount of attention given to the structure of the poem is irrelevant, if not positively bad. In particular, he may find the emphasis on paradox, ambiguity, and ironic contrast displeasing. He has not been taught to expect these in Tennyson, and he has had the general impression that the presence of these qualities represents the intrusion of alien, 'unpoetic' matter.

I have no wish to intellectualize the poem—to make conscious and artful what was actually spontaneous and simple. Nevertheless, the qualities of ironic contrast and paradox *do* exist in the poem; and they *do* have a relation to the poem's dramatic power.

Those who still feel that 'simple eloquence' is enough might compare 'Tears, Idle Tears' with another of Tennyson's poems which has somewhat the same subject matter and hints of the same imagery, the lyric 'Break, Break, Break'.

> Break, break, break,
>   On thy cold gray stones, O Sea!
> And I would that my tongue could utter
>   The thoughts that arise in me.
>
> O well for the fisherman's boy,
>   That he shouts with his sister at play!
> O well for the sailor lad,
>   That he sings in his boat on the bay!
>
> And the stately ships go on
>   To their haven under the hill;
> But O for the touch of a vanish'd hand,
>   And the sound of a voice that is still!

Break, break, break,
　　At the foot of thy crags, O Sea!
But the tender grace of a day that is dead
　　Will never come back to me.

It is an easier poem than 'Tears', and, in one sense, a less confusing poem. But it is also a much thinner poem, and unless we yield comfortably and easily to the strain of gentle melancholy, actually a coarser and a more confused poem. For example, the ships are said to be 'stately', but this observation is idle and finally irrelevant. What relation has their stateliness to the experience of grief? (Perhaps one may argue that the term suggests that they go on to fulfil their missions, unperturbed and with no regard for the speaker's mood. But this interpretation is forced, and even under forcing, the yield of relevance is small.)

Again, consider the status of the past as it appears in this poem: the hand is vanished, the voice is still. It is true, as the poem itself indicates, that there is a sense in which the hand has not vanished and the voice is yet heard; otherwise we should not have the poem at all. But the poet makes no effort to connect this activity, still alive in memory, with its former 'actual' life. He is content to keep close to the conventional prose account of such matters. Memory in this poem does not become a kind of life: it is just 'memory'—whatever that is—and, in reading the poem, we are not forced beyond the bounds of our conventional thinking on the subject.

In the same way, the elements of the line, 'the tender grace of a day that is dead', remain frozen at the conventional prose level. The day is 'dead'; the 'tender grace' of it will never 'come back' to him. We are not encouraged to take the poignance of his present memory of it as a ghost from the tomb. The poet does not recognize that his experience represents such an ironical resurrection; nor does he allow the metaphors buried in 'dead' and 'come back' to suffer a resurrection into vigorous poetic life. With such phenomena the poet is not concerned.

Of course, the poet *need* not be concerned with them; I should agree that we have no right to demand that this poem should explore the nature of memory as 'Tears, Idle Tears' explores it. At moments, men are unaccountably saddened by scenes which are in themselves placid and even happy. The poet is certainly entitled, if he chooses, to let it go at that. Yet, it should be observed that in avoiding the psychological exploration of the experience, the poet risks losing dramatic force.

Mere psychological analysis is, of course, not enough to insure dramatic force; and such analysis, moreover, carries its own risks: the poem may become unnatural and coldly rhetorical. But when the poet is able, as in 'Tears, Idle Tears', to analyze his experience, and in the full light of the disparity and even apparent contradiction of the various elements, bring them into a new unity, he secures not only richness and depth but dramatic power as well. Our conventional accounts of poetry which oppose emotion to intellect, 'lyric simplicity' to 'thoughtful meditation', have done no service to the cause of poetry. The opposition is not only merely superficial: it falsifies the real relationships. For the lyric quality, if it be genuine, is not the result of some transparent and 'simple' redaction of a theme or a situation which is somehow poetic in itself; it is, rather, the result of an imaginative grasp of diverse materials—but an imaginative grasp so sure that it may show itself to the reader as unstudied and unpredictable without for a moment relaxing its hold on the intricate and complex stuff which it carries.

MARSHALL McLUHAN

Tennyson and Picturesque Poetry

In his *Autobiographies* W. B. Yeats mentions that a great advantage which he enjoyed over his fellows of the Cheshire Cheese was his acquaintance with Arthur Hallam's review of Tennyson's poems (*The Englishman's Magazine*, 1831). Hallam's essay is worth close study. It is a manifesto as decisive in the issues it raises as Wordsworth's Preface to *Lyrical Ballads* or Mr. Eliot's 'Tradition and the Individual Talent'. In 1895 Yeats found it invaluable as a key to the French symbolists who were puzzling his friends. Had it been understood in 1831, the energies of the Pre-Raphaelites might have found more direct channels to what in English poetry did not occur until the advent of Joyce, Pound, and Eliot.

Hallam's essay suggests that from his meeting with Tennyson at Trinity in 1829 until his death in 1833 his intense aesthetic interests were of the greatest importance to Tennyson's development as a poet. Until 1842 Tennyson seems to have retained Hallam's insights exclusively. Thereafter he began to admit rhetoric and reflection into his verse, wonderfully purging this admixture from the great 'Rizpah' of 1880 and from several subsequent poems.

Hallam's aesthetic theory was the result of studying Dante through the poetry of Keats. But the extraordinary precision and elaboration of English impressionist criticism and speculation, which had persisted from the 1780s, was still there to sharpen perception and judgement in 1830. The main effort of speculation had been directed towards landscape painting, for reasons which will be mentioned later on. All the Romantic poets were

From *Critical Essays on the Poetry of Tennyson*, edited by John Killham. Copyright © 1960 by John Killham. Barnes and Noble Books, 1960.

nurtured in this speculation; but Hallam's essay draws into a sharp focus some of the neglected implications for poetry:

> Whenever the mind of the artist suffers itself to be occupied, during its periods of creation, by any other predominant motive than the desire of beauty, the result is false in art.

Of course, he goes on, there may be states of mind in which thought and reflection are themselves unified by intellectual emotion:

> But though possible, it is hardly probable: for a man whose reveries take a reasoning turn, and who is accustomed to measure his ideas by their logical relations rather than the congruity of the sentiments to which they refer, will be apt to mistake the pleasure he has in knowing a thing to be true, for the pleasure he would have in knowing it to be beautiful, and so will pile his thoughts in a rhetorical battery, that they may convince, instead of letting them flow in a natural course of contemplation, that they may enrapture. It would not be difficult to show, by reference to the most admired poems of Wordsworth, that he is frequently chargeable with this error; and that much has been said by him which is good as philosophy, powerful as rhetoric, but false as poetry.

This passage arrives at once at the twentieth-century controversy over poetry and beliefs. It implies the Symbolist and Imagist doctrine that the place of ideas in poetry is not that of logical enunciation but of immediate sensation or experience. Rhetoric must go, said the symbolists. Ideas as ideas must go. They may return as part of a landscape that is ordered by other means. They may enter into a unified experience as one kind of fact. They may contribute to an aesthetic emotion, not as a system of demonstration but as part of a total order which is to be contemplated.

So Hallam pronounces in favour of the Cockney School over 'the Lakers':

> We shall not hesitate to express our conviction, that the cockney school (as it was termed in derision from a cursory view of its accidental circumstances) contained more genuine inspiration, and adhered more steadily to that portion of truth which it embraced, than any *form* of art that has existed in this country since Milton... Shelley and Keats were indeed of opposite genius; the one was vast, impetuous, and sublime, the other... does not generalize or allegorize nature; his imagination works with few symbols, and reposes willingly on what is freely given... They are both poets of sensation rather than reflection... Rich and clear were their perceptions of visible forms; full and deep their feelings of music. So vivid was the delight attending the simple exertions of eye and ear, that it became mingled more and more with their trains of active thought, and tended to absorb their whole being into the energy of sense. Other poets seek for images to illustrate their conceptions; these men had no need to seek; they lived in a world of images; for the most important and extensive

portion of their life consisted in those emotions which are immediately conversant with sensation...Hence they are not descriptive, they are picturesque.

The force of this last antithesis depends on knowledge of the aesthetic developments of the eighteenth century, which are summarized in Christopher Hussey's classic *The Picturesque* (1927). 'The picturesque view of nature,' says Hussey, 'led towards the abstract appreciation of colour and light that in painting marks the work of Turner and Constable.' At the end of the epoch of picturesque experiment and exploration there is Cézanne in painting, and Rimbaud in poetry. That is, the impressionists began with sensation, discovered 'abstraction', and achieved, finally, a metaphysical art. The picturesque begins with work like Thomson's *Seasons*, in the search for significant art-emotion amidst natural scenes; and it achieved plenary realization in Rimbaud's metaphysical landscapes—*Les Illuminations*. The early Romantics sought aesthetic emotion in natural scenes; the later Romantics confidently evoked art-emotion from art-situations. The early Romantics ransacked nature, as the Pre-Raphaelites did literature and history, for situations which would provide moments of intense perception. The Symbolists went to work more methodically. As A. N. Whitehead showed, the great discovery of the nineteenth century was not this or that fact about nature, but the discovery of the technique of invention, so that modern science can now discover whatever it needs to discover. And Rimbaud and Mallarmé, following the lead of Edgar Poe's aesthetic, made the same advance in poetic technique that Whitehead pointed out in the physical sciences. The new method is to work backwards from the particular effect to the objective correlative or poetic means of evoking that precise effect, just as the chemist begins with the end-product and then seeks the formula which will produce it. Mr. Eliot states this discovery, which has guided his own poetic activity since 1910 or so, in his essay on *Hamlet*:

> The only way of expressing emotion in the form of art is by finding an 'objective correlative'; in other words, a set of objects, a situation, a chain of events which shall be the formula of that *particular* emotion; such that when the external facts, which must terminate in sensory experience, are given, the emotion is immediately evoked.

Mr. Eliot is saying *à propos* of 'sensory experience' exactly what Hallam was saying about Shelley and Keats: 'They are both poets of sensation rather than reflection.' Clearly Hallam is setting them above Wordsworth in tendency rather than achievement. And the tendency which he approves in them is precisely what we have more recently come to consider as the 'unification of sensibility'. Hallam refused to accept the magnificent rhetoric of Wordsworth as a substitute for such an integral poetry. That such integrity was possible he was sure, because of the poetry of Keats especially. We have the achievement of Joyce, Yeats, Pound, and Eliot to assure us not only that Hallam was entirely right but that Keats had not gone far enough.

What must have been the effect of Tennyson's five years of such conversation and study with Hallam? The volumes of 1830 and 1833 try to surpass Keats in richness of texture and sensuous impact. And 'Mariana' is there to prove that the most sophisticated symbolist poetry could be written fifty years before the Symbolists. On a dependent and uncertain temper such as Tennyson's the effect of the death of the vigorous and clear-headed Hallam was not merely that of personal loss. It was more nearly the loss of his poetic insight and his critical judgement.

Hallam's essay goes on to define the kind of poetry which his age demanded, and which Tennyson was later to provide in such abundance:

> Since then this demand on the reader for activity, when he wants to peruse his author in a luxurious passiveness, is the very thing that moves his bile, it is obvious that those writers will be always most popular who require the least degree of exertion. Hence, whatever is mixed up with art, and appears under its semblance, is always more favourably regarded than art free and unalloyed. Hence, half the fashionable poems in the world are mere rhetoric and half the remainder are, perhaps, not liked by the generality for their substantial merits. Hence, likewise, of the really pure compositions, those are most universally agreeable which take for their primary subject the usual passions of the heart, and deal with them in a simple state, without applying the transforming powers of high imagination. Love, friendship, ambition, religion, etc., are matters of daily experience even amongst unimaginative tempers. The forces of association, therefore, are ready to work in these directions, and little effort of will is necessary to follow the artist. For the same reason, such subjects often excite a partial power of composition, which is no sign of a truly poetic organization. We are very far from wishing to depreciate this class of poems, whose influence is so extensive, and communicates so refined a pleasure. We contend only that the facility with which its impressions are communicated is no proof of its elevation as a form of art, but rather the contrary.

Hallam is insisting, just as much later Mallarmé, Eliot, and Valéry were to insist, that in 'pure poetry', the poetry of suggestion rather than statement, or poetry in which the statements are themselves suggestions and in which the poetic form is the mode of the creative process itself, the reader is co-creator with the poet; since the *effect* depends on the reader's precision of response, and the poet is himself only another reader of his own poetry. So that Harold Nicolson showed himself unaware of this class of poetry, which is often present in Tennyson, when he remarked that 'of all poets, Tennyson should be read very carelessly or not at all'.

When Hallam finally turns to introduce Tennyson, he makes claims which the modern critic is now prepared to accept with little modification:

> Mr. Tennyson belongs decidedly to the class we have already described as Poets of Sensation... We have remarked five distinctive excellences of his own manner. First, his luxuriance of imagination, and at the same time, his control over it. Secondly, his power of embodying himself in ideal characters or rather moods of character, with such extreme accuracy of adjustment, that the circumstances of the narration seem to have a natural correspondence with the predominant feeling, and, as it were, to be evolved from it by assimilative force. Thirdly, his vivid, picturesque delineation of objects, and the peculiar skill with which he holds all of them *fused*, to borrow a metaphor from science, in a medium of strong emotion. Fourthly, the variety of his lyrical measures, and exquisite modulation of harmonious words and cadences to the swell and fall of the feelings expressed. Fifthly, the elevated habits of thought, implied in these compositions, and imparting a mellow soberness of tone, more impressive to our minds, than if the author had drawn up a set of opinions in verse, and sought to instruct the understanding rather than to communicate the love of beauty to the heart.

The fact that Tennyson is in great measure a landscape poet led Hallam to define him in 1831 by the then technical term 'picturesque'. In 1897 Francis Palgrave, another intimate acquaintance, published *Landscape in Poetry from Homer to Tennyson*. It is a poor book, lacking in technical and critical insights, but it makes plain the kind of traditional perspective in which Tennyson set his craftsman's interest in the problem of landscape.

From the first of Thomson's *Seasons* (1726) to the *Lyrical Ballads* of Wordsworth and Coleridge (1798) English landscape art in paint, poetry, and prose had undergone a very great technical development, which was also a growth of awareness at once psychological and naturalistic. Scientific observation and psychological experience met in landscape. Shelley, Keats, and Tennyson, as well as Ruskin and the Pre-Raphaelites, were not only quite conscious of these eighteenth-century discoveries, but set themselves the task of further advance along the same lines. It might be suggested that landscape offered several attractive advantages to the poets of the mid-eighteenth century. It meant for one thing an extension of the Baroque interest in *la peinture de la pensée*, which the study of Seneca had suggested to Montaigne and Bacon and Browne—an interest which reached a maximal development, so far as the technique of direct statement permitted, in Pascal, Racine, and Alexander Pope.

But landscape offered a broader and less exacting course for those who were preoccupied with the new psychological interests on one hand and with means of evading the new insistence on non-metaphorical and mathematical statement as the mode of poetry, on the other hand. With Blake there are many moments when the new landscape interests and techniques are fused with the wit and paradox of Pope. But his success passed unnoticed until it had been reduplicated by the Symbolists. Wordsworth, Shelley, Keats, and Tennyson typically use landscape without the precision and wit provided by apposition of situation without copula. They achieve an exclusive rather than an inclusive consciousness.

Looking back over the landscape developments of a century and more, Ruskin in introducing the Pre-Raphaelites in 1851 summed up what was a commonplace to Wordsworth in 1798 and also to Tennyson in 1830:

> The sudden and universal Naturalism, or inclination to copy ordinary natural objects, which manifested itself among the painters of Europe, at the moment when the invention of printing superseded their legendary labours, was no false instinct. It was misunderstood and misapplied, but it came at the right time, and has maintained itself through all kinds of abuse; presenting in the recent schools of landscape, perhaps only the first fruits of its power. That instinct was urging every painter in Europe at the same moment to his true duty—*the faithful representation of all objects of historical interest, or of natural beauty existent at the period*; representation such as might at once aid the advance of sciences, and keep faithful record of every monument of past ages which was likely to be swept away in the approaching eras of revolutionary change.

This amalgam of moral duty, aesthetic experience, scientific discovery, and political revolution was first effected in the age of Leibniz, Locke, and Newton; and we are still engaged today in contemplating its unpredictable derivatives. For the moment, and in the arts, the terminus appears as the fascinating landscapes of *Finnegans Wake* and *Four Quartets*. So that, if we take our bearings with reference to this new work, it will be easier to assess the intentions and achievement of Tennyson, whose work falls just midway between that of James Thomson and Mr. Eliot. The huge tapestries of the *Wake* are not merely visual but auditory, talking and moving pictures; not just spatial in their unity, but effecting a simultaneous presence of all modes of human consciousness, primitive and sophisticated. Rocks, rivers, trees, animals, persons, and places utter with classical dramatic decorum the kind of being that is theirs. The poet in effacing himself utterly has become a universal Aeolian Harp reverberating the various degrees of knowledge and existence in such a hymn of life as only the stars of Pythagoras were ever conceived to have sung. To this concert there came all the arts and sciences, trivial and quadrivial, ancient and modern, in an orchestrated harmony that had first been envisaged by Joyce's master Stéphane Mallarmé.

Flaubert and Baudelaire had presided over the great city landscape of *Ulysses*. And Mr. Eliot's *The Waste Land* in 1922 was a new technical modulation of *Ulysses*, the latter of which had begun to appear in 1917. The *Quartets* owe a great deal to the *Wake*, as does *The Cocktail Party*. There is in all these works a vision of the community of men and creatures which is not so much ethical as metaphysical. And it had been, in poetry, due to the technical innovations of Baudelaire, Laforgue, and Rimbaud that it was possible to render this vision immediately in verse without the extraneous aids of rhetoric or logical reflection and statement. The principal innovation was that of *le paysage intérieur* or the psychological landscape. This landscape, by means of discontinuity, which was first developed in picturesque painting, effected the apposition of widely diverse objects as a means of establishing what Mr. Eliot has called 'an objective correlative' for a state of mind. The openings of 'Prufrock', 'Gerontion', and *The Waste Land* illustrate Mr. Eliot's growth in the adaptation of this technique, as he passed from the influence of Laforgue to that of Rimbaud, from personal to impersonal manipulation of experience. Whereas in external landscape diverse things lie side by side, so in psychological landscape the juxtaposition of various things and experiences becomes a precise musical means of orchestrating that which could never be rendered by systematic discourse. Landscape is the means of presenting, without the copula of logical enunciation, experiences which are united in existence but not in conceptual thought. Syntax becomes music, as in Tennyson's 'Mariana'.

In the landscapes of the *Quartets* as in those of the *Wake* everything speaks. There is no single or personal speaker of the *Quartets*, not even the Tiresias of 'Gerontion' and *The Waste Land*. It is the places and things which utter themselves. And this is also a stage of technique and experience achieved by Pound in his *Cantos*, and by St. Jean Perse, just as it had earlier been reached by Mallarmé in *Un Coup de Dés*. Browning was groping for it in *The Ring and the Book*. One might say that as the effect of Laforgue had been to open Mr. Eliot's mind to the effects of Donne and the Metaphysicals, so the effect of Rimbaud was to make him more fully aware of the means by which Dante achieved a zoning of states of mind through symbolic landscape.

Facing this unrivalled sophistication and self-awareness of metaphysical landscape in modern poetry, it is easier to observe what the eighteenth century was striving for as well as what effects Wordsworth, Coleridge, and their successors were interested in obtaining. Hitherto the eighteenth century has been examined in retrospect from Wordsworth and Coleridge rather than from Keats and Tennyson. The Lake poets have often been supposed to have exhausted its potencies and to have settled its problems. Such, however, was not the view of Arthur Hallam and Alfred Tennyson. But looked at now across the work of Cézanne and Rimbaud it takes on a different and more impressive character than has usually been allowed it aesthetically. And today we are far from having explored the speculations of Burke and Blake, or even of Knight and Price. What is put forward here as a suggested view of the eighteenth-century attitude to landscape has primarily relevance to what became Tennyson's idea of the function of landscape in poetry. For Tennyson, while accepting much of Wordsworth, certainly differed from him in important respects.

It is plain, for example, that Tennyson did not agree with the author of *The Prelude* in expecting an automatic amelioration of the human condition from the workings of external landscape on passive childhood, youth, and age. Tennyson could see very little valuable truth in Wordsworth's programme for the recovery of a terrestrial paradise. He had many reasons for thinking it what Wordsworth incredulously queried in the preface to *The Excursion*:

> A history only of departed things,
> Or a mere fiction of what never was?

Then Wordsworth takes up the great eighteenth-century theme:

> For the discerning intellect of Man,
> When wedded to this goodly universe
> In love and holy passion, shall find these
> [i.e. 'Paradise and groves']
> A simple produce of the common day,
> I, long before the blissful hour arrives,
> Would chant, in lonely peace, the spousal verse
> Of this great consummation:—and, by words
> Which speak of nothing more than what we are,
> Would I arouse the sensual from their sleep
> Of Death, and win the vacant and the vain
> To noble raptures; while my voice proclaims
> How exquisitely the individual Mind
> ...to the external World
> Is fitted:—and how exquisitely, too—
> Theme this but little heard of among men—
> The external World is fitted to the Mind;

the notion of this pre-established harmony between the individual mind and the external world is the key to the eighteenth-century passion for landscape. Wordsworth naturally underrates the degree to which this 'theme' was rehearsed among men from 1730 onwards, if only because anybody tends to be least aware of the decades immediately before his own time. They are taken for granted, as known. For by then the civilized world had much recovered from the dismay felt by Pascal and his contemporaries at the vision of an infinity of worlds, and had begun to speculate on the possible psychological nexus between man and a geometrically perfect universe. They turned from reflection on man's wretched insignificance to the thought of his sublimity of comprehension, by a simple reversal of the telescope.

Swift spotted the human vanity in the workings of this psychological mechanism and spoofed it at once in *Gulliver's Travels*, but without disturbing the course towards which things were shaping. For it was to be in the main a century of simple psychological mechanisms which were not to break down until Malthus and Darwin had shifted attention to the biological level. It was Leibniz who, as Professor Lovejoy suggests, translated the cosmological and mathematical views of his time into psychological terms. The hierarchy of creatures in his monadology 'is defined primarily in psychological rather than morphological terms; it is by the levels of consciousness which severally characterize them, the degrees of adequacy and clarity with which they "mirror" or represent the rest of the universe, that the monads are differentiated'.

As soon as Newton had added to this view the proof that the universe which we (or rocks, trees, flowers) mirror is a marvel of automatic precision, the road is clear to Wordsworth's therapeutic idea of the educational power of the external world. For it was not enough to know that the mind of man is exquisitely fitted to the external world. It was also necessary to be sure that the external world was exquisitely harmonious with itself. It naturally follows for the early Wordsworth and Coleridge that the best mirrors of the radiant universe of life are those simple, spontaneous natures who have received the least admixture of social artifice and corruption. For it is the necessary operation of traditional society to implant within our natures 'a universe of death'. It has been not uncommon to accept not only this phrase from *The Prelude* but Wordsworth's poetic as expressive of a revulsion from the Newtonian world of science. Professor Willey, for example, says that Wordsworth's 'more positive beliefs, those by which he appears in reaction against the scientific tradition, were built up by him out of his own poetic experiences . . . to animize the "real" world, the "universe of death" that the "mechanical" system of philosophy had produced, but to do so without either using an exploded mythology or fabricating a new one, this was the special task and mission of Wordsworth'.

But neither Wordsworth nor Tennyson rejected science as presenting a 'universe of death'. For if they had done so there would have been no predominance of landscape in their aesthetics, and, most pertinently, there would have been none of Tennyson's celebrated 'accuracy' of observation and description, which, of course, can be matched in the painters and in poets like Barnes and Hopkins. Rather, in their view, science and poetry were near twins, of which poetry was a little the elder. And *The Prelude* passage (Book xiv) not only locates the 'universe of death' as a product of divided aims, selfish passions, mean cares and low pursuits, but goes on to contrast it with that which moves with light and life informed,

Actual, divine, and true.

It is the objective world observed by science and mirrored by simple, loving souls which Wordsworth sets over against the toyshop of vanities that is the soul of man, sensual and dark, under the régime of social custom and private egotism.

The study and discipline of the passions had from the time of Aristotle's *Rhetoric* been a branch of that art. It was the business of the orator to enlist the passions for political ends; and the function of literature was to enlarge, purge, and order the passions for the exercise and solace of the good life. Dr. Johnson was simply expressing this view when he said of Richardson that 'he teaches the passions to move at the command of virtue'. It is important for a grasp of the meaning of landscape in the eighteenth century to see that traditional politics and literature were, in contemporary opinion, being supplanted by science. Men took readily to the notion that the disordered passions of the human heart might be restored to their pristine integrity by the automatic and unconscious operation of landscape on the passive mind—especially when a Newton had guaranteed the exquisite mathematical order of the external world.

The first published essay of Edmund Burke was his ironical *Vindication of Natural Society* (1756), which ridicules the deistic doctrines of Bolingbroke while appearing to utter them. Burke built no political hopes on the new idea that a true social harmony would be born of the direct operation of external nature on the passions of men. Nor could he accept the deistic verdict on human history as an artificial pageant of blood and butcheries perpetrated by 'a few, mad, designing, or ambitious priests'. But he was too intelligent a man of his time not to have made psychology the ground of his inquiry into the origin of our ideas of *The Sublime and The Beautiful*. For that age was committed by its science to the testing of art and external nature as a school of the affections, with landscape art, in particular, cast in the role of teacher of men. The artifice and guile of traditional oratory, art, and politics were to be supplanted by the practice of the contemplation and recollection of the external creation which speaks directly to the human heart.

That Burke's treatise had the greatest effect on the later eighteenth century is admitted by historians. Its influence on Coleridge and Poe, and through them on Baudelaire and the Symbolists, still deserves to be traced very carefully. For its speculations on the nature and effect of landscape art serve to unify the development of poetry from James Thomson to the present. It is in this treatise that are to be found the definitions of 'state of mind' in art, of 'emotions of the mind', of aesthetic emotion, objective correlative, and of the relation between beauty and melancholy as used later by Coleridge, Poe, and Baudelaire. Burke arrived by a single stride at the position that the cognitive process was also the creative process. And it is that awareness in Cézanne and Mallarmé, as later in Joyce and Eliot, which produced the doctrine and practice of 'significant form' in modern art. That this same notion of form was apprehended by Arthur Hallam is plain in the passage already quoted from him concerning Tennyson's *fusion* of objects in the medium of a predominant emotion. Hallam could have had this from Coleridge, but he knew Burke directly.

From the dream of universal social therapy and regeneration which Wordsworth and Coleridge had at first accepted as a necessary consequence of submission of the heart to the pure messages of the external world, Coleridge awakened with his 'Dejection: An Ode' in 1802. The Aeolian lute in his window, type of the poet and the faithful medium of the voices of the external world, now tells him not of the enchantment of a prospective Elysium, but of torture, Devil's yule, and

> ... of the rushing of an host in rout,
> With groans of trampled men ...

If Shelley perhaps persisted in the cosmic optimism, Keats did not. He knew the beauty of the natural order, and the beauty of art, but also the human

> Weariness, the fever, and the fret
> Here, where men sit and hear each other groan...

There had been not only the wreck of the French Revolution, but the vision of the 'hungry generations' in the doctrine of Malthus and the first fruits of the industrial towns to digest by this time. There had come the end of the notion of the external universe as a great clock which could order the inner passions of those who fed their minds on landscape in a wise passiveness. Nature was soon to be officially accepted as 'red in tooth and claw', and the age of private enterprise to get under way. Biological automatism was ready to take over educational and political theory after a century of psychological automatism. Byron, however, was the appointed spokesman of disenchant-ment with the Newtonian sleep, which had sealed the spirits of the landscape idolators, when he proclaimed himself 'a link reluctant in a fleshly chain'. He was not in the least charmed by the great deist doctrine that 'I live not in myself but I become portion of that around me'. And he gave a cue and a credo to the new race of aristocratic dandies from Lytton to Disraeli, Poe, Baudelaire, and Wilde. They took up again the burden of individual consciousness which had been systematically relinquished in the first landscape era. And it is this which links them to the Augustans. The young Tennyson was a bohemian devotee of Byron. The young Arnold was a dandified gentleman, whose muse deserted him with his dandyism. It is hard to see how there could have been any nutriment for the development of Wordsworth's poetic sensibility along his first lines in a milieu that had suddenly abandoned Newton and cosmic automatism. Faced with an equally dramatic reversal of milieu, W. B. Yeats remade himself as a poet. Wordsworth instead settled down to edit his own work.

It was in this milieu that Tennyson was shaped as a poet. His predecessors, expecting to be made whole, had immersed themselves in a cosmic landscape bath certified by Newton. His contemporaries had begun to suspect that the bath was poisoned. His successors, such as Hardy, were sure it was.

When the eighteenth century plunged into the cosmic landscape it was consciously and scientifically seeking to reunite itself with primal energies from which it felt remote. The dim past, the age-old face of the earth, the primitive, the child-like, the pastoral were alike landscapes in which the sophisticated sought to merge themselves. But this merging was also, for civilized men, an act of symbolic suicide, a wilful extinction of personality. So that there is over the eighteenth century both the light of natural reason and a cloud of intense melancholy, which led the French to call eighteenth-century England the 'land of spleen and suicide'. (Karl Polanyi's *The Great Transformation* traces the effect of the Newtonian and deist doctrines of cosmic harmony on the idea of a self-regulating market in land, labour, and capital. Quite unaware of the artistic parallels, Polanyi's work is yet of the greatest interest for aesthetics.) Similar ambivalence attends nineteenth-century England, but for opposite reasons. It was the re-awaking of the individual ego after the self-forgetful plunge into landscape that produced both the social optimism and the personal melancholy which Tennyson reflects. To have awakened in the lap of a trusted Nature that now seemed diseased and malignant brought on a new suicidal gloom which the century never resolved or dissipated.

If this were just a question of the 'history of ideas' there would be little excuse for pursuing it in connection with Tennyson. But the interest in landscape had, from the time of Claude and Poussin in the seventeenth century, been closely associated with the new science. So that when landscape was no longer supported by Newtonian physics for Coleridge and Keats, it was reinforced by botany, biology, and geology for Tennyson, Ruskin, and the Pre-Raphaelites. Science remained as an important prop for interests which were primarily aesthetic. But unlike the later Hopkins and Cézanne, Tennyson and the Pre-Raphaelites were unable to achieve the intensity of contemplation which led to the metaphysical break-through of that later art. They remained picturesque. That is, they devoted themselves to the means of prolonging the moment of aesthetic emotion or of arrested experience, and failed to accept such moments as the thread through the labyrinth of cognition. They substituted immediate feeling and emotion for the process of retracing.

Tennyson began, and, for the most part, remained at the very interesting Constable level. Hopkins, pursuing 'inscape', as Joyce did 'epiphanies', broke through to the life which restored body and solidity to art in an existential vision that is truly metaphysical:

> It is the forged feature finds me; it is the rehearsal
> Of own, of abrupt self there so thrusts on, so throngs the ear.

But, thoroughly trained in the picturesque school, Tennyson never fails to compose his larger pictures with the utmost care for the texture and placing of objects (and words as objects), light and shade. So that the enjoyment of his best poetry calls for the most patient and alert attention. The derision which was once shed indiscriminately on his 'accuracy' and his flag-waving reflects a recent period when, for various reasons, it was thought that art could be taken at the gallop. We are not likely to repeat that mistake. But Tennyson now deserves to be re-read and revalued with the aid of recovered reading ability. And it will be the Tennyson of the precise ear and eye who will provide the most unexpected and persistent enjoyment.

The gallery of pictures which is 'The Palace of Art' is a recreation of the 'worlds' discovered by painters like Wilson, Turner, Danby, and Martin. They are not just descriptions of scenes or paintings but immediate impressionistic evocations of situations in which it is the state of mind of the protagonist that is central, situations which as in Maturin's tales, present 'those struggles of passion when the soul trembles on the verge of the unlawful and the unhallowed'. So that each brief vista is an objective correlative for a moment of concentrated awareness:

> One seem'd all dark and red—a tract of sand,
>   And some one pacing there alone,
> Who paced for ever in a glimmering land
>   Lit with a low large moon.

Tennyson is here practising the art of compression which Mr. Eliot carried even further in such effects as

> Madame de Tornquist, in the dark room
> Shifting the candles, Fraulein von Kulp
> Who turned in the hall, one hand on the door.

This concentration, which requires the utmost precision of eye, of phrase, and rhythm, Tennyson never ceased to exercise. 'Mariana' is a triumph of the sustaining of such concentration; and 'Enone' is only less successful because of the admixture of the narrative flash-back which Tennyson could never handle. But in 'The Voyage of Maeldune' (1881) he solved the problem by only appearing to narrate. It is because of his habitual definition of a moment of awareness in terms of objective landscape that Tennyson found his strength in the short poem such as the sections of *In Memoriam* tend to be. And his longer poems are always risky expansions of these moments, as is plain in the *Idylls of the King*. But the short tale in verse, of which Crabbe was the master Tennyson admired, never ceased to tempt him.

It is in this matter of the landscape or episode which defines and concentrates an intense experience, that Tennyson both inspired and surpassed Rossetti, Morris, and the Pre-Raphaelites. Browning, too, was, in a more dramatic mode, concerned with rendering the intense 'immortal moment' which unified a lifetime of awareness. And Proust, the student and admirer of Ruskin, also lavished his art on the expansion of the 'immortal moment'. Staying close to the lyric mode in which he was so great a technician, Tennyson impresses many today as more successful because less tempted merely to decorate and comment on an experience which commonly eludes us in Browning and the Pre-Raphaelites when they fail to 'force the moment to its crisis'. At his frequent best he never departs from the critical insights that Hallam arrived at concerning rhetoric, Wordsworth, and the slackening effect of intellectual comment.

But the best of Wordsworth is also landscape in the picturesque mode, and 'The Solitary Reaper' is not unrelated in theme and technique to 'La Figlia che Piange'. Modern criticism with its tools ready for the anatomy of verbal wit and dramatic ambiguities will have to go to school to the painters again before it can do justice to the variety and skill of conscious landscape art in prose and poetry after Thomson. Modern verbal criticism finds itself equally mute before Dante's visual art and that of Spenser. Spenser was, inevitably, a master of the picturesque poets from Thomson to Tennyson. Music would appear to be a resource of the poet seeking visual and plastic effects with words—much more so than in the case of the kinæsthetic and dialectical verbal drama of a Donne or Hopkins. For subtleties and ambivalence of mood are managed less by tropes than impressionistic devices. 'She was a phantom of delight' is, for example, a triptych of condensed impressions which rival a cinematic rapidity and nuance. And so it is with the best of the Romantics. Looked at with the camera eye 'The Ancient Mariner' or 'Resolution and Independence' seem to be immediately contemporary with ourselves. The Romantics had nothing to learn from cinema. It is rather cinema that can learn from them.

If anybody ever had and consciously cultivated a movie-camera eye it was Tennyson. But if one asks what it was of landscape art that the Romantics and the Victorians did not achieve, it must be replied, *le paysage intérieur*, which had to wait for Baudelaire, Laforgue, and Rimbaud. It was this discovery that gave the later poets and painters alike, the power to be much more subjective and also more objective than the Romantics. For all their skill in discovering and manipulating external-nature situations by which to render states of mind, the Romantics remained tied to the object when they wished only to present it as a point from which to leap to another kind of vision. So they repeatedly bog down in reflection just at the moment when they are ready to soar. They could not discover the technique of flight. It would be interesting to inquire how far the cessation of the poetic activity of Wordsworth and Coleridge was connected with this technical frustration. By means of the interior landscape, however, Baudelaire could not only range across the entire spectrum of the inner life, he could transform the sordidness and evil of an industrial metropolis into a flower. With this technique he was able to accept the city as his central 'myth', and see it as the enlarged shape of a man, just as Flaubert did in *The Sentimental Education*, Joyce in *Ulysses*, and Mr. Eliot in *The Waste Land*. (It is noteworthy that the English novel also preceded English poetry in the management of the city as 'myth'. Dickens was the first to make London a character or a person. And James and Conrad in their different modes preceded Joyce and Eliot in assimilating the urban to the stuff of poesy.) Moreover, the technique of inner landscape not only permits the use of any and every kind of experience and object, it insures a much higher degree of control over the effect; because the arrangement of the landscape is the formula of the emotion and can be repeatedly adjusted until the formula and the effect are in precise accord. Whereas the romantic poet and painter were much more dependent on the caprices of external nature, sketching, as Ruskin says of Turner, 'the almost instantaneous record of an *effect* of colour or atmosphere taken strictly from Nature . . .', the romantic and picturesque artists had to take advantage of accidents. After Baudelaire there is no need for such accidents. The picturesque artists saw the wider range of experience that could be managed by discontinuity and planned irregularity, but they kept to the picture-like single perspective. The interior landscape, however, moves naturally towards the principle of multiple perspectives, as in the first two lines of *The Waste Land*, where the Christian Chaucer, Sir James Frazer, and Jessie Weston are simultaneously present. This is 'cubist perspective' which renders, at once, a diversity of views with the spectator always in the centre of the picture, whereas in picturesque art the spectator is always outside. The cubist perspective of interior landscape typically permits an immediacy, a variety, and solidity of experience denied to the picturesque and to Tennyson.

But the Romantics and Victorians, lacking this comprehensive and elastic technique, were compelled to remain 'nature' poets whether they liked it or not. They were certainly conscious of having new 'art-emotions', but they were unable to achieve art-conditions for them, and so continued to use external nature as a vehicle for art-emotions. It was the science of their time that taught them to like nature, just as it is the science of our time that has freed us from their particular kind of bondage to external nature. For it is, perhaps, a mistake to regard nature as the subject matter of the Romantics. They wanted not just to see it but to see through it; and failing that they made it an objective correlative for states of mind that are independent of it.

ROBERT LANGBAUM

The Dynamic Unity
of "In Memoriam"

In *Science and the Modern World*, Alfred North Whitehead compares Tennyson's *In Memoriam* to Milton's *Paradise Lost* and Pope's *Essay on Man*, in that *In Memoriam* "exactly," like these earlier long poems, "expressed the character of its period." Its period runs from 1833—when Tennyson's gifted young friend Arthur Hallam died suddenly in Vienna, and Tennyson to express his grief began writing the individual lyrics—to 1850, when the lyrics written during the intervening seventeen years were finally organized and published as presumably one long poem. The mid-Victorian poem is especially comparable to the early eighteenth-century *Essay on Man*, because Tennyson like Pope summarizes the scientific knowledge of his time and relates it to questions of religious and moral judgment. Pope, however, is optimistic about the implications of Newtonian physics; whereas Tennyson, who was thinking about geology, biology and the new astronomy, is for most of the poem pessimistic. The difference is that for the Victorians, scientific knowledge was antithetical to, rather than productive of, a religious and ethical position. And it is this antithesis—this characteristically Victorian controversy between science and religious faith—that Whitehead had in mind in speaking of *In Memoriam* as expressive of its age.

In composing an elegy for Arthur Hallam, who died before he could fulfill his promise of a brilliant political career, Tennyson faced the question of all elegists. If this can happen, what is the value of life? Just as in Milton's

From *The Modern Spirit: Essays on the Continuity of Nineteenth And Twentieth Century Literature*. Copyright © 1970 by Robert Langbaum. Oxford University Press, 1970.

elegy, *Lycidas*, this question leads to general questions of the age (in Milton, the bad state of the church); so, to an even greater degree, in Tennyson. The difference is that Milton could draw upon his age—upon its Renaissance humanistic and its Christian tradition—for an answer. But Tennyson could not easily take over a Christian or even a humanistic answer, because the latest science—mainly Lyell's geology, which taught the vastness of geological time and the extinction of species, and the Herschels' astronomy, which demoted the sun to a minor star in our galaxy and taught the evolution of stars out of nebulae—made it difficult to believe in a purposeful, moral universe, or in the importance of man, much less individual man. If man, too, the poet asks, were to be "seal'd within the iron hills," were to leave as his only trace fossils in the rocks, what hope for the immortality of Hallam's soul or for the enduring value of one's love for him? One could no longer, like the Deists and Wordsworthians, find evidence in nature for the existence of God. But one could—these are the answers Tennyson arrives at—rely on the testimony of the heart and see, in the natural evolution of species, an analogue to social progress and man's spiritual evolution. Thus, Tennyson anticipated the discussion that was to follow the publication of Darwin's *Origin of Species* in 1859.

But the age in which he found himself was inimical to an answer. The age had to be overcome. Tennyson does, it is true, finally draw upon answers already prepared by Carlyle and by Coleridge—Coleridge as filtered through that society founded by Coleridgians, the Cambridge Apostles, to which both he and Hallam had belonged. But Tennyson makes these earlier answers his own, because he took science more seriously, knew much more about it, and coped with a more modern science than did Coleridge and Carlyle. Tennyson wins his victory—if we agree that he wins it—over far more intractable material than theirs. *In Memoriam* is generally called—and I have so called it—a mid-Victorian poem. But it derived from the early Victorian period, the tormented 1830's and 40's. In the questions it raised and the answers it proposed, *In Memoriam* helped shape the affirmative attitudes that characterized the relatively complacent mid-Victorian period—the period that began about the time *In Memoriam* appeared in 1850.

That is why *In Memoriam* came under attack as later generations reacted against the mid-Victorian affirmations—against what G. K. Chesterton, writing in 1913, called "the Victorian compromise," in this case the compromise between science and religion. Victorian humanists, a liberal Anglican like F. D. Maurice, a skeptic like Henry Sidgwick, together with leading scientists, Sir John Herschel and others, thought Tennyson had managed to re-establish the possibilities of faith precisely by taking into account the scientific difficulties and "through almost the agonies of a death struggle." But in 1923, Hugh l'Anson Fausset attacked Tennyson's simple-minded and timid attempt to reconcile science and religion as doing justice to neither. "The synthesis which Tennyson affected was too easy and superficial to excite in him either profound emotion or passionate thought, the two forces out of which poetry is born. He never faced the darkness, and fought his way out into daylight, but... [remained] safe in the citadel of traditional belief." Harold Nicolson, who published in that year the book that started the modern rehabilitation of Tennyson, considers that Tennyson did face the darkness. Nicolson finds the emotion profound, inasmuch as the emotion is despair, but objects to the structure, "the artificially constructed synthesis," that betokens a movement toward affirmation.

T. S. Eliot carries the appreciation of Tennyson up through *In Memoriam*, when in his essay of 1936 he calls it the work in which "Tennyson finds full expression." But Eliot, too, is interested in *In Memoriam* as a poem of despair. "I get a very different impression from *In Memoriam* from that which Tennyson's contemporaries seem to have got. It is of a very much more interesting and tragic Tennyson." Tennyson's feelings were more honest than his thought, and therefore *In Memoriam* is a religious poem, not "because of the quality of its faith, but because of the quality of its doubt. Its faith is a poor thing, but its doubt is a very intense experience. *In Memoriam* is a poem of despair, but of despair of a religious kind." And Eliot says about *In Memoriam* a kind of thing that he has said about his own poem of religious despair, *The Waste Land*. "It happens now and then that a poet by some strange accident expresses the mood of his generation, at the same time that he is expressing a mood of his own which is quite remote from that of his generation." Now *The Waste Land* is a poem that stands up against the first two decades of the twentieth century, that exposes the boredom and terror of the age's faithlessness. And to the extent that *In Memoriam* is about the 1830's and 40's, it stands up against the age—makes the age face the religious impasse to which it has been brought by all the revolutionary forces of the age but mainly by science.

When on the first Christmas after Hallam's death the Tennysons sing the traditional hymns, teaching that the dead "do not die / Nor lose their mortal sympathy" (xxx), it is clear that they cannot really believe these words. And in the moving section that follows, "When Lazarus left his charnel-cave, / And home to Mary's house return'd," we are told that even Lazarus who returned from the grave has left no record of what it was like there. His sister Mary, whose "eyes," we are told in the next section, "are homes of silent prayer," is content to accept without question the miracle of resurrection and adore the Savior who wrought it. And in the section following, the sophisticated reader is told not to despise those present-day Marys whose faith is simple and literal; but it is clear that the present-day

Marys are not modern, have not got the age in their bones.

Not only has Christianity been exploded; so has its romantic substitute—the faith in the benevolent life of nature. It is because the romantic faith is the most proximate and potent that the scientific devaluation of nature plays so important a part in this poem. Section III, in which Sorrow whispers conclusions drawn from the new astronomy, marks the crucial dividing line between romantic and modern nature poetry.

> "The stars," she whispers, "blindly run;
>   A web is wov'n across the sky;
>   From out waste places comes a cry,
> And murmurs from the dying sun:
>
> "And all the phantom, Nature, stands—
>   With all the music in her tone,
>   A hollow echo of my own,—
> A hollow form with empty hands."

The nature that used to echo Wordsworthian joy has lost all vitality; it is now a ghost, echoing Sorrow's voice and teaching only death. "A web is wov'n across the sky" suggests that nature now conceals, instead of revealing, God.

This theme is taken up again in section LVI, the most famous of the nature poems. Having in the previous section come full circle from the Wordsworthian belief in God in nature:

> Are God and Nature then at strife,
>   That Nature lends such evil dreams?
>   So careful of the type she seems,
> So careless of the single life;

Tennyson now remembers Lyell's fossils in the rocks:

> "So careful of the type?" but no.
>   From scarpèd cliff and quarried stone
>   She cries, "A thousand types are gone;
> I care for nothing, all shall go."

Is this then to be the fate of man, who managed to believe in a God of love, though nature "red in tooth and claw" gave no evidence to support such belief? He concludes:

> What hope of answer or redress?
> Behind the veil, behind the veil.

These lines recall Goethe's idea, taken over by Carlyle, that nature can be for the wise the revealing garment of God, only to say that nature has now conclusively drawn the veil over God. The lines represent the low point of *In Memoriam*; they carry the problem raised by science to the point of impasse. Afterwards, the poet can only say "Peace; come away," thus introducing a group in which he consoles himself along lines that evade the issue of science, and which leads to the muted despair of the section on the Second Christmas.

The view of nature here is modern, in that the problems raised by the science of Tennyson's time are still with us, only more so. The universe seems even vaster, more dangerous and less hospitable than in the 1840's; our landings on the dead and ugly moon, our approaches to Mars and Venus, suggest the infinity of waste, of inanimate unconsciousness, that surrounds us. Tennyson also looks toward our century in his recognition that love cannot endure as a purely humanistic value, that the scientific view must inevitably reduce love to sex. In the section that ends the Lazarus group, he says that even if some voice could tell us from the grave that there is no life beyond it:

> Yet if some voice that man could trust
> Should murmur from the narrow house,
> "The cheeks drop in, the body bows;
> Man dies: nor is there hope in dust:"

might I not say that love still gives value to such life as we have on earth? No, the thought of perpetual geological change:

> The moanings of the homeless sea,
> The sound of streams that swift or slow
> Draw down Æonian hills, and sow
> The dust of continents to be;

the thought of inevitable oblivion must change love's "sweetness more and more, / Half-dead to know that [it] shall die" (xxxv). Without some conviction of its permanence, love must be devalued. That prediction has been amply fulfilled in our time.

Why then does *In Memoriam* not seem pressingly modern? Not only in its affirmations, but even in its doubts, the poem seems a bit old-fashioned. We can admire it, but with a certain amount of historical projection—as a poem of its time. Partly, there is the difference in idiom. Tennyson does not say, in the section I have been discussing, that love will turn into sex; he says it will take on its "coarsest Satyr-shape," it will turn into lust—and that is not the way we talk about sex nowadays. But the important thing is that the whole question of religion versus science has ceased to interest us. Most of us never had any faith to lose, and we do not *think* that the lack of religion has left a hole in our lives. As for those who really do believe, my impression is that they have long since given up any hope of reconciling their faith with scientific evidence. In this, of course, they are following Tennyson's main prescription, as well as Kierkegaard's (Teilhard de Chardin seems anachronistic in his present-day attempt to reconcile evolution and religion).

Graham Hough, in his article of 1947, "The Natural Theology of *In Memoriam,*" is more willing than T. S. Eliot to accept some of Tennyson's affirmations. Inasmuch as Tennyson "wishes to provide an answer in scientific terms," to reconcile religion and evolution by telling us we must evolve spiritually—"Move upward, working out the beast" (cxviii) and thus herald "the crowning race" (Epilogue)—inasmuch as Tennyson is doing that, Hough thinks he is merely "manufacturing a conclusion to the poem which will at least appear to draw the scattered threads together. . . . But the real answer, the one that really satisfied him, is not in those terms at all. It is a thoroughgoing subjectivism which does not meet the difficulties raised by science, but simply bypasses them." And Hough quotes the lines from section cxxiv that seem to offer the central theological answer:

> If e'er when faith had fall'n asleep,
>   I heard a voice "believe no more"
>   And heard an ever-breaking shore
> That tumbled in the Godless deep;
>
> A warmth within the breast would melt
>   The freezing reason's colder part,
>   And like a man in wrath the heart
> Stood up and answer'd "I have felt."

"This seems both honest and extremely moving," says Hough, "but it is this subjectivist attitude in 'In Memoriam' that has received the severest criticism."

This so-called subjectivist answer—which Browning was also working out during these years in "Saul"—runs like this. If we *feel,* when we are feeling most deeply, that there is a loving God and the soul is immortal, then this feeling must correspond to an objective reality.

> The wish, that of the living whole
>   No life may fail beyond the grave,
>   Derives it not from what we have
> The likest God within the soul?
>
> (lv)

Coleridge had already lent philosophical support to this argument: "Throughout animated nature, of each characteristic organ and faculty there exists a pre-assurance, an instinctive and practical anticipation; and no pre-assurance common to a whole species does in any instance prove delusive." And Carlyle declared: "The evidence to me of God—and the only evidence—is the feeling I have, deep down in the very bottom of my heart, of right and truth and justice. . . . Whoever looks into himself must be aware that at the centre of things is a mysterious Demiurgos—who is *God*, and who cannot in the least be adequately spoken of in any human words."

Tennyson's subjectivist answer, then, is not arbitrary; he arrived through personal experience at what was becoming the characteristic answer of the age. Tennyson's answer in scientific terms was also becoming characteristic of the age. Having in 1837 studied Lyell's *Principles of Geology* (1830–1833), Tennyson seems to have found an answer to its gloomy implications in the popularized science of Robert Chambers's *Vestiges of the Natural History of Creation* (1844). Chambers interprets evolution in terms of progress and as evidence of a benevolent Providence—a line Browning had already taken in *Paracelsus* (1835). In his doubts and answers, Tennyson like all great writers was able to help bring a new age into being by telling the present age what its preoccupations were. His answers helped provide the staple of liberal opinion during the 1850's and 60's. According to the dramatic action of *In Memoriam*, the answers are not there but have to be evolved. Hallam, it is true, had already worked out the answers; but Hallam, we are told, was ahead of his time, was even the herald of a higher race than ours.

The fact that Tennyson's answers are characteristic of the mid-Victorian age he helped bring into being makes them seem more dated than some of them—the subjectivist answer, or the suspicion that science's latest findings are not the last word—really are. If we abstract from *In Memoriam* the doubts and answers as ideas, then we must ask whether they are convincing. We know they *were* convincing—that Queen Victoria and George Eliot were representative of many, in that after their husbands' deaths they read *In Memoriam* along with the Bible for consolation. But to ask whether the abstracted ideas are *still* convincing is to treat *In Memoriam* as a tract for the times to which we can no longer subscribe.

There is, however, another way of approaching the poem, the way of literary criticism. The literary critic wants to know whether, taken as a poem of its age, *In Memoriam* can still be considered a great poem. And the proper question for him is not whether the doubts and affirmations, especially the affirmations, are convincing in themselves, but whether they are justified and sustained by the dramatic action and by the texture or undersong of emotion and imagery. The question, in other words, is whether the feeling is honest and, if it is, whether there is a sufficiently genuine shift of feeling to justify the finally affirmative movement of the thought. It is to this question that I shall now turn, in order to show that *In Memoriam* is a great poem and that it has a dynamic unity of thought and feeling dependent on a dialectical principle of growth of a single consciousness. The backtrackings, the changes of mood, style and levels of intensity, even the apparent contradictions, are all signs of the genuineness of the experience and coherent aspects of a single developing consciousness.

We have to study *In Memoriam* carefully from beginning to end to be struck by the remarkable coherence of a poem the art of which is to look like a diary. The coherence shows not only within the groups into which most of the sections fall, but also in the progress—what Tennyson called "the way of a soul"—through the groups. The curious thing is that when we have understood this coherence, we realize that it derives from an epistemological sophistication that renders the affirmations more substantial than they seem in the abstract, and renders even the subjectivist answer less simply subjectivist.

About the genuineness of the grief projected in the poem, there is no disagreement. No one at all sensitive to poetry can fail to be moved by section VII in which the poet, after a sleepless night, compulsively creeps at daybreak to Hallam's door on Wimpole Street.

> Dark house, by which once more I stand
>   Here in the long unlovely street,
>   Doors, where my heart was used to beat
> So quickly, waiting for a hand,
>
> A hand that can be clasp'd no more—
>   Behold me, for I cannot sleep,
>   And like a guilty thing I creep
> At earliest morning to the door.
>
> He is not here; but far away
>   The noise of life begins again,
>   And ghastly thro' the drizzling rain
> On the bald street breaks the blank day.

Ghosts are guilty spirits that cannot rest; and the poet, haunting the street, seems a ghost mourning a ghost. This is one of two themes that give texture or sensuous substantiality to *In Memoriam*. One is the theme of reciprocal death: the poet has died vicariously with Hallam. The other is the erotic theme of touching: "Doors, where my heart was used to beat / So quickly, waiting for a hand." The poet's heart, like a lover's, used to beat quickly as he anticipated clasping Hallam's hand; and his grief in these early sections is concentrated in a desire for physical contact. His grief is compared, to take only two examples, to that of a maiden whose fiancé has died (VI); and to that of a widower who on waking "moves his doubtful arms" only to feel that the place beside him in bed is empty (XIII). So fixated is the poet at this stage on Hallam's physical presence that if Hallam should step off the ship returning his corpse to England, and "Should strike a sudden hand in mind," the poet would "not feel it to be strange" (XIV).

This erotic theme carries in section XL adumbrations of an answer having to do with rebirth: the poet tries to look upon Hallam's departure as parents do when they send a bride off to enter "other realms of love" to produce children who will knit present to future. But alas the analogy will not hold; the bride, after all, comes back to visit,

> But thou and I have shaken hands,
> Till growing winters lay me low;
> My paths are in the fields I know
> And thine in undiscover'd lands.

Yet the last line suggests that Hallam's death may nevertheless serve some still undiscovered purpose; and, indeed, in the Epilogue we see that it has served, through the experience of the poem, to set Tennyson's and the reader's face toward the future. *In Memoriam* has dramatic validity just because the answers proposed early in the poem cannot be sustained until the poet has himself undergone a total revolution in perception.

The theme of reciprocal death carries its adumbrations of an answer when Tennyson, standing at Hallam's burial, thinks of resuscitating him according to the prophet Elisha's method—by breathing into Hallam's mouth the last breath of his own almost expiring life.

> Ah yet, ev'n yet, if this might be,
> I, falling on his faithful heart,
> Would breathing thro' his lips impart
> The life that almost dies in me;

but no, it is the expiring Tennyson who will have to be resuscitated by the dead Hallam:

> That dies not, but endures with pain,
> And slowly forms the firmer mind,
> Treasuring the look it cannot find,
> The words that are not heard again.
>
> (XVIII)

Resuscitation or rebirth means learning to accept Hallam's death.

The theme of reciprocal death leads into the question of religion. For "the Shadow fear'd of man," who broke our physical contact and rendered formless the image of you that gave life form for me, "spread his mantle dark and cold, / And wrapt thee formless in the fold." Somewhere in the formless waste, that "Shadow sits and waits for me" (XXII); and is "The Shadow cloak'd from head to foot, / Who keeps the keys of all the creeds" (XXIII)—

the creeds that try to give life form.

The theme of reciprocal death leads also to the first statement of the question of nature. In section II, the yew is addressed as symbolizing the death principle in nature, a principle into which the poet feels utterly absorbed: "I seem to fail from out my blood / And grow incorporate into thee." Out of this mood, Sorrow in the next section whispers that the stars blindly run. But this scientific truth is whispered from Sorrow's "lying lip" and in the last stanza the poet resists Sorrow's view of the world, calling her a blind thing.

> And shall I take a thing so blind,
> Embrace her as my natural good;
> Or crush her, like a vice of blood,
> Upon the threshold of the mind?

"Vice of blood" connects with "I seem to fail from out my blood," suggesting that Sorrow's view of nature emerges from the death instinct inside us, and is therefore as much a pathetic fallacy as the view of nature that emerges from the Wordsworthian sense of joy. Even in the climactic statements of the nature question, the views of nature as "careless of the single life" and "red in tooth and claw" are presented as "evil dreams" (LV, LVI). But in the preceding section, the opposite view of nature—"Oh yet we trust that somehow good / Will be the final goal of ill, / . . . That not a worm is cloven in vain"—is summed up: "So runs my dream." The oscillation belongs to the strategy of realism and sincerity at the heart of In Memoriam. But it reflects also an epistemological sophistication that provides the dramatic action and the adumbrations of an answer. For the poet, when he dies vicariously with Hallam, has to admit into his mind, though he struggles against it, the view of nature as purposelessly destructive. But the struggle signifies a contrary movement toward the internal change that will transform Hallam's death into a life-enhancing force and will enable the poet to see the very same facts as having quite a different meaning.

A group of metaphysical speculations on the state of the soul after death suggests that we are reborn into this world and the next, and that we evolve in this world the self that can be reborn in the next (XLIV, XLV). But it is the "lying" Sorrow of section III who now tries to comfort us with such fancies (XLVIII); and such fancies are mere ripples on the deep pool of the poet's grief (XLIX). The final answer will have to emerge from the depths, and we are therefore returned to the deep grief of:

> Be near me when my light is low,
> When the blood creeps, and the nerves prick
> And tingle; and the heart is sick,
> And all the wheels of Being slow,

(L)

which leads to the climactic statement of the nature question.

There follows a group offering conceits (the superficiality is dramatically right) on Hallam in heaven and a group on consolatory dreams—all of which show the poet moving toward surface cheerfulness though deep down the grief remains. The grief, however, rushes back to the surface in the powerful section LXXII, where the stormy first anniversary of Hallam's death reminds the poet of the day he received the devastating news. The grief increases as he thinks in the next two sections of the fame Hallam would have had and says, in the next three, that he can only write these verses for his own relief though he knows they will not endure or have any effect. (Throughout, there are enough references to pastoral motifs to remind us that the pastoral elegy has been abandoned in the interest of realism and sincerity, and that the traditional themes of pastoral elegy are reversed: nature does not mourn the dead man, who will not have fame and will not be immortalized by this poem.) All these sections help define the quality of the grief by the time of the second Christmas—when grief's "deep relations are the same, / But with long use her tears are dry" (LXXVIII).

The three Christmases, which stand for almost seventeen years, are the most obvious markers of spiritual development. In the dull group immediately following the second Christmas (the only really uninteresting group in the poem), there are two sections that seem extraneous but are there, I think, to fill out the general scheme. In one, the poet declares his love for his favorite brother, Charles, even though he has written of Hallam: "More than my brothers are to me" (LXXIX); in the other, the poet offers to Edmund Lushington a friendship that will substitute in his heart for Hallam's though it cannot be as intense (LXXXV). Both sections show the poet turning back to life, realizing that Hallam can be fulfilled through living men. This prepares us for the Epilogue in which Hallam will be reborn through Lushington's wedding with one of Tennyson's sisters (Hallam had been engaged to another); for the child of this marriage will make a link to that future from which Hallam, as herald of "the crowning race," beckons. It is right that the Epilogue descends to domestic life, where the sublime principle of Love perceived in the closing sections, must be made operative.

But the turning to Charles and Lushington is only preparatory. The next magnificent group leads to the real turning point of In Memoriam, section XCV, where in a mystical trance the poet has the epiphany that transforms and transcends all the problems of the poem. I am inclined to start this group with the charmingly poignant section LXXXVII, where the poet, on a visit to Hallam's rooms at Cambridge, makes the last important revival of Hallam as a vital individual; Hallam is from now on to be revived through diffusion into forms other than his bodily form. The group in any case starts with the next very beautiful section, in which the wild bird's song is understood as combining opposites through total vision—"The glory of the sum of things"—which adumbrates the final answer of the group and the poem.

> Wild bird, whose warble, liquid sweet,
>   Rings Eden thro' the budded quicks,
>   O tell me where the senses mix,
> O tell me where the passions meet,
>
> Whence radiate: fierce extremes employ
>   Thy spirits in the darkening leaf,
>   And in the midmost heart of grief
> Thy passion clasps a secret joy.

Just as the bird's answer to grief is beyond its own understanding; so the poet hopes that even if his harp begins with woe, some force beyond his understanding ("I cannot all command the strings") will take over, so that:

> The glory of the sum of things
> Will flash along the chords and go.

There emerges again the question of Hallam's revival. Come in spring in your bodily form, says the poet, but in summer:

> Come, beauteous in thine after form,
> And like a finer light in light.
>   (xci)

And in section xcii—which parallels section xiv where we were told that if Hallam stepped off the ship alive, the poet would not think it strange—in section xcii, we are told that if a vision should reveal Hallam in his bodily form, and even if Hallam spoke prophecies that came true, the poet would understand the experience as only the action of his own mind. The poet now locates spiritual reality in his own consciousness. "I shall not see thee," he says in the next section, but long to meet

> Where all the nerve of sense is numb,
> Spirit to Spirit, Ghost to Ghost,

but to achieve such communion with the dead, one's spirit must be like theirs "at peace with all" (xciv). At the opening of section xcv, where the communion takes place, the poet is at peace, and he learns to be "at peace with all."

Section xcv is constructed like a Wordsworthian dramatic lyric, in

that the thought develops out of and as a counterpart to the natural setting.
"By night we linger'd on the lawn." The Tennysons are gathered outside
their house at Somersby, during one of those long hushed English summer
twilights in which things remain half-visible:

> ... and o'er the sky
> The silvery haze of summer drawn;
>
> And calm that let the tapers burn
>   Unwavering: not a cricket chirr'd:
>   The brook alone far-off was heard,
> And on the board the fluttering urn:
>
> And bats went round in fragrant skies,
>   And wheel'd or lit the filmy shapes
>   That haunt the dusk ...
>
> While now we sang old songs that peal'd
>   From knoll to knoll, where, couch'd at ease,
>   The white kine glimmer'd, and the trees
> Laid their dark arms about the field.

When the others withdraw, "A hunger seized my heart," and he reads
Hallam's letters—finding in them "love's dumb cry defying change" and
Hallam's ability to look through doubts and "wordy snares" to the positive
"suggestion" behind them. Like the wild bird's song, the letters turn
negation into affirmation; their words turn into an epiphany, a manifestation of Hallam's living soul.

> The living soul was flash'd on mine,
>
> And mine in this was wound, and whirl'd
>   About empyreal heights of thought,
>   And came on that which is, and caught
> The deep pulsations of the world,
>
> Æonian music measuring out
>   The steps of Time—the shocks of Chance—
>   The blows of Death.

The epiphany reveals "The glory of the sum of things"; it is a vision of
process, turning the geological aeons into "Æonian music." "With the flash
of a trembling glance," says St. Augustine in the *Confessions*, the mind
"arrived at *that which is.*"

When the trance is over, doubt returns and we are returned to the
same landscape:

> Till now the doubtful dusk reveal'd
> The knolls once more where, couch'd at ease,
> The white kine glimmer'd, . . .

But the landscape is not the same. For "suck'd from out the distant gloom / A breeze"—Wordsworth's "correspondent breeze," corresponding to inner rebirth—now animates the trees and flowers, saying:

> "The dawn, the dawn," and died away;
> And East and West, without a breath,
> Mixt their dim lights, like life and death,
> To broaden into boundless day.

The breeze shows that the epiphany has transformed the poet's perception, even if he can now only reflect upon the epiphany through inadequate forms of speech and thought. The climactic counterpart to the internal transformation is the transformation of the doubtful twilight dusk into the doubtful dusk of dawn. The glimmering white kine seem to symbolize the Truth that can be apprehended only through doubtful dusks; while the two dusks, which seem in the short Northern summer night to mix into each other, are in the boundless light of Eternity seen, as like life and death, two necessary aspects of a single reality.

Graham Hough defines three major elements in In Memoriam—the influence of science, the influence of Coleridge to which I would add the influence of Wordsworth and Carlyle, and Tennyson's own religious intuitions based on his capacity since childhood to experience mystical trances. Hough finds these elements "not completely unified and the balance between them . . . unstable." I would suggest that these elements are unified according to a scheme showing what I have called Tennyson's epistemological sophistication. For In Memoriam is organized to show that after the poet has undergone a total transformation of perception, all the old facts and problems are transvaluated and absorbed into the affirmative movement that dominates the poem from section xcv on.

In section xcvi, the doubt Hallam engaged in is shown to be a religious virtue: Moses on Sinai stood "in the darkness and the cloud," whereas the Israelites below insisted on seeing "their gods of gold." The second anniversary of Hallam's death brings consolation through his diffusion in, and assimilation to, the natural cycle. But the Tennysons are to move from Somersby and the landscape associated with Hallam. This problem is resolved in the important section ciii, which restates allegorically the resolution of section xcv. The poet had a dream of the dead from which he woke—a sign of how far we have come—"content." He saw in his dream a "statue veil'd" round which maidens sang; and though he recognized "The shape of him I loved," the veil and the word "shape" suggest that Hallam has transcended his earthly identity. The maidens wept but accompanied the poet, as he sailed in a little boat down a river, overhung with vegetation, into an ocean—where he felt himself growing bigger, stronger, more masculine, and where on a great ship they saw the "man we loved" but "thrice as large as man." The poet's growth in size is a sign that he has grown in perception to the point where he can now see Hallam as superhuman. "Up the side I went / And fell in silence on his neck." The maidens wept, thinking they were to be left behind; but Hallam bade them enter in, and they all sail away from shore toward "a crimson cloud" that is like another shore. Clearly, Hallam is no longer to be tied to a physical image or location; his death, in this new realm of value, turns into a positive good. The maidens can be understood as the melancholy, backward-looking, feminine, erotic muses of the earlier sections, which are in the boundless ocean, the poet's trip from sensuous to transcendental perception, subsumed into the masculine, affirmative, forward-looking muses of the concluding section.

This spiritual development is marked by the third Christmas on which the Tennysons, now removed from Somersby, break entirely with the past—with "grief" that abuses "the genial hour," even with old Christmas customs—and turn their thoughts to the future: "The closing cycle rich in good" (CV). Instead of the vegetation cycle that offered consolation in the old elegies, we now have Hallam's faith in progress. That is why, in the next three sections, the New Year bells are asked to "Ring out the darkness of the land, / Ring in the Christ that is to be"; Hallam's birthday can be celebrated with "festal cheer"; and the poet declares: I will no longer "eat my heart alone," but turn my private sorrow into compassion for humanity. There is a diffusion, which Hallam would approve, of values originally concentrated in Hallam.

A new group characterizes Hallam as he was in life, with greater detail and poignancy than before. The purpose is to recall by implication the elegiac theme, "Alas, he is dead," in order to return with even stronger affirmations—the affirmations discussed earlier in this essay. But the affirmations have not, as I have tried to show, been plucked out of the blue. They have been prepared from the start by a submerged counter-movement of the instincts, that offered all along adumbrations of an answer, and led finally to the total revolution in perception that has given to the same facts a different meaning. We can see this through certain deliberately planted parallels. Section CXIX parallels section VII on Wimpole Street. Again, the poet stands at daybreak before Hallam's door. But this time "not as one that weeps"; for he no longer needs the physical pressure of Hallam's hand, it is enough that "in my thoughts with scarce a sigh / I take the pressure of thine hand."

In the lovely section CXXI, "Sad Hesper," the evening star, is blended with the morning star, "Bright Phosphor" to make "Sweet Hesper-Phosphor, double name"—in the manner of the wild bird's song and the blending of twilight and dawn in section XCV. The epiphany of section XCV is alluded to in section CXXII, which parallels the moving pessimism of section L: "Be near me when my light is low." In section CXXII, the poet now asks Hallam: were you with me in that moment of vision when I understood the unity of all things?

> Oh, wast thou with me, dearest, then,
>   While I rose up against my doom,
>   And yearn'd to burst the folded gloom,
> To bare the eternal Heavens again,
>
> To feel once more, in placid awe,
>   The strong imagination roll
>   A sphere of stars about my soul,
> In all her motion one with law;
>
> If thou wert with me, and the grave
>   Divide us not, be with me now,

transform my thoughts, turn grief into joy, so that "As in the former flash of joy," the epiphany of section XCV, "I slip the thoughts of life and death," and "every thought breaks out a rose."

Thus, Lyell's geology is transformed into a gorgeous poetic vision of earth's fluidity, perhaps the most beautiful rendition in English poetry of a modern scientific theory.

> There rolls the deep where grew the tree.
>   O earth, what changes hast thou seen!
>   There where the long street roars, hath been
> The stillness of the central sea.
>
> The hills are shadows, and they flow
>   From form to form, and nothing stands;
>   They melt like mist, the solid lands,
> Like clouds they shape themselves and go.

The last stanza seems to stand in simple opposition to these two:

> But in my spirit will I dwell,
>   And dream my dream, and hold it true;
>   For tho' my lips may breathe adieu,
> I cannot think the thing farewell.
>   (CXXIII)

But the point is, as in Hopkins's "Pied Beauty," that when one sees change as beautiful, one is seeing through to a principle of permanence behind change.

The point is reasserted in the next section after a restatement both of the problem—that the principle of permanence, God, cannot be found either in nature or through reason—and the solution:

> . . . like a man in wrath the heart
> Stood up and answer'd, "I have felt."

An earlier subjectivist assertion of this sort was dismissed:

> So runs my dream: but what am I?
> An infant crying in the night.
>
> (LIV)

Now the assertion is sustained. "No," says the poet, I did not answer like a man in wrath but "like a child in doubt and fear." Yet "that blind clamour made me wise"; I was like a child that "crying, knows his father near." Crying made real the thing I was crying for; it taught me what I truly am. And when "what I [truly] am beheld again / What is, and no man understands," then

> . . . out of darkness came the hands
> That reach thro' nature, moulding men.
>
> (CXXIV)

Hallam's *hand* has been transformed into mystical *hands*.

In other words, the assertion "I have felt" is not so simple-mindedly subjectivist as it seems in isolation. For it is not made against an unyielding reality, but against a reality that the beholder has transformed. The transformation has validity to the extent that the beholder has reached a state of perception that brings to the surface his deepest instincts (the poet says in section CXXV that instinctive Hope and Love were never absent from his song)—instincts which, when they are deep enough, connect with external reality. Thus, internal and external reality are connected through the love of Hallam. The poet must have a personal, which is to say a genuine, experience of love and value to be able to diffuse love and value throughout nature and society, and thus restore the sense of nature's life and the sense of connection with the rest of the world, which Hallam's death killed in him. As the poet works this restoration, he finds he can answer those early nineteenth-century scientific theories that rationalized for him his own despair; and he finds he can reinforce the transcendental philosophies of Coleridge and Carlyle which rationalize his new mood of affirmation.

No wonder Tennyson got the idea, as he organized *In Memoriam*, of modeling his poem on the *Divine Comedy*. For in Dante, too, it is a personal experience, love of Beatrice in life, that leads to a diffusion of value—to the love of Beatrice in death that leads in turn to visions of the Virgin and God. And Dante, too, used the available science and philosophy to help create the world-view of his time by envisioning it. In section cxxx, the sense that the spirit of Hallam lives in nature blends, through a principle of love, with the sense that God lives in nature.

> Thy voice is on the rolling air;
>   I hear thee where the waters run;
>   Thou standest in the rising sun,
> And in the setting thou art fair.
>
> What art thou then? I cannot guess;
>   But tho' I seem in star and flower
>   To feel thee some diffusive power,
> I do not therefore love thee less!
>
> My love involves the love before;
>   My love is vaster passion now;
>   Tho' mixed with God and Nature thou,
> I seem to love thee more and more.

And in the last numbered section (cxxxi), which is pure prayer, I hear the echo of Dante's last passage in *Paradiso*. (Hallam venerated Dante, especially his *Paradiso*.) Dante's intellect retreats before the direct Vision of God, which is beyond his understanding. But he discovers through his deepest instincts, his own desire and will, the desire and will that roll through all things and move the visible universe. "Here imagination failed," says Dante, "but already my desire and will were rolled...." Tennyson begins:

> O LIVING will that shalt endure
>   When all that seems shall suffer shock,
>   Rise in the spiritual rock,
> Flow thro' our deeds and make them pure,
>
> That we may lift from out of dust
>   A voice as unto him that hears,

that we may pray *as though* God exists. There is still the equivocation characteristic of Tennyson's theology. But Tennyson explained "O living will" as referring to individual free will that connects with Divine Will and the visible universe. Free will was, he said, the "main miracle, apparently an act of self-limitation by the Infinite, and yet a revelation by Himself of

Himself." The last stanza shows the influence of Carlyle and of Hallam's "Theodicaea Novissima" based on love:

> With faith that comes of self-control,
>> The truths that never can be proved
>> Until we close with all we loved,
> And all we flow from, soul in soul.

But those last two lines reflect Dante's discovery that his own desire and will were blended (as in Tennyson's "O living will") with God's:

> . . . but already
> my desire and will were rolled—as a wheel
> that is turned evenly—by the Love that moves
> the sun and the other stars.

Dante's discovery led back, we know, to an established and public theology. But Tennyson, too, makes connection with the developing liberal or Broad Church theology of F. D. Maurice and others. Eleanor Mattes speaks of Maurice's influence on the Prologue, dated 1849, which is apparently Christian, but still relativist:

> Our little systems have their day;
>> They have their day and cease to be:
>> They are but broken lights of thee,
> And thou, O Lord, art more than they.

But Tennyson's faith beyond the forms of faith has still wider application, in that it remains the unstated eclectic religion of liberals who are even vaguely theistic—though we allude to our faith in new terms, terms borrowed from depth psychology and anthropology. Among church members, too, Tennyson's faith informs the new ecumenical spirit which recognizes all creeds as possible responses to an ultimate reality that can be experienced but not known. What matters for such a faith—as it matters for gauging the success of In Memoriam—is not the creed but its undersong or symbolic texture, and that the creed really be arrived at through a process of personal discovery.

CHRISTOPHER RICKS

"The Days That Are No More"

In 1931 Sir Charles Tennyson drew attention to "one curious characteristic of Tennyson's methods of composition":

> I have noted in these early poems a number of lines which the poet used again, often years afterwards, in quite different contexts, in his published work. It is known and has been remarked that Tennyson often stored observations and similes for long periods before finally working them into his poems, and this storage of actual lines from early compositions is a fresh illustration of the same tendency. The remarkable thing is that the lines, when finally taken from storage, fit so naturally and aptly into their new context that they are often among the best passages in the poems in which they are employed.

Such self-borrowings are relevant to Tennyson's most impassioned subject: Time. "He was," said Humphry House, "an Aeonian poet; one on whom the consciousness of time bore like a burden." It was on the subject of time that Tennyson wrote those lines of his which are most likely to stand against time.

The point is implicit in a famous example of self-borrowing in Wordsworth. His sonnet "Mutability" tells how the outward forms of truth

> ... drop like the tower sublime
> Of yesterday, which royally did wear
> His crown of weeds, but could not even sustain

From *Tennyson*. Copyright © 1972 by The Macmillan Publishing Company.

> Some casual shout that broke the silent air,
> Or the unimaginable touch of Time.

Why is it moving to learn that the last line, "the unimaginable touch of Time," had been part of a "Fragment of a 'Gothic' Tale" about thirty years earlier? Mainly because of the sureness of Wordsworth's sense of context, the life which here pours into the cliché "the touch of Time." But perhaps we are moved too by the poem's subject, "Mutability," by the fact that despite mutability and the touch of time, for Wordsworth something important endured unchanging and still new: the line of poetry which he had written thirty years before.

Of course, the point is not, strictly, literary criticism; it is a point about biography, or methods of composition—it concerns the question why, of all the good lines which Wordsworth had available from his juvenilia, it should have been this one which later meant so much to him and which he was able to use so beautifully. Again and again Tennyson's self-borrowings explicitly concern time, even the mystical wish to be "Out of the sphere of Time."

Yet there is nothing a poet can use which he cannot also abuse, and *Maud* provides important evidence that Tennyson's self-borrowings can lead to the heart of his failures as well as of his successes. It is not an accident that one reaches for an organic metaphor like "germ" to describe the relationship of "Oh! that 'twere possible" to the completed monodrama. What we find is not the changing but the providing of a context. As originally published, "Oh! that 'twere possible" had no dramatic or psychological setting; itself a cry, it cried out for one. That Tennyson was dissatisfied with it, is clear from his not including it in his volumes of 1842; by 1855, he had created its context.

Maud, then, shows the success of this method of composition, but it also shows us a failure. One section of *Maud* was bitterly ridiculed by many critics on publication, as falling far below the lyrical and psychological force of the rest: the song "Go not, happy day" (I. xvii), which the hero exclaims in his love of Maud:

> Go not, happy day,
>   From the shining fields,
> Go not, happy day,
>   Till the maiden yields. . . .
> Pass the happy news,
>   Blush it through the West;
> Till the red man dance
>   By his red cedar-tree,
> And the red man's babe
>   Leap, beyond the sea.

> Blush from West to East,
>> Blush from East to West,
> Till the West is East,
>> Blush it through the West . . .

The objection to this song is not to its happiness but to its being ill written: the graceless hyperbole which has the red man's babe leaping because of a love-match in England, and the cumbrous repetitions, uncharactistically devoid of lyrical feeling.

There are indeed true moments of happiness in *Maud*—the section which follows this song ("I have led her home, my love, my only friend") is one of them. But "Go not, happy day" is written in the wrong style; why does the hero fall into this nursery-rhyming? If we ask where we have met such a tone before, the answer is in some of the songs which Tennyson interpolated in the third edition of *The Princess* (1850). "Go not, happy day" was originally one of the songs for *The Princess*; Tennyson found no place for it there, and rather than waste it he made a place for it in *Maud* (made, not found). The tone resembles that of this song from *The Princess*:

> And blessings on the falling out
> That all the more endears,
> When we fall out with those we love
> And kiss again with tears!

The affinity is evident in the two poems which Tennyson published as "Child-Songs" in 1880, but which he notes were originally for *The Princess*:

> Minnie and Winnie
> Slept in a shell.
> Sleep, little ladies!
> And they slept well.

But such a tone was not right for *Maud*—and we can now see why the red man's babe appeared. Not because of any aptness to *Maud* but because of the babe in *The Princess*. But in transferring "Go not, happy day," Tennyson was for once under the ill influence of his habit.

For the habit at its best, we may turn to some of the finest lines he ever wrote, from "Ulysses":

> To follow knowledge like a sinking star,
> Beyond the utmost bound of human thought.

In their context as Ulysses speaks (a context soaked in a consciousness of time):

> Life piled on life
> Were all too little, and of one to me

> Little remains: but every hour is saved
> From that eternal silence, something more,
> A bringer of new things; and vile it were
> For some three suns to store and hoard myself,
> And this gray spirit yearning in desire
> To follow knowledge like a sinking star,
> Beyond the utmost bound of human thought.

In a Trinity notebook, these two lines form part of quite a different poem, "Tiresias," which Tennyson did not complete and publish until 1885 but which he had begun at the same time as "Ulysses": October 1833, the month in which he heard the news of Hallam's death. As published, "Tiresias" begins:

> I wish I were as in the years of old,
> While yet the blessèd daylight made itself
> Ruddy through both the roofs of sight, and woke
> These eyes, now dull, but then so keen to seek
> The meanings ambushed under all they saw....

But a Trinity manuscript begins:

> I wish I were as in the days of old,
> Ere my smooth cheek darkened with youthful down,
> While yet the blessèd daylight made itself
> Ruddy within the eaves of sight, before
> I looked upon divinity unveiled
> And wisdom naked—when my mind was set
> To follow knowledge like a sinking star,
> Beyond the utmost bound of human thought.

(Again, in "Tiresias," the oppressive sense of time.) It is the context which triumphantly justifies Tennyson's decision as to where to use his resonant lines. What has a star to do with Tiresias? But Ulysses is speaking to his mariners, and mariners do indeed watch and follow stars. And what had Tiresias to do with bounds and horizons? Whereas in his last voyage Ulysses yearns

> To sail beyond the sunset, and the baths
> Of all the western stars, until I die.

Again, notice how the contrast between Ulysses' aged frame and his burning spirit comes out in a juxtaposition absent from the context in "Tiresias": the play of "this gray spirit" against the "sinking star" (and of the "suns" against the "star"). All these details bind the lines into their context, and so does the echo of Dante in "knowledge." "Ulysses" has as its primary source the speech by Ulysses in Dante's *Inferno*, urging his companions to their last voyage. Tennyson's "knowledge" calls up Dante's *conoscenza*. The difference between the use of those two lines in "Tiresias" and in "Ulysses" is the difference between talent and genius. It is Tennyson's sense of context which releases all the energies of the lines.

The same is true of another of his great lines, again in a context heavy with time: "The phantom circle of a moaning sea." The scene is the last battle in "The Passing of Arthur" (1869)—a scene likely to bring out the best in a poet whose enterprise had shown itself more than forty years earlier in a poem on Armageddon.

> Then rose the King and moved his host by night,
> And ever pushed Sir Modred, league by league,
> Back to the sunset bound of Lyonnesse—
> A land of old upheaven from the abyss
> By fire, to sink into the abyss again;
> Where fragments of forgotten peoples dwelt
> And the long mountains ended in a coast
> Of ever-shifting sand, and far away
> The phantom circle of a moaning sea.

Could any location be more apt to "this last, dim, weird battle of the west"?—where the fighters are themselves phantoms in the mist, where not only the sea is moaning, and where the life of the king completes its phantom circle? And yet only a year before (1868), Tennyson had printed, though not published, the line as part of the last section of "The Lover's Tale." In the trial edition, which he suppressed once more, we hear of

> A dismal hostel in a dismal land,
> A world of reed and rush, and far away
> The phantom circle of a moaning sea.

How fortunate that Tennyson somehow knew not to waste the line on such a context. Not, in fact, that he had created the line for "The Lover's Tale" either. More than thirty years before, about 1833, it had formed the climax of his little poem describing Mablethorpe on the Lincolnshire coast. In 1850 he published these "Lines," but without the second stanza which survives in a Trinity manuscript, and which speaks of "The phantom-circle of the moaning main." In the fullness of time, Tennyson ameliorated the alliteration and found for the line the right fullness of context.

For Tennyson, context often meant the fusion of a landscape with a mood. The Harvard manuscript of *The Princess* includes these lines in its Prologue:

> Within, the sward
> Was kept like any lawn, but all about
> Large ivy sucked the joinings of the stones,
> Beneath like knots of snakes.

No fusion, because that muscularity, that mood, answers to nothing in *The Princess*. In "The Marriage of Geraint," Tennyson fuses description and mood, a mood haunted by time:

> And high above a piece of turret stair,
> Worn by the feet that now were silent, wound
> Bare to the sun, and monstrous ivy-stems
> Claspt the gray walls with hairy-fibred arms,
> And sucked the joining of the stones, and looked
> A knot, beneath, of snakes, aloft, a grove.

Sometimes such a gift for placing may crystallize into a discreet pun. The *Memoir* (i. 465) says that the following fragment was jotted down at Torquay:

> . . . as the little thrift
> Trembles in perilous places o'er the deep.

But this jotting about the plant thrift was not used by Tennyson until he could engage with the other sense of thrift. His poem "Sea Dreams" deals with his disastrous investing of all his funds in Dr. Matthew Allen's wood-carving scheme:

> Small were his gains, and hard his work; besides,
> Their slender household fortunes (for the man
> Had risked his little) like the little thrift,
> Trembled in perilous places o'er a deep. . . .

At the other extreme from such a tiny instance of self-borrowing comes the incorporation *en bloc* of a whole passage of blank verse. Context here means pace—Tennyson is a master of pace. Who would have thought that the finest lines in the magnificent closing passage of *The Princess* were originally part of another poem written fifteen years before? The tempo, with its superb rallentando and its tranquil finality, is perfect:

> . . . the walls
> Blackened about us, bats wheeled, and owls whooped,
> And gradually the powers of the night,
> That range above the region of the wind,
> Deepening the courts of twilight broke them up
> Through all the silent spaces of the worlds,
> Beyond all thought into the Heaven of Heavens.
>   Last little Lilia, rising quietly,
> Disrobed the glimmering statue of Sir Ralph
> From those rich silks, and home well-pleased we went.

Tempo depends here on time as well as timing. "Last," "quietly": the full potentialities of the lines emerge only in this context, as can be seen if we look back at them in "The Lover's Tale" of 1832, which Tennyson suppressed before publication:

> When thou and I, Cadrilla, thou and I
> Were borne about the bay or sitting gazed
> Till gradually the powers of the night
> That range above the region of the wind
> Deepening the courts of twilight, broke them up
> Through all the silent spaces of the worlds
> Beyond all thought, into the Heaven of Heavens.
> When thou and I, Cadrilla, thou and I
> Were moored by some low cavern, while without
> Through the long dark . . .

And so on, in a deft passage of Tennysonian verse. But those central lines needed to be something more than merely one among many memories; it was not till the end of *The Princess* that they found the placing which, as it were, they were made for.

Such self-borrowings not only revealed Tennyson's sense of context and his preoccupation with time; they also underline the extreme rashness of the generalizations as to his development, the growth or decline of his powers. The little poem "Poets and Critics" was not published till his posthumous volume of 1892, and its manner suggests that it encapsulates his long battling with the reviewers:

> Year will graze the heel of year,
> But seldom comes the poet here,
> And the Critic's rarer still.

Yet it was written sixty years before, and is Tennyson's reaction, not to a lifetime of reviewing, but to the reviews of his earliest volumes. And for Tennyson, year had indeed grazed the heel of year before he came to publish it.

It is the same with the honeymoon song that introduces the late poem "The Ring," published in 1889, a song which must not be taken as evidence that his lyrical gift had astonishingly survived (or sadly declined) since it in fact dates from 1833.

> Shall not *my* love last,
> Moon, with you,
> For ten thousand years
> Old and new?

Love may last, as the poem itself had lasted—though this could be known to none but the poet and his immediate circle. The "Ode on the Death of the

Duke of Wellington" (1852) is imbued with a sense of the passing of an era:

> For though the Giant Ages heave the hill
> And break the shore, and evermore
> Make and break, and work their will...

But this vision of time was one which had come to Tennyson far back in time, twenty years before; it is the Soul, in a manuscript of "The Palace of Art," who sees this vision:

> Yet saw she Earth laid open. Furthermore
>   How the strong Ages had their will,
> A range of Giants breaking down the shore
>   And heaving up the hill.

The convergence for Tennyson of self-borrowings and a preoccupation with time is implicit in two examples furnished by Sir Charles Tennyson. The early unpublished poem "An Idle Rhyme" provided a line for In Memoriam (XCV. 40)—the line is "The deep pulsations of the world," which in In Memoriam goes on: "Æonian music measuring out / The steps of Time." And the early poem "Sense and Conscience" provided a simile for "The Lover's Tale"—the simile ponders youth and age:

> Even the dull-blooded poppy-stem, "whose flower,
> Hued with the scarlet of a fierce sunrise,
> Like to the wild youth of an evil prince,
> Is without sweetness, but who crowns himself
> Above the naked poisons of his heart
> In his old age."

Yet, as these examples bring out, this is not the case of an artist who has outlived his gift and who is forced to clutch at his unpublished juvenilia—rather as James Thurber, when blind and unable to draw, is said to have devised new captions for his old drawings. In Tennyson the habit was a lifelong one, as is well known from the composition of his first notably successful poem, "Timbuctoo," with which he won the Chancellor's Gold Medal at Cambridge in 1829. For this, "he patched up an old poem on 'The Battle of Armageddon' "; in fact the Trinity manuscript shows that about 120 lines, or roughly half of "Timbuctoo," was lifted whole from "Armageddon." It is characteristic of Tennyson that he went on to borrow from "Timbuctoo" itself; one of its lines turns up in "The Lover's Tale," and two lines in the "Ode to Memory." What is also characteristic is the subject of these further self-borrowings: "A centered glory-circled memory," and "the lordly music flowing from / The illimitable years."

There is no breach between the young Tennyson and the old. His first political pronouncement as a peer was the poem "Freedom," published in, and dated, 1884. Its closing stanza was taken from the poem "Hail Briton," which Tennyson had written but not published fifty years before. And it is not just the closing stanza which was taken over; the Trinity manuscripts make clear that much of "Freedom" was culled from political poems of 1832–33. The political viewpoint is altogether consistent. Robert Frost wrote:

> I never dared be radical when young
> For fear it would make me conservative when old.

But Tennyson had no need of this "Precaution"; when he wished to speak as a septuagenarian, he simply published at last the words which he had written in his twenties.

For Tennyson there was never a breach between the political and the personal. Yet when a man's son dies, and he writes a poem about the death, one would expect all of that poem at least to be newly created. When Tennyson's son Lionel died on his way home from India in 1886, Tennyson's funeral poem began with a stanza which he had written more than fifty years before in "Hail Briton." "To the Marquis of Dufferin and Ava" thanks the Viceroy for all he had done for Lionel.

> At times our Britain cannot rest,
>   At times her steps are swift and rash;
>   She moving, at her girdle clash
> The golden keys of East and West.
>
> Not swift or rash, when late she lent
>   The sceptres of her West, her East,
>   To one, that ruling has increased
> Her greatness and her self-content.

And so through masterly transitions to personal thanks.

But if we look back fifty years, we see that in the earlier context "East and West" was no more than a ringing description of the British Empire; it had none of the personal aptness here found for it. Dufferin had been ambassador in Constantinople and viceroy in India; Lionel Tennyson had died visiting India on his work for the India Office. And once again the lines seem to have risen to Tennyson's mind because of their sense of time, of an era. "Not swift or rash"—the words may, without flippancy, be applied to the habit of composition itself.

For Tennyson, there had never been an era's end so unforgettable as the French Revolution—from his first to his last poems, it preys upon his mind. In "Hail Briton," he has eight lines on revolution and time; these eight lines he transferred to *In Memoriam*, CXIII, where they became some of the noblest lines which he wrote in praise of Hallam, whose death had removed a man of great political promise:

> Should licensed boldness gather force,
>> Becoming, when the time has birth,
>> A lever to uplift the earth
> And roll it in another course,
>
> With many shocks that come and go,
>> With agonies, with energies,
>> With overthrowings, and with cries,
> And undulations to and fro.

The political and the personal are here truly joined, in the converging of self-borrowing and the sense of time.

The deep biographical roots of his self-borrowing (its being not a convenience but a cast of mind) are evident in the impulse to borrow from similar contexts. Take these lines about time, from *The Princess*:

> . . . all the rich to-come
> Reels, as the golden Autumn woodland reels
> Athwart the smoke of burning weeds.

Tennyson created these lines from the conclusion to *In Memoriam*, which in the Lincoln manuscript includes this stanza:

> We pace the stubble bare of sheaves,
>> We watch the brimming river steal
>> And half the golden woodland reel
> Athwart the smoke of burning leaves.

When Tennyson's mind went back and rescued those lines he was not simply gleaning natural description, he was reaching to the context of ideal married love (itself golden and autumnal). In *The Princess*, the lines go on to "My bride, / My wife, my life." In the manuscript of *In Memoriam*, they describe how the wedding guests stroll through the countryside after the marriage of Tennyson's sister. The change from "burning leaves" to "burning weeds" is a fine one, in its slight unexpectedness, and in the way in which it transforms "weeds" into part of the golden scene.

It seems important that so many of these self-borrowings have to do with time, but there are three counter-arguments. First, that there are dangers in even speaking of Tennyson's "characteristic" preoccupation with time—everybody is preoccupied with time, and literary critics are always fudging up "characteristics" of an author or a period which are simply common to humanity. Second, that if most of Tennyson's poems are about time, it is hardly surprising or significant that most of his self-borrowings are also about time. Third, that time is so elastic a concept that it is hard to imagine a poem which couldn't in some sense be claimed as "about" time.

Yet it still seems that Tennyson writes about time with an unusual depth and imagination; that, even so, unexpectedly many of his self-borrowings are concerned with time; and that no far-fetched meaning has to be sought for "time" in order to accommodate them. The habit of self-borrowing manifests both an awareness of, and a means of countering, time. It has the "emotional importance" which Humphry House brilliantly picked out in Tennyson's fascination with description:

> Many of Tennyson's poems—*Maud* most notable among the longer ones—totter on the edge of madness. Constantly the one rallying-point in them as poems is the description of external things. . . . In a number of poems he uses description as if it were in itself the final aim of poetic art. . . . These descriptions . . . had for him a central emotional importance. They stabilised his mind in the contemplation of unending processes, and allayed the restlessness of the searching and journeying involved in his view of what poetry should do.

Does self-borrowing (a method of composition which became a means of composition) have for Tennyson a comparable function? The dangers of melancholia, even of madness, were not remote from Tennyson; in a world of unending flux, a world where all seemed ephemeral (even the works of the greatest poets), a world where personal identity was a mystery and often a burden, Tennyson found some rallying point in the continuity of his own creativity. What helped to "stabilize his mind" was the reassurance offered by his own past (as in his "Passion of the Past"), and nothing was more reassuring in that past than the surviving, and still living, evidences of his powers. To revise a published poem was to show that the past was not done with, irrevocable, immutable. To quarry from his unpublished work was to show that the past was indeed a quarry, its geological obduracy the source of its riches. The threatening melancholia crystallizes in two lines in the poem "Walking to the Mail" about the "morbid devil in his blood":

> He lost the sense that handles daily life—
> That keeps us all in order more or less. . . .

Is it just a coincidence that those lines too had originally been part of another poem ("The Gardener's Daughter")?

Tennyson's self-borrowings, then, seem to have the same emotional importance as his preoccupation with description. Just how important this continuity was to him can be seen from the Tennyson *Concordance*. Self-borrowing needs to be related not only to the word "time" (over 300 times in the *Concordance*) or the favorite adjective "slow," but also to his persistent need for the prefix "re-", itself a signal that the past still lives, can revive. "The blossom that rebloomed"; "Remade the blood and changed the frame"; "Rewaken with the dawning soul"; "Remerging in the general Soul"; "Can I but relive in sadness?"—there are innumerable examples. For Tennyson, revision is truly a second vision. "So that, in that I *have* lived, do I live" ("The Lover's Tale").

Tennyson's self-borrowings go to the heart of his poetic skill and of his preoccupation with time. They also bring out the conflict which is often felt in reading Tennyson, the conflict between confidence in his extraordinary expertise and faint uneasiness about the extent to which the expertise is verbal or purely verbal. There is something strange about the predicament of a poet whose wife had continually to urge his friends to provide him with subjects or stories for poems. Yet the end-products are sheer Tennyson.

The oddity of Tennyson's sources is analogous to that of his style: how is it that such apparently dangerous habits so often resulted in something magnificently personal? Certainly the habit of self-borrowing leads to a central point: Tennyson's verbalism. The best criticism of Tennyson is by Walt Whitman:

> To me, Tennyson shows more than any poet I know (perhaps has been a warning to me) how much there is in finest verbalism. There is such a latent charm in mere words, cunning collocutions, and in the voice ringing them, which he has caught and brought out, beyond all others—as in the line, "And hollow, hollow, hollow, all delight," in "The Passing of Arthur."

It comes agreeably to hand that even that line, "And hollow, hollow, all delight," had originally been fumbled for in a line which Tennyson rejected from "Locksley Hall": "hollow, hollow, hollow comfort."

JOHN ROSENBERG

"Idylls of the King": Evolving the Form

"Perfection in art," Tennyson re-marked, "is perhaps more sudden sometimes than we think; but then the long preparation for it, that unseen germination, *that* is what we ignore and forget." The unseen germination of the *Idylls of the King* goes back at least to that moment in Tennyson's early youth when he first read Malory and "the vision of Arthur as I have drawn him...had come upon me." The vision remained with him until his death, within a few months of which he made the last of the innumerable revisions of the *Idylls*. As Kathleen Tillotson observes, the poem, which is so richly concerned with time and change, was itself subject in the long course of its composition to the pressures of time and change.

Yet despite its tortuous evolution, the *Idylls* displays a remarkable unity. The germ of the whole, the fragmentary "Morte d'Arthur," drafted in 1833, revised in 1835, and published in 1842, was so instinctually right in tone and design that over a quarter of a century after its first publication Tennyson could incorporate it without change into the still-unfinished *Idylls* of 1869. During the next two decades he continually altered and expanded the design of the larger poem without violating the verbatim integrity of this first-composed but last-in-sequence of the idylls. With the hindsight the completed poem grants us, we can see that this last of the idylls had come first, or at least that no other segment of the Arthurian cycle could have fit with fewer complications into Tennyson's ultimate design. At this stage in

From *The Fall of Camelot*. Copyright © 1973 by the President and Fellows of Harvard College. The Belknap Press of Harvard University Press, 1973.

the decline of the Round Table, the cast of characters has dwindled to Arthur and the sole surviving knight who witnesses his passing, and the overriding theme of the poem—the wasting away of human aspiration in the face of time—is felt at its keenest. Drawn to that part of the Arthurian myth which most compelled his imagination, Tennyson begins abruptly upon a conjunction—"So all day long the noise of battle rolled"—which implies everything that comes before it yet leaves him the maximum freedom in later developing the full story.

In 1833 the coincidence of a personal catastrophe with what can only be described as a lifelong obsession led Tennyson to begin his two "Arthur" poems, the "Morte d'Arthur" and In Memoriam. The obsession concerned some apocalyptic upheaval—of a city, a civilization, of the earth itself—and is present in Tennyson's earliest writing. The catastrophe was the sudden death of Arthur Hallam, the news of which reached Tennyson on October 1, 1833, and his response to which he made public seventeen years later in In Memoriam. The "Morte d'Arthur" was as much a reaction to the actual Arthur's death as was In Memoriam. The earliest manuscript fragments of the two poems appear in the same notebook, and Tennyson himself strongly hints at their common origin in the autobiographical "Merlin and the Gleam" (1889):

> Clouds and darkness
> Closed upon Camelot;
> Arthur had vanished
> I knew not whither,
> The king who loved me,
> And cannot die . . .
>   (st. VII)

The king who "loved *me*" and cannot die is clearly Arthur Hallam, yet he is also the Arthur of the *Idylls*. The two are virtually indistinguishable: "Thou art the highest and most human too," Guinevere says of her king (G, 644); and Tennyson addresses the king of In Memoriam as "Known and unknown; human, divine" (sec. CXXIX). Given the internal and external evidence, Sir Charles Tennyson's comment on the connection between Hallam's death and the "Morte d'Arthur" strikes me as indisputable: Tennyson in part "sublimate[d] in *Morte d'Arthur* his own passionate grief at the death of Arthur Hallam." Beneath the measured cadences of Bedivere's lament for Arthur's passing, one senses the urgency of personal statement, as if Tennyson himself were forced to "go forth companionless" into an alien world. His profoundly personal quest for reunion with Hallam in In Memoriam—"Descend, and touch, and enter" (sec. XCIII)—becomes in the Idylls a profoundly impersonal despair for the passing not only of a hero but of civilization.

Haunted all his life by the ghosts of such passings, Tennyson was understandably drawn to the story of the doomed king who falls with the death of his kingdom. In his boyhood, before he had read Malory, Tennyson had written a whole series of poems whose titles alone betray his preoccupation with the subject: "The Fall of Jerusalem," "The Vale of Bones," "Babylon," "Lamentation of the Peruvians." The Library of Trinity College, Cambridge, contains the manuscript of a poem far more ambitious than these which is remarkably premonitory of the apocalyptic close of the *Idylls*. Written when Tennyson was probably not more than fifteen, "Armageddon" draws in its climactic passage upon the chapter in Revelation (16) in which the angels of the Lord pour out His wrath upon mankind on the Day of Judgment. The confused shoutings and "dark terrific pall" that obscure the battle of the Last Day in "Armageddon" also mark Arthur's last dim battle in the West. And the "dim cries/ . . . As of some lonely city sacked by night" that accompany Arthur's passing, echo the passage in "Armageddon" in which is heard

> . . . the long low moaning
> Of inarticulate thunder like the wail
> Of some lost City in it's [sic] evil day.

The pervasiveness of the apocalyptic mode of vision throughout Tennyson's works has never been sufficiently appreciated. Previsions of some fiery fall—of Troy in "Oenone," of Camelot throughout the *Idylls*, of the earth itself in the early and astonishing "Kraken"—are among the most striking motifs in his verse. The "annihilating anarchy" of "Armageddon" reappears near the end of *In Memoriam*, where the ice-capped mountains topple,

> And molten up, and roar in flood;
> The fortress crashes from on high,
> The brute earth lightens to the sky,
> And the great Aeon sinks in blood.
> (sec. CXXVIII)

This same apocalyptic landscape reappears in the great close of the *Idylls*, where Arthur moves his host by night

> Back to the sunset bound of Lyonnesse—
> A land of old upheaven from the abyss
> By fire, to sink into the abyss again;
> Where fragments of forgotten peoples dwelt,
> And the long mountains ended in a coast
> Of ever-shifting sand, and far away
> The phantom circle of a moaning sea.
> (PA, 81–87)

The image of some catastrophic upheaval figures crucially in Tennyson's earliest outline of an Arthurian poem. The sketch is remarkable in that it contains no narrative action whatsoever, yet its very stasis foreshadows one of the central symbols of the *Idylls*, the towering, illusory city poised on the brink of the abyss:

> On the latest limit of the West in the land of Lyonnesse, where . . . all is now wild sea, rose the sacred Mount of Camelot. It rose from the deeps with gardens and bowers and palaces, and at the top of the Mount was King Arthur's hall, and the holy Minster with the Cross of gold. Here dwelt the King in glory apart, while the Saxons whom he had overthrown in twelve battles ravaged the land, and ever came nearer and nearer.
>
> The Mount was the most beautiful in the world, sometimes green and fresh in the beam of morning, sometimes all one splendour, folded in the golden mists of the West. But all underneath it was hollow, and the mountain trembled, when the seas rushed bellowing through the porphyry caves; and there ran a prophecy that the mountain and the city on some wild morning would topple into the abyss and be no more. . . .

The hollowness of the mountain figures in the finished *Idylls* as the mists which enshroud the sacred Mount and symbolizes the whole series of interlocking illusions and betrayals that finally bring Camelot down in flames. Tennyson remains true to this earliest image of a fair appearance succumbing to a fatal reality, but his conception of Arthur "dwelling in glory apart" undergoes a significant change. The isolated Arthur of the prose sketch recalls one aspect of Tennyson himself in the 1830's, torn between his attraction to the "golden mists" of the imagination and the claims of social responsibility (the ever-encroaching Saxons). The Arthur of the *Idylls*, however, must abandon the "Palace of Art" in order to do the work of this world. Yet the "many-corridored complexities" of Camelot (MV, 730) also enshrine the aesthetic imagination, which Tennyson felt was threatened by the rationalist-materialist bias of his age. In reanimating the myth of Arthur he was deliberately trying to conserve ancient modes of thought and feeling that he knew to be vital not only to his private activity as a poet but to the continuity of our culture. This conviction informs the close of the very early "Timbuctoo," in which the Spirit of Fable praises

> The permeating life which courseth through
> All the intricate and labyrinthine veins
> Of the great vine of *Fable*, which, outspread
> With growth of shadowing leaf and clusters rare,
> Reacheth to every corner under Heaven,
> Deep-rooted in the living soil of truth.
>
> (216–221)

The Spirit surveys the splendid domes and gardens of a city that symbolizes the poetic imagination, and laments that they must all soon fall victim

> To keen *Discovery*: soon yon brilliant towers
> Shall darken with the waving of her wand;
> Darken, and shrink and shiver into huts,
> Black specks amid a waste of dreary sand,
> Low-built, mud-walled, Barbarian settlements.
> How changed from this fair City!
>
> (240–245)

The fall of this fair city of the imagination is one of the most striking anticipations in Tennyson's early verse of the fall of Camelot; in both "Timbuctoo" and the *Idylls* the "brilliant towers" of the mind's own building give way to a desolate, post-civilized landscape of forgotten peoples and waste sands.

I have tried to suggest why Tennyson's imagination was so strongly predisposed to the story of Arthur, and why in the year of Hallam's death he was moved to begin his first major poem on what he called "the greatest of all poetical subjects." It remains for us to see how, having found his subject, he reshaped it in the light of his own genius.

A clue to Tennyson's earliest intentions appears in the introductory verses to the "Morte d'Arthur," where we learn that the poet has burnt his epic on "King Arthur, some twelve books," for they were mere "faint Homeric echoes, nothing-worth." Only the "Morte" was plucked from the flames in the conviction that "its use will come." The imaginary burning of the books is more than a device for introducing, in medias res, the isolated fragment on Arthur's passing. It symbolizes Tennyson's rejection, sometime between the drafting of the "Morte" in 1833 and its publication nine years later, of an epic model for the *Idylls*. "At twenty-four I meant to write an epic or drama of King Arthur," he remarked after the *Idylls* was nearly completed: "I said I should do it in twenty years; but the Reviews stopped me." Hypersensitive to criticism, Tennyson was doubtless distressed by the mixed reviews of the "Morte"; if they in fact stopped him, one can only be grateful. Eleven more books in the ostensibly epic form of the "Morte" might indeed have produced "Homeric echoes, nothing-worth." As is, he began with that part of the Arthurian cycle which, together with "The Coming of Arthur," most lends itself to epic treatment: the national hero who creates a kingdom and dies in single combat in its defense. Tennyson himself pointed out that the form and style of these two frame poems are "purposely more archaic" than the ten Round Table idylls which they enclose. Once the final design completed itself in his mind, he turned the initial disparity to aesthetic advantage. He added to the original epic fragment the great opening lines of "The Passing" (1–169) that draw together all the dominant symbols of the *Idylls*, thereby binding the "Morte" to all that precedes it. And by setting off from the Round Table idylls the paired poems which mark Arthur's coming into the mutable world and passing into another, Tennyson incorporates into the very structure of the *Idylls* its cyclic themes of change and permanence, of time and eternity.

Despite its evident excellence, one detects a certain unevenness in the "Morte." Its most moving moments are elegiac rather than epic, pictorial rather than narrative, such as Arthur's eulogy to his fallen knights or Bedivere's lament as he watches the barge vanish, knowing that he must

> . . . go forth companionless,
> And the days darken round me, and the years,
> Among new men, strange faces, other minds.
> (PA, 404–406)

One suspects that Tennyson's abandoned prose sketch, in which absolutely nothing happens but everything is seen with fixed intensity, was in fact closer to his essential genius than the more conventionally epic portions of the "Morte." Yet the Arthurian story to which he had committed himself was crowded with actions of all kinds, some suited to epic treatment, such as Arthur's last battle, some to the highly mannered conventions of romance, such as the tale of Lancelot and Elaine, some to a more allegorical handling, such as the story of Merlin and Vivien, which Tennyson recast as a medieval debate of body and soul. The reviewers doubtless slowed his progress, but the seventeen-year hiatus between the publication of the "Morte" and that of the first four idylls of 1859 was due far more to Tennyson's uncertain quest for a form that would encompass the inherent diversity of his subject.

In addition to the prose sketch for an Arthurian work, Tennyson considered two other schemes, both fortunately abandoned. One was for a drama or masque in five acts; the scenario, with its projected "Chorus of Ladies of the Lake," disastrously suggests a sort of Christmas pantomime set to music. The second, more fragmentary outline calls for an allegorical rendering in which Arthur is to stand for "Religious Faith," Merlin for "Science," and the Round Table for "liberal institutions."

Although Tennyson very soon gave up the idea of structuring the *Idylls* as a strict allegory, his commentators persisted in interpreting the poem as such, provoking him to remark: "They have taken my hobby, and ridden it too hard, and have explained some things too allegorically, although there is an allegorical or perhaps rather a parabolic drift in the poem." Tennyson appears to have been both flattered by the finding of allegorical significances in the *Idylls* and deeply apprehensive that such readings were reductive of his whole intention. Hence his revealingly ambiguous reply to those who asked whether or not the Three Queens who appear at Arthur's coronation stand for Faith, Hope, and Charity: "They are right, and they are not right. They mean that and they do not. They are three of the noblest of women. They are also those three Graces, but they are much more. I hate to be tied down to say, 'This means that,' because the thought within the image is much more than any one interpretation." By "parabolic drift" and "thought within the image," Tennyson means precisely what we mean by *symbol*, the antithesis of the reductive, this-for-that equivalence which his commentators have found in the *Idylls*. The point is not that allegory is simplistic—a patent absurdity—but that the *Idylls* is not an allegory and that those who so read it are forced into simplistic conclusions.

Yet in a curiously conspiratorial way Tennyson encouraged such misreadings: "By King Arthur I always meant the soul, and by the Round Table the passions and capacities of a man." But if, as Tennyson writes in the Epilogue, the *Idylls* is about "Sense at war with Soul," why is the "sinful" Lancelot, usurper of the Soul's bed, the secular hero of the poem? The answer lies in a confusion of intention in Tennyson and of perception in his critics. An allegorical residue remains embedded in the overall symbolic structure of the poem, although only once—when Arthur ("Soul") denounces Guinevere ("Sense")—does the mixture of modes jar on the reader. Elsewhere, this residue results in a certain deficiency of realization, as with the Lady of the Lake or those

> ...three fair queens,
> Who stood in silence near his throne, the friends
> Of Arthur, gazing on him, tall, with bright
> Sweet faces, who will help him at his need.
> (CA, 275–278)

The difficulty with the trio is that they have no narrative function and no real connection with the poem's central characters or symbols, and so they stand in idle silence. They are simply part of the magical donné of Arthurian legend, to which Tennyson remains perhaps too diffidently faithful. His awareness of this dilemma always shows itself in a failure in his craft as a poet: the verse either becomes portentous or, as in the cited passage, lapses into the *contrivedly* prosaic (unlike Wordsworth, Tennyson is incapable of being unwittingly prosaic).

At the other extreme from an abstraction such as the Lady of the Lake ("The Church") are those characters who so richly embody the poem's moral and psychological complexities that any attempt to tag them with allegorical labels at once breaks down. Lancelot, for example, is larger than any didactic formula we might devise to contain him, and it is his greatness as a character that . . . compels us, in our attempts at explanation, to enlarge

our terms of moral definition. His love for his king is as absolute as his love
for his queen, and it is his tragedy that loyalty to one must be disloyalty to
the other:

> The great and guilty love he bare the Queen,
> In battle with the love he bare his lord,
> Had marred his face, and marked it ere his time.
> (LE, 244–246)

The whole force of this passage lies in the juxtaposed "great *and* guilty": the
guilt of the love is indisputable, but so too is its greatness, by which
Tennyson means not only intensity but nobility. Indeed, the guilt is a
function of the nobility; were it not for Lancelot's nobility, he would feel no
guilt, and without the guilt, there would be less greatness. The paradox of
the adultery of Lancelot and Guinevere is that it not only "mars" them (and
the kingdom) but ultimately ennobles them (and the kingdom), as Tennyson
emphasizes by contrast with another adulterous triangle—the guiltless,
peculiarly modern and joyless affair of Tristram and Isolt.

Yet in a recent book on the *Idylls* we read that Lancelot's guilty love of
Guinevere "has coarsened not only his moral sensibilities but also his
appearance." Nothing could more starkly illustrate the pitfalls consequent
upon reading the *Idylls* as a war of Sense versus Soul, in which certain
characters represent the vices of the first and others the virtues of the
second. The warfare, as James D. Merriman has brilliantly shown, "is not
between individuals, but rather within individuals, and the various characters in the *Idylls* illustrate at any given time some stage of victory or defeat in
that inner struggle." Gawain's losing inner battle exactly parallels the outer
struggle of the kingdom. His progressive degeneration from idyll to idyll is so
beautifully integrated with that of the realm, from its founding in the spring
to its barren end in the winter, that we scarcely notice him, for the changes
in the character's moral foliation all but merge with those of the kingdom.
Lancelot's far more tempestuous struggle moves in the opposite direction,
toward salvation, and even those characters at the moral extremes of
humanity—the harlot Vivien, for example—have an energy and solidity
that elude any reductive personification such as "The Flesh." Only Galahad
stands outside the arena of moral combat, and his victory over the flesh, as
Merriman points out, "comes at the expense of simply abandoning the
world, the real battleground of the war between Sense and Soul."

The *Idylls* dramatizes on all levels the only conflict that can engage
the mature moral imagination—the clash not of right versus wrong but of
right versus right. Allegorical interpretations of the *Idylls* obscure this
distinction and substitute didactic solutions for the moral dilemmas it poses.
Thus one critic assures us that the *Idylls* represents the triumph of "the high

soul of man" over the passions, while another describes the poem as an allegory of the collapse which "must follow the rejection of spiritual values." Yet the moral of the *Idylls* is not that men must abide by spiritual values, any more than the moral of *Othello* is that wives should look to their linen. In this sense, the poem is totally without a moral but explores instead the ambiguous results of man's quest for such values, and the disastrous effects of abandoning them. In "Lancelot and Elaine" *denial* of the flesh proves fatal, and as "The Holy Grail" makes clear, spiritual values can drive men as mad as sexual obsession. Tennyson suggests a possible connection between the two: the color red, which throughout the *Idylls* symbolizes sexuality, is also associated with the Grail itself, first seen as "rose-red" by a nun in a condition of erotic ecstasy, then as "blood-red" by Galahad—as is fitting for the vessel that bore Christ's blood.

Even of this simplest of the poem's thematic antitheses—white as purity, red as passion—we cannot say "*this* means *that*." The lily maid of Astolat, white in purity, is at first glance a personification of Virgin Innocence; but her dreams are insistently sexual and the sleeve she gives Lancelot is scarlet, for her purity, like the nun's, is profoundly passionate. Because the lily maid is not a conventional figure in an allegory, our impulse is to distort her into a modern simplism of our own: seeming purity masking a libidinous reality. Yet like the symbols associated with her, she is neither this nor that, but both pure *and* passionate, sexual *and* innocent, embodying the same intense conjunction of contrary elements that draws her instantly—and fatally—to Lancelot.

In 1859, when "Lancelot and Elaine" was published, Tennyson for the first time grouped his new series of Arthurian poems under the general title *Idylls of the King.* An idyll is a "little picture" of a character or mood colored by a single, dominant emotion. Tennyson's choice of the plural *idylls* stresses his intention, as Jerome Buckley points out, to portray "not a single unified narrative but a group of chivalric tableaux selected from a great mass of available legend....Each of the Idylls moves through a series of sharply visualized vignettes toward its pictured climax, its moment of revelation." Yet true as this is, one's experience of the *Idylls* is less static than it suggests. The sharply visualized vignettes which characterize so much of the poem— Lancelot kneeling before Guinevere in the vine-clad oriel window, Balin and Balan "sitting statue-like" by the fountain—are not simply pictures but *actions*, or rather their pictorial intensity is so great that we experience them as actions. The very early "Mariana" consists entirely of this hypercharged description. Imprisoned in her moated grange, Mariana is an animate extension of the setting, the setting a symbolic embodiment of her mental entrapment. The *Idylls* is filled with such moments of fixed intensity in which the energy of outward action turns in upon itself and narration becomes a kind of dramatized vision. The first critic to perceive this quality in Tennyson's verse was Arthur Hallam, and there is a certain ghostly aptness in summoning Hallam to illuminate the poetry in which he later figures so largely. Reviewing the volume in which "Mariana" first appeared, Hallam remarks on Tennyson's

> power of embodying himself in . . . moods of character, with such extreme accuracy of adjustment, that the circumstances of the narration seem to have a natural correspondence with the predominant feeling, and, as it were, to be evolved from it by assimilative force. . . . These expressions of character are brief and coherent: nothing extraneous to the dominant fact is admitted, nothing illustrative of it, and, as it were, growing out of it, is rejected. They are like summaries of mighty dramas. . . . We contend that it is a new species of poetry, a graft of the lyric on the dramatic.

Although the phrase was not in Hallam's vocabulary, he comes astonishingly close to saying in 1831 what we are only now recognizing in the 1970's: Tennyson is essentially a symbolist poet. Donald Smalley has noted the anomalous fact that while on one side of the Channel middle-class Victorians were finding the *Idylls* congenial to their taste, on the opposite shore the poem was being appreciated by an audience that "the Laureate would scarcely have anticipated or been likely to welcome—the French Symbolists." The influence of Tennyson on Poe ("I regard him as the noblest poet who ever lived") and, through Poe, on Baudelaire and Mallarmé constitutes one of the vital currents flowing into the poetry of our century. Mallarmé translated "Mariana," Baudelaire borrowed from Tennyson, and Yeats, who read Hallam's essay in the 1890's, found it indispensable to an understanding of the French Symbolists.

The symbolist technique that Hallam recognized in "Mariana" reaches its furthest development in the *Idylls*. The solitary Elaine in her tower, dreaming of Lancelot and stripping the silken case from his naked shield, is a more complex version of Mariana in her moated grange. Tennyson's whole problem in structuring the *Idylls* consisted in getting Elaine, as it were, down from her tower and onto the poem's field of action. A long narrative poem made up of separate vignettes, however sharply visualized, would collapse of its own static weight. Tennyson solved the problem by incorporating individual characters into the larger landscape of the *Idylls*; as in "Mariana," he obliterates the gap between self and scene and frees himself from bondage to conventional narrative. Building on the techniques of the classical idyll, with its intensification of mood, its highly allusive texture, its startling juxtapositions, flashbacks, and deliberate discontinuities, Tennyson creates an inclusive psychological landscape in which all the separate consciousnesses in the poem participate and in which each action is bound to all others through symbol, prophecy, or retrospect.

Seen from this perspective, the first lines Tennyson composed for the *Idylls* take on a singular significance. The "Morte" begins with the simplest and apparently slightest of alterations from Malory:

> So all day long the noise of battle rolled
> Among the mountains by the *winter* sea ...

Tennyson's shift in the setting of Arthur's death from summer to winter suggests that from the start he had in mind the symbolic season in whose cycle of florescence and decline every scene and character in the *Idylls* is enmeshed. It is impossible to exaggerate the fullness of consequence this single alteration bears. Throughout Malory, with the exception of the closing chapters, one feels the suspension of time characteristic of romance. In such a world everything is possible, coincidence abounds, and spring is eternal. Only in "Gareth and Lynette," the first of the Round Table idylls, does Tennyson allow his reader this primal fantasy of romance. By linking the separate idylls to the cycle of seasons, Tennyson transposes the dominant mode of Arthurian myth from romance to tragedy, in which the only release from time is death.

The symbolic season, then, enabled Tennyson to control the random, timeless sequence of events in Malory. In the *Morte d'Arthur*, for example, the tragedy of Balin and Balan precedes the romance of Gareth and Lynette. Tennyson reverses the order of the two tales, as elsewhere he compresses the more diffuse episodes in Malory or cuts them altogether. What remains of this distillation from the *Morte d'Arthur* Tennyson orders along a strict narrative sequence in which the clock of Arthur's fall ticks at a steadily accelerating rate. Yet this *linear* movement through time, while it lends a propulsive thrust to the narrative, tends to make of each idyll a separate episode spaced out along the temporal chain. And so Tennyson superimposes upon this strict chronological sequence a much more fluid temporal movement in which events that are narratively sequential appear to take place simultaneously in the reader's mind. Thus although "Balin and Balan" comes quite early in the chronological sequence and is set in the time of the lady-fern and the lily, we are made to feel a sudden acceleration of the symbolic season, in consonance with this first of the idylls that ends tragically. By implying early in "Balin and Balan" that Arthur's youth has passed, Tennyson ages his hero and the kingdom in a single line:

> Early, one fair dawn,
> The light-winged spirit of his youth *returned* ...
>   (18–19, italics added)

The very brevity and symmetry of "Balin and Balan"—it is less than half as long as "Gareth and Lynette," one third as long as the Geraint idylls that precede it—reinforce this sense of propulsive doom.

Tennyson's manipulation of time in the *Idylls* produces an effect akin to that of syncopation in music or, closer to his medium, to departures from regular meter in a line of verse. When the stress falls unexpectedly, it falls with twice the weight. The annual Tournament of Diamonds, spaced over nine years, establishes the normal temporal rhythm of the poem. But in "The Holy Grail," when the knights seek violent escape from the diurnal world to the world of eternity, Tennyson causes time to run amok: the narrative is deliberately discontinuous and kaleidoscopic; lightning and darkness, droughts and floods, replace any recognizable moment of day or year; apocalyptic time—in which all times are simultaneously present—displaces chronological time.

Throughout the *Idylls* leitmotifs of all kinds cut across the linear narrative and connect past and future. "Merlin and Vivien" opens with an impending storm that finally bursts in the closing lines; recurrent images of tempests and waves gather to a climax the storm of warring passions internalized in Merlin and externalized in nature. Before Vivien seduces him, indeed before the "present" in which the idyll is narrated, Merlin has

> . . . walked with dreams and darkness, and he found
> A doom that ever poised itself to fall,
> An ever-moaning battle in the mist,
> World-war of dying flesh against the life.
>
> (188–191)

The wave poised to break symbolizes the seer's prevision of his own doom, but his fall is both a cause and prophecy of the larger fall of the kingdom. And so the dreams and darkness through which he walked later become the clouds of self-doubt that enshroud Arthur at the end; the moaning struggle in the mist foreshadows the last dim battle in the West, when the "wave" of heathen at last engulfs the kingdom, and it reverberates back to the founding, when Arthur pushed back the heathen wave and "made a realm and reigned" (CA, 518).

Like each of the idylls, "Merlin and Vivien" tells a self-contained story that is also interwoven into the central story of Arthur's coming and passing. Through dreams, prophecy, and retrospect, through recurrent symbols, characters, settings, and verbal echoes, any part of the poem imples all other parts. Guinevere's marriage vow to Arthur, itself ironic— "King and my lord, I love thee to the death!" (CA, 469)—is ironically echoed much later by the vow of Tristram to Isolt:

> Come, I am hungered and half-angered—meat,
>
> Wine, wine—and I will love thee to the death—
> (LT, 713–714)

a lie made true by Tristram's murder the instant after it is sworn, as Guinevere's lie is finally proven true by her repentance in the convent of Almesbury.

The major characters reappear from idyll to idyll, forming a "human chain of kinship" whose linkages serve the same unifying function as the poem's clusters of symbols. Minor characters who appear only once, or rarely, are in turn incorporated into the larger story by a kind of analogical patterning through which one character reenacts the role previously played by another. The early idylls present special problems of narrative continuity, for happy endings are by definition self-contained, as the tag-phrase "they lived happily ever after" makes clear. "Gareth and Lynette" has just such an ending: Gareth's fearsome adversaries prove to be mock-monsters in disguise, and the novice knight wins the scornful lady. "Pelleas and Ettarre" tells the same story in reverse, the later idyll retrospectively enriching the earlier. Fair appearance conceals a hideous reality, and the sadistic Ettarre drives the young Pelleas impotent and mad. Gareth tests and finds himself at a time when the integrity of the kingdom and his own naive idealism are in perfect accord. Pelleas is Gareth reborn in decadent times; the clash between his idealism and the corruption of the kingdom destroys him, for he can find no supporting matrix for his fledgling identity. "What name hast thou?" Lancelot asks as Pelleas bears down upon him in blind rage. "No name, no name," he shouts, "I am wrath and shame and hate and evil fame" (551–556).

As certain characters seem to exchange identities, so certain settings recur throughout the *Idylls*. Early in "Balin and Balan," for example, Balin observes a meeting between Lancelot and Guinevere in a garden of roses and lilies. The queen walks down the path of roses toward Lancelot but he pauses in his greeting, for he has dreamed the previous night of "That maiden Saint who stands with lily in hand/In yonder shrine" (256–257), and the dream restrains him, just as his praise of the perfect purity of the lilies chills Guinevere:

> "Sweeter to me," she said, "this garden rose
> Deep-hued and many-folded! sweeter still
> The wild-wood hyacinth and the bloom of May.
> Prince, we have ridden before among the flowers
> In those fair days—not as cool as these,
> Though season-earlier."
>
> (264–269)

Guinevere nowhere more richly expresses the sensuousness which first drew Lancelot to her than in these lines, "deep-hued and many-folded." The consequences of that first, fatally joyous meeting reverberate throughout the poem, as here, when the sight of the lovers shocks Balin into his former "violences," and he rides off from the orderly garden into the wilderness where he meets his death. The garden scene works perfectly within the narrative of "Balin and Balan" at the same time that it takes us back, through Guinevere's reminiscence, to the time before the founding of the Round Table and forward to "Lancelot and Elaine." The scene opens out to become the entire setting of the later idyll, in which Lancelot again must walk the same divided path and choose between the rose of Guinevere and the lily-maid of Astolat.

In the light of such subtle architectonics one is at a loss to understand much of the twentieth-century criticism of the *Idylls*: "Utterly wanting in unity and coherence of structure...strikingly uneven...a collection of episodes....Tennyson could not tell a story at all...he failed signally to bring out the underlying, archetypical significance of the ancient mythological symbols he was employing." Tennyson could of course tell a story perfectly well. He handles the conventional narrative devices with virtuosity, ranging from the first-person monologue of Percivale in "The Holy Grail" to the omniscient narrator in "Lancelot and Elaine," from the simple plot of "Merlin and Vivien" to the complex interweavings of the two adulterous triangles in "The Last Tournament." Yet however skillfully he might retell the tales in Malory or the *Mabinogion*, he would end where he began, with "a collection of episodes." And so he developed, in Hallam's phrase, "a new species of poetry" in order to convey his vision of Arthurian myth to the contemporary world. Like every great long poem, the *Idylls* draws on traditional forms and is itself a new genre. Shakespeare had Seneca and Marlowe; Milton had Homer; but tragedy and epic radically redefine themselves in their works. Tennyson bears this same innovative relation to tradition, but we have yet to assimilate into our literature this poem which is at once epic and lyric, narrative and drama, tragedy and romance. Our difficulty with Tennyson's "medieval charade" is not its derivativeness but its novelty.

JOHN HOLLANDER

Tennyson's Melody

U nlike his contemporary Browning,
Tennyson was no musician, either by training or by inclination, and the
treatment of vocal and instrumental music in his poetry reflects none of the
interest in its structure and history in Europe which engaged Browning's
imagination so well. The consciousness of horizontal and vertical music
patterns; the ability to comprehend dialectic and erotic dimensions in the
unfolding development of a musical piece; the nature of the energy and the
intellect which are jointly attuned in that unique state of attentiveness of
informed listening—with respect to these Tennyson is no closer to Browning or Gerard Manley Hopkins than he is to Mann or Proust. Instead, we
can perceive at work in his poetic world the typical English nineteenth-
century split between the distanced, ahistorical, purely emblematic music
of mythology and romance, and the imaginatively authentic but figurative
music of natural sound: on the one hand, the music of the lutes and
dulcimers (which the poets who wrote of them had never heard, but invoked
because their names were most resonant) and, on the other hand, the sound
of the wind in the trees. Above all, this tradition features the authentication
of actual, contemporary vocal and instrumental music by a process of blending it with the noises of nature, a figure which I have referred to elsewhere,
following Collins and Coleridge, as the "mingled measure." What makes
Tennyson's engagement of the tradition unique is the way in which he
eventually comes to handle both musics—the sounds of myth and the
melodies of nature. In Keats and particularly in Shelley, sound and noise,
music and the eloquence of brooks, are realized in modes of the visual.

From *The Georgia Review* 3, vol. 29 (Fall 1975). Copyright © 1975 by the University of
Georgia.

In Tennyson they are represented by the pictorial, and enter his world of pictures sometimes as with a prefiguring of film underscoring, and sometimes, more remarkably, as if entering directly into the delineated scene.

In his interesting juvenilia, Tennyson came to grips with the dominant tradition of romantic musical imagery in a characteristically accomplished way, trying out his hand on the full range of conventional themes. A little exercise in the manner of Tom Moore, for example (published in 1827), celebrates the cliché of the abandoned Celtic harp in the appropriately elegiac meter of the anapestic tetrameter:

> I will hang thee, my Harp, by the side of the fountain,
>   On the whispering branch of the lone-waving willow:
> Above thee shall rush the hoarse gale of the mountain,
>   Below thee shall tumble the dark breaking billow.
> The winds shall blow by thee, abandoned, forsaken,
>   The wild gales alone shall arouse thy sad strain;
> For where is the heart or the hand to awaken
>   The sounds of thy soul-soothing sweetness again?
>   Oh! Harp of my fathers!
>   Thy chords shall decay,
>   One by one with the strings
>   Shall thy notes fade away;
>   Till the fiercest of tempests
>   Around thee may yell,
>   And not waken one sound
>   Of thy desolate shell!

The convention of hanging an instrument on a tree and thereby abandoning it derives, in romantic lyric, from a characteristic misreading of the 137th Psalm, "By the waters of Babylon," a misreading in which the instrument is not shelved in a gesture of defiance against a captor, but with a kind of *Weltschmerz*; the invariable consequence is that the wind will play gently or fitfully through the strings that the human fingers can no longer elicit music from. The abandoned biblical or neoclassical instrument, in effect, becomes reanimated as the aeolian harp of romantic poetry. Tennyson has combined this figure with the silent harp of Tara and other halls, the lost authentic Celtic minstrelsy, to evoke not (as for Moore) the ruined Ossian, but the ruined Moore. The "wild gales" which, alone, can make the old harp sing, are not enough to harmonize with the mountain wind above and the sound of the sea below, completing the conventional concert of blended instrumental music and natural noise. In the second strophe, the young, ambitious poet seeks to wreath the instrument with flowers, and succeeds in composing a picture that commemorates his own achievement— making a posy out of the old song—without violating the harp's silence: " . . . the roses are twining/ Thy chords with their bright blossoms glowing and red." (It is not as if the roses are bluebells or morning-glories, about to break into music of their own as in some frenzied version of this image in George Darley's at that time unpublished *Nepenthe*, for example.) The poet ends

> One sweep will I give thee,
> And wake thy bold swell;
> Then, thou friend of my bosom
> For ever farewell.
>
> (29–32)

He will not try that bit again, although the sweep is excellent pastiche (save for the naturalistic term "strings" which should not coexist with the purely visionary musical language of "chord" and "shell").

Tennyson's early experiments abound in imitations of this sort which embody the divergent strains of natural noise on the one hand and the emblematic minstrelsy of harp and ode of lyre on the other. He reworks Ossian ("Midnight") and Scott ("Inverlee"); he quickly bores through an unsuccessful lode of exultant sound rendering. The imitation could be Keatsian, as in the "Leonine Elegiacs" ("Over the pools in the burn water-gnats murmur and mourn"—the gnats coming from the rising sounds at the end of "To Autumn" which haunted Tennyson so, and not from the natural scene, the hour being too late). Or it could smack of Darley, as in the absolutely awful sound texture of "When Claribel low lieth" ("At eve the beetle boometh/ Athwart the thicket lone" may be the worst two lines he ever wrote) where he attempts to render one of those resonant landscapes in an onomatopoeic thickening of archaic third-person-singular verb forms. He would learn to do this with great success later on; at this stage, his descriptions of sound would have to imitate their subject by sounding like Wordsworth's and Shelley's and Keats' response to it.

In the 1829 Cambridge prize poem "Timbuctoo," Tennyson's angel of vision speaks to him "In accents of majestic melody,/ Like a swoln river's gushings in still night/ Mingled with floating music" (188–90), and here, amid the flood of Miltonic, Wordsworthian, Shelleyan and Keatsian echoes in which the poem nearly drowns, a reminiscence of Coleridge flashes across the surface. This, at any rate, is the canonical blending of music and noise that romantic poetic tradition makes its own. A few lines further on, the Spirit tells of his gifts to man:

> I play about his heart a thousand ways,
> Visit his eyes with visions, and his ears
> With harmonies of wind and wave and wood,
> —Of winds which tell of waters, and of waters
> Betraying the close kisses of the wind. . . .
>
> (201–5)

"His eyes with visions"—symmetry would demand, "his ears with auditions"; unfortunately, there is no equivalent term in the phonetic realm for "visionary" (as opposed to "visual") in the optical one, a want which Tennyson himself seems to perceive in these very lines. The "harmonies of wind and wave and wood" which must fill in for these unnamable "auditions" are as authentic in their literary, derived aspects as are the visionary phenomena. The interlock and chiasm of the winds and the waters comes ultimately from Spenser's intricate musical-natural concert in the Bower of Bliss, although filtered through the conventional post-Spenserian treatment of that concert by which all of the possible dangers lurking in the blended sounds from different sources have vanished. Only the metaphorically musical polyphonic organization of what Geoffrey Hart-man has called, with reference to Wordsworth's use of this device, the soundscape, remains. The substitution of the mythologized natural sound for the long-since silenced music of the spheres, another widely used romantic figure, is on the verge of occurring here, too; the Spirit tells the poet that he has raised him toward the "spheres of Heaven": "and thou with ravished sense/ Listenest the lordly music flowing from/ The illimitable years. . . ." Whether that lordly music derives from the music of nature heard a few lines earlier by all men, or from the resonances of the Spirit's own motion through "All the intricate and labyrinthine veins/ Of the great vine of *Fable*," it is invoked in the archaic, Elizabethan language of ravishing sense and so forth. In either case, it is the voice of poetry itself.

"Before I could read," Tennyson is quoted as saying in his son Hallam's *Memoir*, "I was in the habit on a stormy day of spreading my arms to the wind, and crying out 'I hear a voice that's speaking in the wind.' " One may of course wonder if the utterance did not cast itself into a perfect iambic pentameter only in afterthought, and if the poet had not read yet of the voice of nature, he may most likely have been read to of it. In any event, it constitutes a later avowal of an early encounter with poetic tradition after which never again would birds' song be the same. The representation of that voice in the body of Tennyson's poetry would evolve from the extremely skillful handling of the received devices for the poetic treatment of sound, and two early instances point out the directions this evolution would take.

The first of these is chiefly important for its pictorial effect: in the very early "Ode to Memory" there is mention of "the waterfall/ Which ever sounds and shines/ A pillar of white light upon the wall/ Of purple cliffs, aloof descried" (52–54), and although later on in the poem Tennyson will underscore one of his most characteristic landscapes—the wasteland stretching away to the distantly sounding sea—it is the doubled "sounds and shines" that marks out a mode of visualization he would soon start to develop. In the wonderful "Recollections of the Arabian Nights" the sound is pictorialized in just such a manner, but more energetically. As the voyager-poet wanders through a day in the visionary Baghdad, successive banquets of sense appear before him in almost Spenserian presentations. As his Alastor-like journey takes him through a clear canal "rounded to as clear a lake,"

> From the green rivage many a fall
> Of diamond rillets musical,
> Thro' little crystal arches low
> Down from the central fountain's flow
> Fallen silver-chiming, seemed to shake
> The sparkling flints beneath the prow.
>   (46–51)

Here (as with the later "And many a shadow-chequer'd lawn/ Full of the city's stilly sound") the soundscape is embodied in the visual texture: for example, the diamonded, crystalline, and finally "silver-chiming" quality of the falling water. It has been observed that this silveriness becomes central in Tennyson's imagery, not because of its associations with a Keatsian mode of moonlit enchantment, but more perhaps because the visionary metal of moonlit bells both tinkles and twinkles. "Rillets" is a Keatsian word, but probably placed here for its phonetic linkage with the sequence *rivage—rillets—little crystal—silver—flints*. What is usually called the "music" of Tennyson's verse itself helps build here the motion picture of the fountains at night, which in turn paint the pictures of the music their motion makes. At the heart of the vision in "Recollections of the Arabian Nights" there is heard, not surprisingly, the voice of the nightingale—not a bird of hammered gold and gold enamelling, but the source of a voice which transcends in essence and power the natural music even of such a perfectly contrived *locus amoenus* as this great garden city of total art. Using an inevitable, low-keyed pun employed as such from Milton on, we are shown how

> Far off, and where the lemon grove
> In closest coverture upsprung,
> The living airs of middle night
> Died round the bulbul as he sung;
> Not he, but something which possess'd
> The darkness of the world, delight,
> Life, anguish, death, immortal love,
> Ceasing not, mingled, unrepress'd,
>   Apart from place, withholding time,
>   But flattering the golden prime
>   Of good Haroun Alraschid.
>   (67–77)

The "living airs" are breezes and songs both, and they are mingled; they die because the song of the mythological songbird of Persian lyric, at this point in the journey into Imagination, supplants them. It is as if they were to be left behind, as sight must be abandoned while the Keatsian protagonist follows the earlier poet's nightingale into his shadowed forest of touch and sound.

The other early instance of Tennyson's treatment of sound is in the great "Mariana," in which for the first time he is able to move past the received modes of soundscape. Indeed, in the opening stanza there is a frightful blanketing of sound into an ominous, pregnant silence. The first sound designated in the poem is the absence of an expected one—"Unlifted was the clinking latch"—and the core words for the associative sound patternings of the word-sounds themselves are "thickly crusted," just as the buildup of the alveopalatal fricatives and affricates and the unvoiced clusters underscore the sense of hush and thickening:

> With blackest moss the flower-plots
>   Were thickly crusted, one and all;
> The rusted nails hung from the knots
>   That held the pear to the gable-wall.
> The broken sheds look'd sad and strange:
>   Unlifted was the clinking latch;
>   Weeded and worn the ancient thatch
> Upon the lonely moated grange.
>
>   (1–8)

The deferred clinking is the most conventionally "musical" of the sounds in the landscape of the moated grange. In the third stanza, what should be bells ringing round the hours of the day are replaced by animal sounds of night-bird, cock and lowing oxen; in the fifth, the shrill and wild winds are marked not by their voices, but by their visual resonance in the image of the poplar tree with its affrighted branches and its shadow (not even a demon lover) in her bed. But it is in the final two stanzas that the oppressive stuffiness of the air is cut by a consort of sounds, and a failed and antithetical consort it is. As if to emphasize the recurrent refrain rhyme of "said:dead" (rather, even, than "sigh:die," which at least suggests wind and breathing)—for Mariana never sings or chants—all we hear in the inside of her house which becomes more and more like the inside of her head are the noises. The one instance of the verb "sing" occurs in a form and a context that robs the word of any music in its meaning:

> All day within the dreamy house
>   The doors upon their hinges creaked;
> The blue-fly sung in the pane; the mouse
>   Behind the mouldering wainscot shrieked,
>   Or from the crevice peered about.

> Old faces glimmered through the doors,
>   Old footsteps trod the upper floors,
> Old voices called her from without. . . .
>
>   (61–68)

The final consort of sounds "within" and "without," the layered contrasting textures of the last stanza, act not to confirm the harmoniousness of pastoral landscape here. Rather, they make up the part-song of the *locus horribilis*, leading to silence and darkness and, inevitably, to a reminder of the stultifying *thickness* of the opening:

> The sparrow's chirrup on the roof,
>   The slow clock ticking, and the sound
> Which to the wooing wind aloof
>   The poplar made, did all confound
> Her sense; but most she loathed the hour
>   When the thick-moted sunbeam lay
> Athwart the chambers, and the day
> Was sloping toward his western bower.
>   Then, said she, "I am very dreary,
>   He will not come," she said;
>   She wept, "I am aweary, aweary,
>   O God, that I were dead!"
>
>   (73–84)

The symphony confounds her sense (in this instance, of hearing), and the music moves toward a travesty of the end of Keats' *To Autumn*, where light dissolves into darkness and unseen sound. As an underscoring to Mariana's moated house of unfulfilled ripeness, the orchestration of the noises is superb. In turn, it is underscored by the onomatopoeic music of the opening stanza, playing in the key of a conventional fiction of English verse which distinguishes between consonantal clusters and vowels as between noise and musical tone.

In "The Dying Swan," also from this period, we again get a landscape which generates a music; but in this case, the song is monodic—a single melodic line; and the equivalent of layered harmony (even in the anti-symphonies of "Mariana") is in this poem an extension of surface and texture, rather than a filling of space. The music engulfs the landscape, and it is the elements of the responding scene which become the various musical parts. The bleak, gray scene with which the poem begins is full of wind, and "With an inner voice the river ran,/ Adown it floated a dying swan/ And loudly did lament." In the normal pastoral landscape, the sound of moving water is the *locus classicus* of eloquence (as, indeed, standing water, with its surface of reflection and its depths, is a picture of thought); here, the river's inner voice is silent, and only the almost emblematic swan (the local swan standing, in classical tradition, for the local poet) breaks the silence. In the second strophe, the initial response to the dying swan's eloquence is in the intransigence of a landscape dominated by cold and unregarding distant peaks, and a bit of sighing wind, already established as "weary" in the ninth line. But then, as if this bit of deadened picture were functioning as a kind of grand pause, the full power of the poetic voice to animate nature frozen into landscape becomes clear:

> The wild swan's death-hymn took the soul
> Of that waste place with joy
> Hidden in sorrow: at first to the ear
> The warble was low, and full and clear;
> And floating about the under-sky,
> Prevailing in weakness, the coronach stole
> Sometimes afar, and sometimes anear;
> But anon her awful jubilant voice
> With a music strange and manifold,
> Flowed forth on a carol free and bold....
>
> (21–30)

And here, with the masterful interjection of a Homeric simile but with markedly Biblical resonance, the swan-song is given the force of prophecy, and its subsequent representation, in the closing catalogue of the music's listeners, flies beyond fancy:

> As when a mighty people rejoice
> With shawms and with cymbals, and harps of gold,
> And the tumult of their acclaim is rolled
> Through the open gates of the city afar,
> To the shepherd who watcheth the evening star.
> And the creeping mosses and clambering weeds,
> And the willow-branches hoar and dank,
> And the wavy swell of the soughing reeds,
> And the wave-worn horns of the echoing bank,
> And the silvery marish-flowers that throng
> The desolate creeks and pools among,
> Were flooded over with eddying song.
>
> (31–42)

Reeds, horns, flowers and mosses and weeds—a "manifold" consort surely, and closed off and completed in the marvelous echo of the final line, "*flooded:eddying.*"

This method of picturing sound, whether formally musical or not, Tennyson applied throughout the lyrical and meditative poems. Sometimes it is a matter of an acoustical effect in a scene or action doubling a visual one; in "The Lady of Shalott," for example, most of the sound in the poem is what is heard by the outside world. The "song that echoes cheerly/ From the river winding clearly,/ Down to towered Camelot" is the Lady's, and Tennyson wisely altered, in 1842, the original lines 46–48 of the 1832 version: "She lives with little joy or fear./ Over the water, running near,/ The sheepbell tinkles in her ear." The effect of the revision was to make the first sound that reaches her the sound of Lancelot's bridle-bells and ringing armor. And when she actually sees him (and the effect is the same whether or not one accepts Christopher Ricks' ingenious suggestion that the protective effect of her mirror reversal is nullified by the fact that she sees an image of his image in the river, as well as an image of himself)—when she actually sees him, she hears his song, which is a mere refrain, except that refrains in romantic poetry are seldom "mere." The erotic "tirra-lirra" of the lark in Autolycus's song from *The Winter's Tale* serves in the present context not only for its literary resonance, but in its extrapolated form as a phonetic mirror image:

> From the bank and from the river
> He flashed into the crystal mirror,
> 'Tirra lirra,' by the river
> Sang Sir Lancelot.
>
> (105–8)

Tennyson's fondness for chiasmus, for the *abba* pattern that emerges in the rhyme scheme of the *In Memoriam* stanza, shows up here in the sequence *river—mirror—lirra—river*; the Miltonic syntax allows a hovering over the line-break at 106, reinforced by the assonance of *lirra* and *river*, the effect being to make us hear Lancelot's song as going "Tirra lirra by the river." In the immediate context of mirroring, the doublings in *tirra lirra*, and of it by *river* are most prominent. The river is itself a mirror (the word rhyming with itself), the sound and light mirror each other, the "tirra lirra" flashes into her hearing as Lancelot and Lancelot's image flash into the Lady's mirror.

Sound thus answers sound, image answers image; in "Mariana in the South," Tennyson's revision of "One dry cicala's summer song/ At night fill'd all the gallery" allows a rich evocative pairing, the small "dry" sound answered quasi-echoically by the vast moist one: "At eve a dry cicala sung,/ There came a sound as of the sea"—and not only is the characteristic tone of the first Mariana poem regained, but the conclusion of the second is now inevitable.

These doublings of sound and picture—shadow answering noise, echo mirroring image—seem to compose, throughout Tennyson's poetic world, a music of landscape. His poetic act is the association of the sound and sight, the rendering of the former not so much by direct pseudo-onomatopoeia in the sounds of words, but in the pattern we have been discerning, of a sound-rich description of a visual phenomenon which itself stands for an auditory one. In Walter Pater's poetry about Venetian pictures in *The Renaissance*, we get what purports to be iconological analysis, but which dissolves into just this mode of Tennysonian poetry. Pater is evoking the landscapes of Giorgione:

> But when people are happy in this thirsty land water will not be far off; and in the school of Giorgione, the presence of water—the well, or marble-rimmed pool, the drawing or pouring of water, as the woman pours it from a pitcher with her jewelled hand in the *Fête Champêtre*, listening, perhaps, to the cool sound as it falls, blent with the music of the pipes—is as characteristic, and almost as suggestive, as that of music itself.

In the Tennysonian landscape, sound and silence both can be rendered by these doublings. In "Oenone," for example, the representation of the acoustical silence depends upon the deadening, rather than the quickening, effect of repetition:

> For now the noonday quiet holds the hill:
> The grasshopper is silent in the grass:
> The lizard, with his shadow on the stone,
> Rests like a shadow, and the winds are dead.
> (24–27)

We know that we can hear nothing because we are told this in linguistic structures that parallel those in which we learn that we can see and feel nothing either.

Sometimes the pairings of sight and sound are more delicate. "The lights begin to twinkle from the rocks:/ The long day wanes: the slow moon climbs: the deep/ Moans round with many voices..." ("Ulysses," 54–56). The pictorialized echoes in the lyric from *The Princess* ("The Splendor Falls") are almost too familiar to need comment. The effect is clearly enhanced by the verse structure: the internal rhymes are made by the context to represent the echoing ("The long light shakes across the lakes"), as is the terminal rhyme pair "flying:dying." The visual correlative throughout the poem is the power of the reddening, dying sunlight to pick out resonant visions, elements in the landscape haunted by dead romantic fictions. The reddening and the dying comprise a strange, accidental anticipation, incidentally, of a Doppler shift.

Elsewhere in the songs from *The Princess*, we can see the intensification of Tennyson's use of the pseudo-music of verse itself to do what he accomplishes elsewhere with doubling: thus, for example, in the narrative of the Prologue to the poem, we find a domesticated, almost low-mimetic scene, in which picnic noises, a "twanging violin," etc., blend, while "overhead/ The broad ambrosial aisles of lofty lime/ Made noise with bees and breeze from end to end" (86–88). Tennyson had been long haunted by Keatsian hummings and buzzings ("The murmurous haunt of flies"; "the small gnats" in "To Autumn," "in a wailful choir," etc.), and in an undergraduate fragment, "Sense and Conscience," he had responded to them with one of his more elaborate youthful soundscapes. It is one of

> ... deep shades,
> A gloom monotonously musical
> With hum of murmurous bees, which brooded deep
> In ever-trembling flowers, and constant moan
> Of waterfalls i' the distance, and low winds
> Wandering close to earth, and voice of doves,
> Which ever bowing cooed and cooing bowed
> Unto each other as they could not cease ...
>
> (44–51)

The devices are familiar; the literal and blatant chiasmus of line 50 would give way in his later poetry to more subtle adaptations of the classical figure. In the inset Idyl from *The Princess*, Part VII, the valley of Love is contrasted with the alpine heights of Death, and its single, warm visual image of hearth-smoke dissolves in a very Keatsian fashion into sounds. But the sounds are rendered by the verse, rather than depicted, in one of Tennyson's most famous tours de force:

> ... and sweet is every sound,
> Sweeter thy voice, but every sound is sweet;
> Myriads of rivulets hurrying through the lawn,
> The moan of doves in immemorial elms,
> And murmuring of innumerable bees.
>
> (203–7)

The traditional pastoral soundscape is nowhere better rendered, the "immemorial elms" phrase doing the work of the more usually designated wind in the leaves, the alliterations all centering on the word "murmuring," the "moan" of the waterfalls from the earlier poem being transferred not only to the doves, but to the alliterating environment of the last two lines generally. The line about the rivulets is a simple matter of augmenting the assonance with extra syllables (only two, but there seem to us to be myriads of them) and, even more cleverly, by the palatalizations of "myriads" and "rivulets" (if the words were "myrids" and "rivlets," consider how less dense the hastening motion of enunciation would seem).

Consider, on the other hand, the combined images of amplification in "Tears, Idle Tears," where the senses fade as the sensibilia strengthen. This is done by image, rather than verbal music:

> Ah, sad and strange as in dark summer dawns
> The earliest pipe of half-awaken'd birds
> To dying ears, when unto dying eyes
> The casement slowly grows a glimmering square....
>   (IV, 31–35)

Local pairings of picture and sound can give way to more elaborate associations. There is the kind of visual phantasmagoria that lets us hear the "low voluptuous music" of "The Vision of Sin," for example:

> Then methought I heard a mellow sound,
> Gathering up from all the lower ground;
> Narrowing in to where they sat assembled
> Low voluptuous music winding trembled,
> Woven in circles: they that heard it sighed,
> Panted hand-in-hand with faces pale,
> Swung themselves, and in low tones replied;
> Till the fountain spouted, showering wide
> Sleet of diamond-drift and pearly hail;
> Then the music touched the gates and died;
> Rose again from where it seemed to fail,
> Stormed in orbs of song, a growing gale;
> Till thronging in and in, to where they waited,
> As 'twere a hundred-throated nightingale,
> The strong tempestous treble throbbed and palpitated;
> Ran in its giddiest whirl of sound,
> Caught the sparkles, and in circles,
> Purple gauzes, golden hazes, liquid mazes,
> Flung the torrent rainbow round....
>   (14–32)

This bursting fountain of erotic energy is blown through by the winds of the music, and the gauzes, hazes, and mazes entangle the votary listeners, who

> ... started from their places
> Moved with violence, changed in hue,
> Caught each other with wild grimaces,
> Half-visible to the view,
> Wheeling with precipitate paces
> To the melody, till they flew,
> Hair, and eyes, and limbs, and faces,
> Twisted hard in fierce embraces,
> Like to Furies, like to Graces,
> Dashed together in blinding dew....
>   (33–43)

Then, reflecting the momentarily spent energies of the hearers (and the word "some" in the following lines, instead of being simply a definite or indefinite article, is *really* coy), the poem continues, "... killed with some luxurious agony,/ The nerve-dissolving melody/ Fluttered headlong from the sky." This is not an image like that at the beginning of the "Choric Song" from "The Lotus Eaters" where the sweet music

> ... softer falls
> Than petals from blown roses on the grass
> Or night-dews on still waters between walls
> Of shadowy granite, in a gleaming pass. . . .

Here, rather, the melody falls in detumescence, like a shot bird, and completes the series of roles—motive, source, action, scene, agent—it has played in the tiny *Gesamtkunstwerk*.

Closest of all to what we would think of as actual underscoring comes the rendering of sound in the dream in "Sea Dreams" called by its narrator "one/ That altogether went to music." It involves a mixture of vision and audition accompanying a destruction:

> —But round the North, a light,
> A belt, it seemed, of luminous vapour, lay,
> And ever in it a low musical note
> Swelled up and died; and as it swelled, a ridge
> Of breaker issued from the belt, and still
> Grew with the growing note, and when the note
> Had reached a thunderous fulness, on those cliffs
> Broke, mixt with awful light. . . .
>
> (201–8)

The action is elicited by the music, as much as being accompanied by, or releasing it:

> ... and then the great ridge drew,
> Lessening to the lessening music, back,
> And past into the belt and swelled again
> Slowly to music. . . .
>
> (213–16)

It is antithetical to the masque-like music which, as we shall see, is associated with the building of Camelot in the *Idylls*; this is a visionary music of undoing.

It is in *In Memoriam*, though, that the widest possible range of acoustical presences make themselves known. The poem's meditative patterns, its cycles of visualization and envisioning, of thought and memory, of enlightened and darkened perception, are all haunted by accompanying sounds. The invocation of music and noise can be purely emblematic, in the first place, as in section XXXVII, standing in a simple classical way for poetry itself, as when Urania tells the poet to

> "Go down beside thy native rill,
>   On thy Parnassus set thy feet,

> And hear thy laurel whisper sweet
> About the ledges of the hill."
>
> (5–8)

It can, on the other hand, exemplify the more usual kind of doubling we
have seen before, as in XXXVI; the closing lines describe the Pacific
islanders whom the power of the Gospel may yet reach. The alliterations
grouped around /w/ in the word "watch" and /r/ in "roar" underscore the
pairing very neatly:

> Which he may read that binds the sheaf
> Or builds the house, or digs the grave,
> And those wild eyes that watch the wave
> In roarings round the coral reef.
>
> (13–16)

The sounds of a near or distant sea or brook are almost constant in
the poem, and the ceremonial bells occur at cyclical points. They may be
the hardly "merry merry bells of Yule" which, in XXVIII, "Swell out and
fail, as if a door/ Were shut between me and the sound," where the image
evoking the acoustical condition carries so much more weight. And there
are those bells which, at a corresponding point in the yearly cycle in CIV
(which again begins "The time draws near the birth of Christ"), first heard
as "A single peal of bells below," now waken "A single murmur in the
breast," an image not in the least auditory.

More complex is the kind of figure that we get in the representation of
the silence of death. In XIX, Hallam's body, brought from Vienna for burial,
was laid, the poet remembers, "by the pleasant shore/ And in the hearing of
the wave." The next two quatrains enforce a pair of parallels: the tidal sea-
water filling and silencing the river Wye, and the eloquence of the poet
drowned in its reservoir of tears and then, implicitly, the relation of what we
might call acoustical silence (soundlessness, inaudibility) and rhetorical
silence (the cessation of utterance):

> There twice a day the Severn fills;
> The salt sea-water passes by,
> And hushes half the babbling Wye,
> And makes a silence in the hills.
>
> The Wye is hushed nor moved along,
> And hushed my deepest grief of all,
> When filled with tears that cannot fall,
> I brim with sorrow drowning song.
>
> (5–12)

It is obvious that the particular strophic form of the In Memoriam lyrics lends
itself beautifully to these patterns of doubling and contrast. In CXV, for

example, the *abba* rhyme scheme embraces both lexically and schematically an image structure of sound—sight—sight—sound:

> Now rings the woodland loud and long,
> The distance takes a lovelier hue,
> And drowned in yonder living blue
> The lark becomes a sightless song.
>
> (5–8)

Sound calls up vision, vision elicits sound, and the English country cliché of the skylark's power to fill the world with noise from no apparent source is strikingly reanimated.

Perhaps the most elaborate symphony of audition and vision in the poem, however, occurs in the paradisal recollections of a Hallam-hallowed world in sections LXXXVII–LXXXIX, ushered in by the visual "tumult of the halls" at Trinity and mirrored immediately by the heavenly tumult of the sounds of chapel—"The storm their high-built organs make,/ And thunder-music, rolling, shake/ The Prophet blazoned on the panes." The poem and its speaker perambulate past these sounds to a "noise/ Of songs, and clapping hands, and boys/ That crashed the glass and beat the floor." The meditation culminates with the cadences of Hallam's discourse, "The rapt oration flowing free// From point to point, with power and grace/ And music in the bounds of law," this last music being metaphoric and ceremonial—a type of music in Tennyson's poetry that I shall examine in a moment.

The following brief lyric to the nightingale, "Wild bird, whose warble, liquid sweet,/ Rings Eden through the budded quicks," asks the heavily emblematic bird for a moment of imaginative transfusion, almost like a Miltonic turn to the Muse for the power needed in modulating tone or subject:

> O tell me where the senses mix,
> O tell me where the passions meet,
>
> Whence radiate: fierce extremes employ
> Thy spirits in the darkening leaf,
> And in the midmost heart of grief
> Thy passion clasps a secret joy. . . .
>
> (3–8)

The bird traditionally sings out of the darkness, and here joy sings out of grief; if the passions meet in this central stanza, then the senses mix finally in the last one, where the older form of aeolian harp emblem is transformed, as light, rather than wind, plays through the strings of the poetic instrument which cannot always yield joy, but must respond to reality:

> And I—my harp would prelude woe—
>   I cannot all command the strings;
>   The glory of the sum of things
> Will flash along the chords and go.
>   (9–12)

But this is only a prelude to a more fully recollected vision of perfection. In section LXXIX a glimpse of chequer'd shade leads back to visual and auditory memories of Hallam in the countryside. A triad of stanzas harmonizes three modes of music, the natural noises of the cultivated *locus amoenus*, the figurative "music" of recited Italian poetry, and the actual music of song and instrument, voice and string aligned with their appropriate heavenly bodies and conditions of light:

> O sound to rout the brood of cares,
>   The sweep of scythe in morning dew,
>   The gust that round the garden flew,
> And tumbled half the mellowing pears!
>
> O bliss, when all in circle drawn
>   About him, heart and ear were fed
>   To hear him, as he lay and read
> The Tuscan poets on the lawn:
>
> Or in the all-golden afternoon
>   A guest, or happy sister, sung
>   Or here she brought the harp and flung
> A ballad to the brightening moon. . . .
>   (17–28)

Returning to this bower of bliss, at the end of the poem, from the glade in the distant woods where Tennyson and Hallam had discoursed and where "the stream beneath us ran,/ The wine-flask lying couched in moss,// Or cooled within the glooming wave," we hear, finally, the sounds of paradise unmediated. In an astonishing image connecting the lowest of literal farm noises with a totally imaginary sort of film underscoring, the promises of Exodus 3:8 sound together:

> And brushing ankle-deep in flowers,
>   We heard behind the woodbine veil
>   The milk that bubbled in the pail,
> And buzzings of the honied hours.
>   (49–52)

The milk and honey bubble and buzz, in the making, but it is the hours, in the syntactic ambiguity, which themselves buzz and hum in the memory. In the part of "The Lover's Tale" done when Tennyson was nineteen, he had written of "a land of love!/ A land of promise, a land of memory,/ A land of promise flowing with the milk/ And honey of delicious memories" (325-8); in the *In Memoriam* lyric, the proverbial image is reanimated with magnificent imaginative tact, providing an undersong to the actual remembered experience.

The many modes of sound and music in the remainder of the poem are quite varied. The association of sound and odor in section CI: "And many a rose-carnation feed/ With summer spice the humming air" is not merely Keatsian, but connected with a much older trope going back to the Renaissance. A strange version of the aeolian harp image haunts the close of the dream vision of CIII: as the great ship of death bears Hallam, Tennyson, and the former's complement of graces out onto an eternal sea, the underscoring wind plays not merely upon the rigging, but upon the gently punning winding sheets as well:

> And while the wind began to sweep
> A music out of sheet and shroud,
> We steered her toward a crimson cloud
> That landlike slept along the deep.
>
> (53-56)

It is this interplay between the figurative and the literal which is put to such effective use in section XCV. The amazingly erotic quality of the sound of the landscape as the poetic faculty returns to the poet, toward the end of the lyric, makes manifest what was latent in the intercourse of poet and Hallam's ghost earlier on. The not wholly barren leaves of Hallam's letters are associated with acoustical, but not rhetorical, silence:

> A hunger seized my heart; I read
> Of that glad year which once had been,
> In those fallen leaves which kept their green,
> The noble letters of the dead:
>
> And strangely on the silence broke
> The silent-speaking words. . . .
>
> (21-26)

But after his communion with Hallam's spirit, when "The living soul was flashed on mine," and after their entwined spirits have heard "The deep pulsations of the world,/ Aeonian music measuring out the steps of Time. . . ." the unfallen leaves in the trees, which had enfolded the nostalgic singing of friends at the opening, respond to the caresses of the wind:

> The white kine glimmered, and the trees
> Laid their dark arms about the field.

> And sucked from out the distant gloom
> A breeze began to tremble o'er
> The large leaves of the sycamore
> And fluctuate all the still perfume....
>
> (51–58)

As the lyric closes, the breeze breaks out into a last *alba* for the two commingled souls, and vanishes in a doubling of its sound in light:

> And gathering freshlier overhead,
>   Rocked the full-foliaged elms, and swung
>   The heavy-folded rose, and flung
> The lilies to and fro, and said
>
> "The dawn, the dawn," and died away;
>   And East and West, without a breath,
>   Mixt their dim lights, like life and death,
> To broaden into boundless day.
>
> (57–64)

The auditory phantasmagoria with which the mad ears of the protagonist of *Maud* are assailed employs many of the devices noted above. The earlier lyric, "O that 'twere possible" (first published 1837), which forms section IV of the completed monodrama represents urban noises in the almost canonical Tennysonian manner: "When all my spirit reels/ At the shouts, the leagues of lights,/ And the roaring of the wheels." Elsewhere, there are the sounds of burglary and commercial crime in the unjust city (I, 41–44), of brook and distant sea calling at the edges of the protagonist's sanity (I, 97–108; 516–20), of half-hallucinated readings of echo and of birdsong (I, 4; 412–15). A passage reminiscent of "Mariana" harmonizes noises that resound in emptiness—noises that are either wholly fancied, amplified by maddened attention, or as in the last instance, magnificently indeterminate in the purity of the image:

> Living alone in an empty house,
> Here half-hid in the gleaming wood,
> Where I hear the dead at midday moan,
> And the shrieking rush of the wainscot mouse,
> And my own sad name in corners cried,
> When the shiver of dancing leaves is thrown
> About its echoing chambers wide....
>
> (257–63)

But the speaker's perceptions of sound decay into more desperately fancied images: "Just now the dry-tongued laurels' pattering talk/ Seem'd like her light foot along the garden walk" (I, 606–7); when the continuing moan of distant waves and the tolling of the silver bell have died, he invokes the starlight: "And ye meanwhile far over moor and fell/ Beat to the silent music of the night!" In the famous rose-garden lyric the hateful sounds of the dance music in the house are contrasted with the natural music sanctified by association with Maud:

> All night have the roses heard
>   The flute, violin, bassoon;
> All night has the casement jessamine stirr'd
>   To the dancers dancing in tune;
> Till a silence fell with the waking bird,
>   And a hush with the setting moon.
>
> (I, 862–7)

Then after the meticulous observation that "Low on the sand and loud on the stone/ The last wheel echoes away," after all the music is done, it returns in remembered agony, only to be washed away by the sounds of the *locus amoenus*:

> And the soul of the rose went into my blood,
>   As the music clashed in the hall;
> And long by the garden lake I stood,
>   For I heard your rivulet fall
> From the lake to the meadow and on to the wood,
>   Our wood, that is dearer than all;
>
> From the meadow your walks have left so sweet
>   That whenever a March-wind sighs
> He sets the jewel-print of your feet
>   In violets blue as your eyes,
> To the woody hollows in which we meet
>   And the valleys of Paradise.
>
> (882–93)

(An unstated trope lurking beneath the surface of the scene might be the conventional association of odor and sound, both carried by breezes; if the flowers are "talking," it is through their scents and emblematic natures.)

Aside from the unsystematic derangements of sense in *Maud*, however, Tennyson's characteristic pattern of underscoring sound with vision and image with sound gives way only in the *Idylls of the King* to another concern with reported, rather than represented, musical sound. True, "The Passing of Arthur," incorporating the "Morte d'Arthur" written some twenty-seven years earlier, shows some of the more typical instances of depicted sound. Arthur's dream, with its voice of Gawain blown in a wind crying "Hollow, hollow, hollow all delight!", passes over with just such a movement:

> And fainter onward, like wild birds that change
> Their season in the night and wail their way
> From cloud to cloud, down the long wind the dream
> Shrilled; but in going mingled with dim cries
> Far in the moonlit haze among the hills,
> As of some lonely city sack'd by night....
>   (38–43)

The visual location of the source, the point of mixture of the sound, the delicate paralleling of "wail their way" with "cloud to cloud" (as if to imply "wail their wail" as well)—these are all familiarly Tennysonian. So, too, the vision of Lyonesse, where

> ... the long mountains ended in a coast
> Of ever-shifting sand, and far away
> The phantom circle of a moaning sea.
>   (85–87)

From the three queens there rises

> A cry that shiver'd to the tingling stars,
> And, as it were one voice, an agony
> Of lamentation, like a wind that shrills
> All night in a waste land, where no one comes
> Or hath come, since the making of the world.
>   (367–71)

And finally, the magnificent conclusion to the earlier version, an amazingly prophetic version of a final movie shot, shows us

> ... Sir Bedivere
> Revolving many memories, till the hull
> Look'd one black dot against the verge of dawn,
> And on the mere the wailing died away.
>   (437–40)

With the same assonance of "wail:away" used earlier, the decaying vision and the dying audition coalesce in their vanishing. It is a magnificent closing, and the somewhat regrettable additions in the final version of the poem are only partially redeemed by the cleverly placed echo of the sounds of Arthur's dream which died, as we have just seen, in a haze of light from which emanate the cries of a ruined city. Bedivere climbs to a final high point of vision and

> Then from the dawn it seem'd there came, but faint
> As from beyond the limit of the world,
> Like the last echo born of a great cry,

> Sounds, as if some fair city were one voice
> Around a king returning from his wars.
>
> (457-61)

This is an effective inversion of the phantasmagoria of the dream vouchsafed in a prophetic vision, as in that long tradition of pastoral poetry where an echo of the poet's utterance authenticates, rather than mocks, his feeling.

But this represented sound is by no means typical of the poetry of the *Idylls*. Throughout, musical and other acoustic description is even more limited to a few set-pieces that are purely visual elaborations. The ceremonial character of music itself, having a magical or otherwise privileged power, severely limits its ubiquity in the other poems of the cycle. When Gareth and his companions set out for Camelot in "Gareth and Lynette," "The birds made/ Melody on branch and melody in mid air" (179-80), almost as a kind of Spenserian narrative premonition of the more remarkable sounds that assail them from the city's gateway, previously envisioned as rising from the mist. "Out of the city a blast of music peal'd" that startles the travellers; yet they soon learn that these are the sounds of the city itself, the region which exudes no din but a scrupulously underdescribed music. Camelot's builders, they hear, "came from out a sacred mountain-cleft/ Toward the sunrise, each with harp in hand,/ And built it to the music of their harps" (256-8). This central vision of the founding of the central locus of order, of The Order, evokes previous Tennysonian descriptions of the creation of Troy. Recent critics such as Ricks and John Rosenberg have pointed out the connection between these lines and those in "Tithonus": "Like that strange song I heard Apollo sing/ While Ilion like a mist rose into towers" (62-63), lines redolent of the masque-like music accompanying the building of Pandemonium (*Paradise Lost* I, 711-12) which "rose like an exhalation." Oeone echoes the Miltonic lines even more precisely, when she announces

> Hear me, for I will speak, and build up all
> My sorrow with my song, as yonder walls
> Rose slowly to a music slowly breathed.
>
> (38-40)

But for the instrumental sounds, the harps playing the stones of the city into place like the stones of Thebes moved by the lyre of Amphion, Tennyson was returning to Ovid, and perhaps in a way to his own early "Ilion, Ilion" fragment, where the melody of mountain rivers yields finally "To a music from the golden twanging harpwire heavily drawn." Camelot cannot be sighed or breathed or sung into place, but must be established by the choir of fairy harps to be an instance of something universal. For, as the travellers are told, "an ye heard a music, like enow/ They are building still, seeing the city is built/ To music, therefore never built at all,/ And therefore built for ever" (271–74).

It is this music of eternal law which, here heard as an auditory actuality, is invoked metaphorically elsewhere in the cycle. Arthur's injunction to Balin "walk with me, and move/ To music with thine Order and the King" (73–74) is echoed in the narration later, when "all the world/ Made music, and he felt his being move/ In music, with his Order and the King" (207–8), and continued on thereafter through a simile of the nightingale. It is the music of internalized order which is broken by Balin's terrible yell at the end of the poem, but it remains undeveloped in imagery, hieratic, given, like an ethical term. In its corrupted form, it is Tristram's "broken music" in "The Last Tournament," and in metamorphosed form it is associated with Arthur's Harp, which "makes a silent music up in heaven," like the lyre of Orpheus. And essentially, it is a purely emblematic music, rather than an acoustical experience like the sounds of benign or maleficent nature, or of human activity, or, as for a very different kind of writer, an example of structure, of syntax *per se,* and only hence a kind of poetry.

The music accompanying the Holy Grail is less abstract. Percivale is told of a sound associated with moonlight "As of a silver horn from o'er the hills/ Blown." The music is clearly supernatural, in the mode of ceremonial or masque music whose source can only be the image it accompanies:

> . . . And the slender sound
> As from a distance beyond distance grew
> Coming upon me—O never harp nor horn,
> Nor aught we blow with breath, or touch with hand,
> Was like that music as it came; and then
> Stream'd thro' my cell a cold and silver beam. . . .
> (111–16)

The music of the descending Grail is like that of Camelot. It is not surprising to find that even the nonmusical sounds in the *Idylls,* even the noises of nature can share this ceremonial quality. There is the rural music sacred to the hermit's cave in "Lancelot and Elaine," lines 409–10, for example, where "in the meadows tremulous aspen-trees/ And poplars made a noise of falling showers." When these sounds are mentioned again, emblematically and almost like a leitmotif, a hundred lines later, it is with a subtle reversal of the lines, which not only separates the tree-voices, with the slighter, thinner (perhaps higher?) one coming afterward, but also underlines the merely implicit roar of the worldliness from which Lancelot retires to recover from his wound: "Hid from the world's wide rumor by the grove/ Of poplars with their noise of falling showers,/ And ever-tremulous aspen-trees he lay" (520–3). By the augmentation of "ever-tremulous," the aspen sounds have been given a character of their own. But the music remains almost magical, authenticating the separateness of place, rather than affecting feelings, evoking memories, or helping to fix visionary moments. We can, in fact, almost imagine the music to be part of the cure, as in medieval and renaissance tradition. It partakes of some of the transcendent qualities of the Camelot and Grail musics; and although it is not to be "moved to," like the first of these which the great city was "built to," it is surely, here, a music to which to rest or be healed.

The so-called "music" of Tennyson's own verse becomes, in the end, part of a curious version of this *Idylls* music. In "Merlin and the Gleam," the visionary gleam of the poet's imagination is continually represented as "Moving to melody," but a melody undefined and unrepresented, save when, in a period of despair in Tennyson's life, "The light retreated,/ The landskip darkened,/ The melody deadened"—the associative effect of the assonance is wonderful here—or when, in a region of imaginative renewal, it dissolves into "warble of water,/ Or cataract music/ Of falling torrents." But the melody is more than merely that of verse; it is a very basic rhythm of active life, and a peculiar situation occurs in section VIII where the Gleam itself is given voice and is thus presumably discernible to Tennyson's adoring multitudes:

> And broader and brighter
> The Gleam flying onward,
> Wed to the melody,
> Sang through the world. . . .
> (95–98)

The wedding is more than one of imagination to utterance, poetry to literature, worth to fame, or any of the other nested readings we might give this visionary unification. It is a final association of vision and audition. The two are "wed" in a characteristic visionary image of English poetry from Spenser on; if they are combined in so apparently stately and bourgeois a fashion (we cannot but remember that Rimbaud's *Une Saison en enfer* was published some seventeen years before "Merlin and the Gleam" was written), the radical quality of the union, occurring near the margin of the allegorical poetic quest, is not to be overlooked. It represents the limits of a certain kind of fulfillment, both in and of poetry. It leads us to wonder whether the musics of Camelot and Grail might not have suffered from remaining contracted or reductive forms of the higher Gleam melody, from being the music of order and belief rather than that of the imagination that they spurn and crave. The wedding of sight and sound can only be reported to us, however, and we can do no more than respect that report, as we respect the sense of the "tide as moving seems asleep" in Tennyson's canonical final vision. But it will always be the doubled "sound and foam" of the poetic achievement, the twilight cut through by the invisible evening bell, that can authenticate in any way the less accessible presentations of the eternal which seek to transcend them.

HAROLD BLOOM

Tennyson: In the Shadow
of Keats

Freud, in his essay on "Repression" (1915), says that psychoanalysis shows us:

> ...that the instinct-presentation develops in a more unchecked and luxuriant fashion if it is withdrawn by repression from conscious influence. It ramifies like a fungus, so to speak, in the dark and takes on extreme forms of expression, which when translated and revealed to the neurotic are bound not merely to seem alien to him, but to terrify him by the way in which they reflect an extraordinary and dangerous strength of instinct. This illusory strength of instinct is the result of an uninhibited development of it in phantasy and of the damming-up consequent on lack of real satisfaction.

Freud emphasized that repression manifested itself particularly in hysteria, but added that it could be observed in "normal" psychology also. Any definition of Freud's notion of "repression" should make clear that what is repressed is not an instinctual drive or desire, but rather the representation of it *in an image*. The repressed image is not wholly confined to the unconscious. However, some aspect of it is, an aspect which distorts, expands, intensifies the aspect still apparent in consciousness. Freud began by using "repression" and "defense" as though they were synonyms, but defense was necessarily always the wider term. Yet, of all the defenses, repression is most sharply differentiated from the others, and again it is the most elaborate of the defenses, being a three-phased process:

From *Poetry and Repression*. Copyright © 1976 by Yale University. Yale University Press, 1976.

1. Primal Repression, directed against representations, but not against the instinct that remains fixated to the representations.

2. Repression proper, which Freud calls "after-pressure."

3. The Return of the Repressed, as dream, or symptom, or lapse in speech or behavior.

Since only representations or images can be repressed, but not desire or drive, we can wonder what motives Freud could ascribe to repression? There can be no repression unless the image threatens unpleasure, Freud insists. We approach therefore, particularly in the context of poetry, a fundamental question, which is doubtless fundamental for psychoanalysis also, but that is not *our* concern. Why must the ego be defended from the representations of its *own* desires? Whatever the answer is in a psychoanalytic context (and Freud is evasive in this area), I am certain that in the context of poetry the answer has to do with the anxiety of influence. The representations that rise up from the id are not wholly the ego's own, and this menaces the poetic ego. For the precursor poem has been absorbed as impulse rather than as event, and the internalized precursor thus rises, or seems to rise, against the ego from what appear to be the alienated representations of the id. It is in this strange area of identity-and-opposition that unpleasure in one's own images becomes a burden for the poetic ego, a burden that provokes defense, which in poetry means misprision, or the trope as a misreading of anteriority.

This essay is to be a discourse on Tennyson and not on Freud, however analogically, and yet I want to keep us in the gray area where poetry and psychoanalysis compete, for a while longer. My concern will be with Tennyson's revisionist genius for internalizing Keats, a process we might have thought impossible but for Tennyson's incredible rhetorical skill. That particular act of revisionary genius, on Tennyson's part, changed poetic history, for it was Tennyson's transformation of Keats that was the largest single factor in British and American poetry from about 1830 until about 1915. I am thinking not only of such various literary phenomena as the Pre-Raphaelites, Pater, aspects of Yeats, and of Wilfred Owen and other Georgians, and Trumbull Stickney and the early Stevens in America, but of hidden, crucial influences such as that of Tennyson on Whitman, and then of Tennyson and Whitman together upon Eliot. But first, I return us to the terrible poetic double-bind relationship of identity-and-opposition, between the formative poetic ego and its internalized precursor.

For the post-Enlightenment poet, identity and opposition are the poles set up by the ephebe's self-defining act in which he creates the hypostasis of the precursor as an Imaginary Other. We can agree with Nietzsche that distinction and difference are humanly preferable to identity and opposition as categories of relationship, but unfortunately strong poets are not free to choose the Nietzschean categories in what has been, increasingly, the most competitive and overcrowded of arts. I am tempted to adopt here the notion of what Jacques Lacan calls the Imaginary Order, which has to do with a world of what Blake called the Crystal Cabinet, a Beulah-world of doubles, illusive images, mirrors and specular identification, except that Lacan says there is no Other in the Imaginary but only others, and for the ephebe there is always the imaginary Other. But I do find useful in poetic, rather than general human terms, Lacan's remark that the ego, the *moi*, is essentially paranoid. The poetic ego is a kind of paranoid construct founded upon the ambivalency of opposition and identity between the ephebe and the precursor. Lacan says also that, in analysis, a passage is made from the "empty word" or Imaginary discourse to the "full word" or Symbolic discourse. Let us adopt our constant subversive principle, which is that many nineteenth- and twentieth-century speculators secretly are talking about poems when they assert that they are talking about people. Translating Lacan, we substitute the word "poet" for the "patient" and the word "poem" for the "analysis," and we arrive at the following: "The poet begins the poem by talking about himself without talking to you, or by talking to you without talking about himself. When he can talk to you about himself, the poem will be over." To this formula, I would add that the blocking agent that gradually gives way here is the imaginary form of the precursor.

The Marxist reply to my way of talking about influence necessarily would have to be that scorn of repetition as overdetermined force which Marx manifests in his powerful *The 18th Brumaire of Louis Napoleon*. Contemporary Marxist theorists, like Althusser or Marcuse or the systems-theorist Wilden, tend to see art as a domain where a return of the repressed can be completed. Thus, Wilden speaks of "transcending the individualistic identities and oppositions of the Imaginary by entering the *collective differences* of the Symbolic." I would say against this Marxist idealizing that the study of poetic misprision demonstrates the necessity of fresher and greater repressions if strong poetry is to survive. The Marxist critics say, in effect: Do not make the mistake of trying to destroy the precursor by taking his place, but rather let the dead bury the dead, and so make the precursor irrelevant. My sad reply must be: No newly strong poet can reduce the significance of the precursor's mastery, because it is not possible for the new or belated poet to transcend the oppositional relationship that is ultimately a negative or dialectical identification with the precursor. That relationship can be transcended only by refusing the perpetual burden and conflict of *becoming a strong poet*. There are no dialectics of liberation that will work in the world of the antithetical, and the dialectics of poetry are never those of nature or of society or of history. I do not know whether psychoanalysis will prove to be the final form or perhaps dubious last achievement of capital-ism, but I suspect that really strong modern poetry may prove to be that form, a suspicion in which I follow again the prophetic lead of Emerson, or of Wallace Stevens in his Emersonian aphorism: "Money is a form of poetry."

I am aware of how incongruous all this seems as an introduction to the poetry of Alfred, Lord Tennyson, but Tennyson was surely one of the most sublimely repressed poets in the language. It is no accident that Tennyson, like his precursor Keats, and like their common ancestor, Spenser, is one of the three most authentically erotic poets in the language. I commence with a marvelous poem of enormous erotic repression, *Mariana*, where I will ask: What does this erotic repression itself repress? Let us recall Freud's profound theory of desire, which speculates that desire always tries to bring about an identity between a present state of nonsatisfaction, and a past state that is recalled as satisfaction, whether truly it was that or not. I am afraid that Freud implies that what desire desires is desire, which means that desire never can be satisfied. In Freud's view, the unconscious compo-nent in desire dooms all erotic quests to the worst kind of repetition. Tennyson was the peculiar master of this insight, and I suggest now that Tennyson's mastery in this regard came out of a beautiful misprision of Keats. With all this as prologue, I come at last to the superb *Mariana*, a genuine perfection of strong poetry, and a work as genuinely alarming in its deepest implications as are even the darkest speculations of Freud.

The "sources," in a conventional sense, of *Mariana* are traditionally and rightly held to include Keats, particularly his rather dreary poem, *Isabella*, which the young Tennyson loved rather more than anyone else has since. Here are stanzas XXX through XXXIV of *Isabella*:

> She weeps alone for pleasures not to be;
> 　　Sorely she wept until the night came on,
> And then, instead of love, O misery!
> 　　She brooded o'er the luxury alone:
> His image in the dusk she seem'd to see,
> 　　And to the silence made a gentle moan,
> Spreading her perfect arms upon the air,
> And on her couch low murmuring, "Where? O where?"
>
> But Selfishness, Love's cousin, held not long
> 　　Its fiery vigil in her single breast;
> She fretted for the golden hour, and hung
> 　　Upon the time with feverish unrest—
> Not long—for soon into her heart a throng
> 　　Of higher occupants, a richer zest,
> Came tragic; passion not to be subdued,
> And sorrow for her love in travels rude.

In the mid days of autumn, on their eves
    The breath of Winter comes from far away,
And the sick west continually bereaves
    Of some gold tinge, and plays a roundelay
Of death among the bushes and the leaves,
    To make all bare before he dares to stray
From his north cavern. So sweet Isabel
By gradual decay from beauty fell,

Because Lorenzo came not. Oftentimes
    She ask'd her brothers, with an eye all pale,
Striving to be itself, what dungeon climes
    Could keep him off so long? They spake a tale
Time after time, to quiet her. Their crimes
    Came on them, like a smoke from Hinnom's vale;
And every night in dreams they groan'd aloud,
To see their sister in her snowy shroud.

And she had died in drowsy ignorance,
    But for a thing more deadly dark than all;
It came like a fierce potion, drunk by chance,
    Which saves a sick man from the feather'd pall
For some few gasping moments; like a lance,
    Waking an Indian from his cloudy hall
With cruel pierce, and bringing him again
Sense of gnawing fire at heart and brain.

Keats's distressed lady is waiting for a murdered man; Shakespeare's Mariana is waiting for a deceiver, who has no intention of arriving. All that Tennyson really wants from *Measure for Measure* is that moated grange; we *know*, all through the poem, *Mariana*, that her lover *could* not arrive, even if he willed to, and that what reverberates in Tennyson's ear are a few lines from *Isabella*: "She weeps alone for pleasures not to be;/Sorely she wept until the night came on... /And so she pined, and so she died forlorn." Besides Keats, Virgil is the presence almost always haunting Tennyson, and somewhere in the background we see Dido resolving to die, and hear the ominous line: "She is weary of glancing at the curve of heaven" (*Aeneid* IV, 451). But these "sources" have little to do with the truly deep or repressed literary anxieties of the poem *Mariana*, just as the tags from Keats scattered through are essentially ornamental allusions ("athwart the glooming flats," line 20, goes back to "athwart the gloom" of *Sleep and Poetry*, line 146, while "Upon the middle of the night," suggests "Upon the honeyed middle of the night" in *The Eve of St. Agnes*, line 49). Such echoes, as I keep saying, are not matters of poetic influence, nor is style much the issue either. A profound ambivalence towards Keats's influence is the true subject of Tennyson's poem, and the rich repression that fascinates the reader throughout is part of the defensive pattern of misprision clearly at work in the poem. To get at that pattern, we need ask only: why does this poem fascinate so much, what makes it as strong and memorable as it is, why is it so important a poem? Important it certainly is; as much as any poem, it can be said to have invented that whole mode of poetry which in the next generation was called, so very oddly, Pre-Raphaelitism. What is the new, uncanny element that we hear in Tennyson's first stanza?

> With blackest moss the flower-plots
>   Were thickly crusted, one and all:
> The rusted nails fell from the knots
>   That held the pear to the gable-wall.
> The broken sheds looked sad and strange:
>   Unlifted was the clinking latch;
>   Weeded and worn the ancient thatch
> Upon the lonely moated grange.
>   She only said, 'My life is dreary,
>   He cometh not,' she said;
>   She said, 'I am aweary, aweary,
>   I would that I were dead!'

There are the naturalistic particularities of Keats, as globed and tactile as they are in the ode *To Autumn*, yet we are troubled by the impression that what we confront is not nature, but phantasmagoria, imagery of absence despite the apparent imagery of presence. The troublesomeness comes from a sense of excess, from a kind of imagery of limitation that seems to withdraw meaning even as it thickly encrusts meaning. The rusted nails appear no more nor less a morbid growth than the moss does, and the overwhelming impression of absence seems irreversible. We are drawn into an internalization that has brought phantasmagoria very close, yet the language gives such pleasure, such a frustrate ripeness, that we are anything but sorry to be so drawn. We have here, I think, a kind of catachresis imposed upon a rhetorical irony, or psychically Tennyson's reaction-formation to the fascination that Keats had for him.

Catachresis is not so much a trope in itself as it is an abuse of the other tropes. It is a kind of tautology to speak of a "false figure," since all figures are necessarily false, but a catachresis, skillfully used, is a subtly imperfect trope, or a peculiarly extended trope, or a forced one. Derrida seems to suggest that all philosophical tropes are catachreses; Tennyson is not a philosophical poet, but he is peculiarly conscious of his own poetic belatedness from the start, and his rhetorical resources were enormous. In one sense, the whole poem of *Mariana* is an exquisite catachresis of Keats's own modification of the Wordsworthian crisis-poem, but we will come to that sense later. First, let us break from the sequence of *Mariana*, so as to consider its seventh and last stanza:

> The sparrow's chirrup on the roof,
>   The slow clock ticking, and the sound
> Which to the wooing wind aloof
>   The poplar made, did all confound
> Her sense; but most she loathed the hour
>   When the thick-moted sunbeam lay
>   Athwart the chambers, and the day
> Was sloping toward his western bower.
>   Then, said she, 'I am very dreary,
>   He will not come,' she said;
>   She wept, 'I am aweary, aweary,
>   Oh God, that I were dead!'

This stanza is manifestly obsessed with time, and indeed with belatedness. But what kind of belatedness is this, erotic or poetic? If there is any validity at all to my theory of misprision, then sexual anguish, in a belated poetic text, would be, frequently, a mask for influence-anxiety, if only because an erotic blocking-agent, if it is to be handled by a poem, must be treated as though it also was a Covering Cherub or precursor-text doing the work of double-binding. Let me again beat upon the obvious; I am *not* taking away from the poem *Mariana* the fine anguish of Mariana's erotic frustration. But I recur to a point I made about the poem in an earlier essay ("Tennyson, Hallam and Romantic Tradition" in *The Ringers in the Tower*): this Mariana is herself a poetess, her true affliction is the Romantic self-consciousness of Keats and Shelley as solitary questers made yet one generation more belated, and no bridegroom, if he ever arrived, would be able to assuage her malaise. Without pulling the poem into our contemporary areas of the war between men and women, we can still note that what Mariana is longing for is not her belated swain but a priority in poetic invention that would free her from her really deadly obsession that nevertheless is giving her an intense quasi-sexual pleasure, a kind of sublime perversion that no sexual satisfaction could begin to hope to match. Mariana is much more than half in love with easeful death, and in the poem's closing lines she all but identifies death with her own primal narcissism.

I urge us, however, in the final stanza, to concentrate on the astonishingly strong but psychically costly transumption or metaleptic reversal of the most characteristic of Keatsian metonymies, which is the substitution of near-stasis or slow-pacedness for the language of the sense, for the sounds and sights of passing time. To Mariana, the sparrow's chirrup, the clock's ticking, the poplar's erotic cry in response to the wind's cry, all "confound her sense," which recalls Shelley's transumption of Wordsworth, in *The Triumph of Life*, when he has Rousseau speak of "many sounds woven into one / Oblivious melody, confusing sense." So Mariana also achieves a synaesthetic vision, yet more in Rousseau's victimized way than in Wordsworth's mode of tranquil restoration. What she hates, the poem ends by telling us, is that final near-stasis of light, when the sunbeam holds on, as thick-moted as the harsh luxuriance that opened the poem. Reversing Keats's heroic and proleptic naturalism, she projects and so casts out all past time, which means all erotic otherness, and introjects death, her own death, in despair of present as of the past. The poem is more deliciously unhealthy than all its Pre-Raphaelite and Decadent progeny were to be, and remains the finest example in the language of an embowered consciousness representing itself as being too happy in its unhappiness to want anything more.

Whatever canonical interpretation has said to the contrary, what he does so superbly in *Mariana* is Tennyson's peculiar greatness as a poet. I want in this discourse to trace that greatness now in a sequence of poems: *The Hesperides, Ulysses* (though very briefly, since I have mapped *Ulysses* in *A Map of Misreading*), and then most elaborately in *Tithonus*, with an after-glance at *Tears, Idle Tears*, after which I will conclude with a reading of Tennyson's repressive masterpiece, "Percivale's Quest," as I have called it, excerpting it from *The Holy Grail* in the *Idylls of the King*. But I will begin this sequence with a final glance at *Mariana*, so as to attempt some conclusion about the nature of Tennysonian repression in that poem. Let us look at that celebrated poplar tree, which Leslie Brisman notes as itself deriving from *Sleep and Poetry*, lines 277–78. It enters in the fourth stanza, dominates the fifth, vanishes in the sixth, and acquires an erotic voice in the seventh. Let us dismiss the grotesque notion that it is a phallic emblem; it is a very lone tree, and it represents the Sublime, so that we can call it, grimly and accurately, itself an emblem of repression, of purposeful forgetting or after-pressure, which always leaves a residue or some slight element of return. Far from being a representation of the lover who will not arrive, the poplar represents the Sublime or repressed element in Mariana herself, her own uncanny solipsistic glory. Its shadow falls not only "upon her bed" but significantly "across her brow" as well. As the solitary height above the level waste, the poplar is the precise equivalent of Childe Roland's dark tower, the internalized negative sublime that the quester will not see until it comes upon him or her. In the final stanza, what is the poplar but the High Romantic aeolian harp, or Mariana's song gathered together in its condensed glory?

What then is Mariana repressing? Why, that she doesn't want or need the other who cometh not. What would she do with him, what mental space has she left for him? And what is Tennyson the poet repressing? Only that the most dangerous and powerful and authentic part of his own poetic mind would like to be as perfectly embowered as Mariana's consciousness is, but of course it can't. And yet, Tennyson *has* surpassed Keats in his misprision of Keats's mode, for even Keats is not, could not be, the sustained artist that Tennyson is. To get beyond *Mariana,* as a poem, you must go the way of Dante Gabriel Rossetti, but that is another story, a story of still greater repression.

Before going on to an even more gorgeous triumph of repression, *The Hesperides,* let us worry the notion of repression just a bit longer, by returning to Freud's central essay on the subject:

> The process of repression is not to be regarded as something which takes place once for all, the results of which are permanent, as when some living thing has been killed and from that time onward is dead; on the contrary, repression demands a constant expenditure of energy, and if this were discontinued the success of the repression would be jeopardized so that a fresh act of repression would be necessary.

The emphasis here is on energy expended, again and again, and that is how we have got to think of repression, particularly in the context of strong poetry. Repression is, as Derrida surely remarks somewhere, a difference in contending forces, and so necessarily is a strong poem such a difference. It is the constant renewal of repression that is, I am convinced, the clue to the magnificence of Tennyson's style. No poet in English, not even Milton, is so consistently Sublime. Tennyson's most characteristic trope is not even the hyperbole, but is a catachresis or extended abuse of that trope of overthrow or overemphasis. Tennyson never stops exaggerating, yet never stops giving pleasure by his leaps beyond limits. Take the Miltonic closing trope of *Mariana:* "and the day / Was sloping towards his western bower." It is an elegant allusion to line 31 of *Lycidas,* where the evening star "Toward heaven's descent had sloped his westering wheel," but Tennyson's or rather Mariana's sun is lingering belatedly, so that the sloper, when he gets there, will be in much the same closed-in condition as the embowered Mariana, so that we are compelled to see that solipsistic damozel as being rather a sloper herself. Keats, in a pungent and somewhat ungracious letter to Shelley, had urged his swifter colleague to be an artist and so serve Spenser's Mammon: load every rift with ore. Tennyson betters Keats's instruction and, as Keats's ephebe, word-paints himself into the most densely inlaid art in the language.

Mariana, as I suggested earlier, can be regarded as a catachresis of the Romantic crisis-ode, as a hyperbolic version of Coleridge's *Dejection* or Keats's *Nightingale.* The catachresis here is the hothouse-forcing of the crisis-situation, since it would be difficult to image a more extreme state of self-consciousness than the one that Mariana so dialectically enjoys. But note Tennyson's curious staging of the poem; he narrates, and she speaks, and yet we find it difficult to keep the narrative and the embowered voices separate from one another. A descendant, odd as it must seem, is Stevens's *Sunday Morning*, where again the narrator and the occasionally speaking woman tend to merge in heightened passages. Let us think of Mariana as Tennyson's Stevensian Interior Paramour or Shelleyan epipsyche, and be prepared to find her hovering elsewhere in his poetry.

It is at the catachresis of internalized quest or Keatsian revised romance that Tennyson is most gifted, a wonderful instance being *The Hesperides*, a poem that the poet always insisted upon suppressing. Why? I suppose because here the repression is not strong enough, so that there is a dangerous and, evidently to Tennyson, disconcerting partial or apparent return-of-the-repressed. Here is the incantation of the repressive daughters of Hesperus at its properly apocalyptic climax:

> Holy and bright, round and full, bright and blest,
> Mellowed in a land of rest;
> Watch it warily day and night;
> All good things are in the west.
> Till midnoon the cool east light
> Is shut out by the round of the tall hillbrow;
> But when the fullfaced sunset yellowly
> Stays on the flowering arch of the bough,
> The luscious fruitage clustereth mellowly,
> Goldenkernelled, goldencored,
> Sunset-ripened above on the tree.
> The world is wasted with fire and sword,
> But the apple of gold hangs over the sea.
> Five links, a golden chain, are we,
> Hesper, the dragon, and sisters three,
> Daughters three,
> Bound about
> All round about
> The gnarlèd bole of the charmèd tree.
> The golden apple, the golden apple, the hallowed fruit,
> Guard it well, guard it warily,
> Watch it warily,
> Singing airily,
> Standing about the charmèd root.

Though this lovely song intentionally induces a languorousness in its readers, it requires of its singers a continual expenditure of repressive energy. As these ladies had sung previously, trying no doubt to keep their drowsy dragon awake:

> If ye sing not, if ye make false measure,
> We shall lose eternal pleasure,
> Worth eternal want of rest.

The pleasure they value so highly must be their pride as poets and as performers, as weavers of an enchantment so sinuous as to block all questers from fulfillment in an earthly paradise. Their closing stanza is a celebration of belatedness, of being perpetually "after the event" by virtue of always being poised in front of it. As a transumption, this is a catachresis of the Keatsian trope that unheard melodies are sweeter, and the Hesperides arrive at a stasis that introjects lateness ("All good things are in the west"). There is an implication, throughout, that poetry and repression are an identity, but there is also a manifest anxiety as to the palpable misprision of Keats that is being enacted. The end of quest is to be not in the quester's merging in the identity of others, or of the poethood, but in the perpetual stasis of an earthly paradise preserved by enchantment from the single gratification it affords, and which would end it.

We pass to mature Tennyson, but before turning to *Tithonus*, where the Keatsian influence is so wonderfully engaged and held to a draw, I want very briefly to re-examine *Ulysses*, which is a companion-poem to *Tithonus*. It would seem odd to speak of repression in regard to a poem like *Ulysses*, whether we mean in the speaker of this dramatic monologue, or in Tennyson himself, for however one wants to interpret the poem, it offers us a vehement and highly expressive selfhood. Whether this Ulysses is a hero, or more likely a hero-villain, or whether he is Tennyson knowing he must go on after Hallam's death, or a more equivocal Tennyson confronting his own ambivalences, in any of these cases he would appear to be a consciousness that has forgotten nothing, even unconsciously. Indeed he seems a total purposefulness, fretting at inaction, and far from burying the representations of any impulse, he seems a man who in the drive to fulfill *all* impulses would welcome all self-representations whatsoever. What can this most sublime of questers not know, or not wish to know, whether about himself or about his relation to others? And, if this is somehow Tennyson himself, why ought we to associate the poem with defensive processes of any kind? Finally, what sort of a poem is this *Ulysses* anyway? Where are we to find its precursors, its brothers, its descendants, in our own quest for those inter-poetic relationships and juxtapositions by which meaning is produced?

Vico, more directly than any other theorist, associated meaning with survival, and rhetoric with defense. Tennyson's Ulysses is not interested in mere survival (thus his heartfelt scorn "as though to breathe were life!") but he cares overwhelmingly about *what he means*, and whether he still means what he used to mean. His rhetoric defends against meaningless or mere repetition, against the reduction of life to the metonymy of breath. In the deep sense, his quest for continued meaningfulness is Vichian, for the meaning he seeks will guarantee his survival as the hero, the perpetually early wanderer, rather than the belated, aged king he has become when we meet him at the opening of his monologue. Surely, this Ulysses is strikingly like one of those magical formalists that Vico describes the primitive godlike men as being. As their lives were what Vico called "severe poems," so this Ulysses had lived a severe poem, and now cannot bear the life he has come home to, in what has turned out to be a mockery of the fulfilled quest. Can it be that by successfully returning home, this Ulysses has understood himself too well, and thus destroyed his own quest for meaning? In Vichian terms, the poet's quest for divination has been ruined in this quester, which is why he must set out again if he is to survive.

I want to quote part of one of what Vico calls his "Corollaries concerning Poetic Tropes, Monsters, and Metamorphoses," because I believe that Vico is a much better guide than Freud to the curious affinity or even identity between strong poetry and a kind of repression. Vico, in his axiom 405, notes that in language most of the expressions relating to inanimate things are formed by metaphor from the human body, senses, or passions. He then cites his own axiom 120: "Beware of the indefinite nature of the human mind, wherever it is lost in ignorance man makes himself the measure of all things." Even so, Vico says, man through rhetoric "has made of himself an entire world." In what follows, Vico suddenly achieves an astonishing insight:

> So that, as rational metaphysics teaches that man becomes all things by understanding them, this imaginative metaphysics shows that man becomes all things by *not* understanding them; and perhaps the latter proposition is truer than the former, for when man understands he extends his mind and takes in the things, but when he does not understand he makes the things out of himself and becomes them by transforming himself into them.

Behind this axiom is the central Vichian principle: you only know what you yourself have made, which means that to know yourself is to have made yourself. Whatever one thinks of the truth of Vico's vision, it certainly applies to Tennyson's Ulysses, who is a severe poet and a Vichian primitive solipsist. When Tennyson's quester says: "I am a part of all that I have met" he means: "I understand only myself, and so everything I have met I have made out of myself, and I have become all things by transforming myself into them." One step further on from Tennyson's Ulysses is Browning's Childe Roland; another step on is Pater's Marius, and the final step is taken by the Hoon of Wallace Stevens who can proclaim triumphantly:

> I was the world in which I walked
> And what I saw or heard came not but from myself
> And there I found myself more truly and more strange.

What Vico saw is that truly poetic metaphysics was founded upon a sacred solipsism, which Vico called "ignorance," or rather that imagination takes its flight when the mind *represses* its own knowing and its own understanding. What Tennyson's Ulysses represses is his own knowledge, of himself and of his relation to others, so that by this repression he can be driven out, away from home, to seek knowledge again. To *know* is to have become belated; not to know, not to understand, is to become early again, however self-deceivingly. What is the relation between this odd catachresis of a transumptive stance, and the celebrated Negative Capability of Keats? Keats spoke of "when man is capable of being in uncertainties, Mysteries, doubts, without any irritable reaching after fact & reason" and added that one must be capable "of remaining content with half knowledge." This is the wisdom of the *aporia*, of knowing we must end in uncertainty, and surely Tennyson's Ulysses is a grand parody of such intellectual heroism. Ulysses asserts he wants full knowledge, and actually wants no knowledge at all, except the Vichian transformation of the self into everything unknown, meaning into everything encountered.

With *Tithonus*, the Vichian repression of understanding achieves an even more intense version of the Sublime, yet one that is also more recognizably in the shadow of Keats. Vico, if I understand him (which in my own terms means if I misread him strongly enough), is saying that poetic repression is a mode of Knowing, or even that rhetoric is a mode of knowing *by negation*. The absolute exquisiteness of the rhetoric of Tennyson's *Tithonus* may mask a profound loss of the self by way of a negation of knowing that becomes a new kind of repressive knowing. Or, more simply, what is Tithonus repressing?

> The woods decay, the woods decay and fall,
> The vapours weep their burthen to the ground.
> Man comes and tills the fields and lies beneath,
> And after many a summer dies the swan.
> Me only cruel immortality
> Consumes: I wither slowly in thine arms.
> Here at the quiet limit of the world,
> A white-haired shadow roaming like a dream
> The ever-silent spaces of the East,
> Far-folded mists, and gleaming halls of morn.

Ostensibly, both *Ulysses* and *Tithonus*, like *Tears, Idle Tears* and the whole of In Memoriam, are poems of grief at the loss of Hallam, and of guilt for going on living without Hallam, the guilt of being a survivor, of being humanly as well as poetically belated. We might apply here the insight of Freud, in his "Mourning and Melancholia" essay, that melancholia begins, like mourning, in the loss of the beloved object, but this loss is not the real cause of the melancholia. Instead, the ego splits, with one part attacking the other, and the attacked portion becomes the repressed representation of the lost object (through "identification"). What is thus exposed is the narcissistic element in the love felt for the lost object, so that mourning becomes a process in which self-love is transformed into self-hatred. Tithonus shows a pattern not wholly unlike this Freudian insight, but I want to place our emphasis elsewhere, upon Vico again, and therefore upon the repression that makes Tithonus the extraordinary poet he is.

Or, should we say "aesthete" rather than "poet," just as we should say "hero-villain" rather than "hero" when we speak of Ulysses? I want to approach Tithonus, including its surpassingly beautiful opening passage, by way of Tears, Idle Tears, a closely related poem, and also like Tithonus an act of defense against the composite precursor, Keats-and-Wordsworth. Just as any sensitive reader will hear Wordsworth's Simplon Pass (from The Prelude) in the opening of Tithonus, so he or she will be haunted by Tintern Abbey while brooding upon Tears, Idle Tears:

> Tears, idle tears, I know not what they mean,
> Tears from the depth of some divine despair
> Rise in the heart, and gather to the eyes,
> In looking on the happy Autumn-fields,
> And thinking of the days that are no more.
>
> Fresh as the first beam glittering on a sail,
> That brings our friends up from the underworld,
> Sad as the last which reddens over one
> That sinks with all we love below the verge;
> So sad, so fresh, the days that are no more.
>
> Ah, sad and strange as in dark summer dawns
> The earliest pipe of half-awakened birds
> To dying ears, when unto dying eyes
> The casement slowly grows a glimmering square;
> So sad, so strange, the days that are no more.
>
> Dear as remembered kisses after death,
> And sweet as those by hopeless fancy feigned
> On lips that are for others; deep as love,
> Deep as first love, and wild with all regret;
> O Death in Life, the days that are no more.

Cleanth Brooks has devoted some brilliant pages in *The Well Wrought Urn* to uncovering the motivation of Tennyson's weeper. I myself would say that we cannot uncover the motivation, because of the patterns of repression in the poem. Whatever else we read it as being, *Tears, Idle Tears* is a lament of belatedness, in which part at least of the poet's burden is his inability to achieve any priority in the wording of his own very authentic grief. The dominant imagery of the poem is hyperbolical *depth*, buried passion, and buried in more than one sense, though the poem's largest trope of representation is the Virgilian noble synecdoche, in which weeping for a particular loss is a part of which the tears of universal nature are the whole. In the poem's closing lines, Tennyson tropes upon Wordsworth's double trope in the *Intimations* Ode, of "Heavy as frost, and deep almost as life!" that ends the first movement of the ode, and "Thoughts that do often lie too deep for tears," the ode's final line. The weight that Wordsworth called "custom," a death-in-life, lay deep almost as life, until it was transumed by thoughts of such depth that they transcended tears. But Tennyson beautifully reverses the trope, by metalepsis; the depth greater than "custom" and greater than thoughts of human sympathy, is the repressed depth of lost first love, the true death-in-life that cannot be reversed into an earliness: "the days that are no more."

Though Tennyson defends against Wordsworth's presence, in a poem actually composed at Tintern Abbey again, the tropes of limitation he employs defend rather against Keats, whose ode *To Autumn* is more deeply involved in the lyric repressions of *Tears, Idle Tears*. In *his* ode, Keats looks on the happy autumn fields, and does not weep, does not lament the loss of earliness, the absence of the songs of spring. The bird songs of late-summer/early-autumn intimate to Keats one of his liminal states, a threshold vision poised or held open to the possibility of tragedy, but above all *open*, to whatever may come. This *aporia*, or beautiful uncertainty, is too strong a limitation for Tennyson to accept. But for Tennyson the bird song is not another metonymy for death, like the glittering beam and the sail in the previous stanza, and like the strange metaphoric transformation of Keats's characteristic open casement in "when unto dying eyes / The casement slowly grows a glimmering square." So gorgeous a lyric is *Tears, Idle Tears*, in its dark undoings of Keats's heroism, that we do not pause long enough to suspect a little how perceptive, how aesthetic a vision, is being achieved despite those tears. They are "idle" enough in that they do nothing to blind this weeper.

I think *that* is where the emphasis falls in Tennyson's even more beautiful reverie of a grieved aesthete, his *Tithonus*, where the mourning is necessarily more primal and terrible, being for the monologist's own lost youth and beauty. But, quite evidently, not for lost love, as the grand link between Tithonus and Ulysses is their palpable, solipsistic inability to have loved anyone but their own former selves. As I have said elsewhere, one would not wish to be in a boat with Tennyson's Ulysses, who has the knack of surviving while others drown. Equally, unlike poor Aurora, one wouldn't wish to be in the same bed with Tithonus. But of course it all depends on how one reacts to a really primal narcissism—which will involve another brief digression into how criticism might set about reclaiming the pirated poetic element from yet another of Freud's fundamental insights.

Freud's final insight in regard to narcissism was his realization that it was a defensive movement against the death-drive. His original insight had seen narcissism as the element in the ego that made the ego an image, an imaginary object, rather than an hypostasis of reason. In the subtle lights of Tennyson's *Tithonus*, it is fascinating to note that Freud began to brood upon narcissistic neuroses in order to explain the psychoses of hypochondria and megalomania, as Tithonus has more than a touch of each. We fall in love, according to Freud, as a defense against a narcissistic cathexis or self-investment when our passion-for-ourself threatens to go too far. But in such falling, we continue to love what represents ourself, whether what we were, or what we would like to have been. If Tithonus had fallen in love with Aurora at all, then it was only to the degree that she was a narcissistic representation of himself. But she has remained splendidly herself, he has withered, and now he loves only death.

I repeat Freud's belated insight, that ultimately narcissism is a defense against the death-instincts. If Tithonus genuinely wants to die, as he asserts, then he has ceased to be a poet (if ever he was one) and he has abandoned also the primal megalomania of his own narcissism. His monologue belies both these assertions, and so is either self-deceptive or rhetorically deceptive towards ourselves, or both together, as would be normal in the characteristic Browning monologue. Something is therefore very equivocal about this dramatic monologue, and so I want to return again to its really gorgeous opening lines. Let us regard this first verse-paragraph as the poem's *clinamen*, its swerve away from the naturalistic affirmations of Wordsworth and of Keats. What is absent in these opening ten lines is simply all of nature; what is present is the withered Tithonus. As Tennyson's reaction-formation against his precursors' stance, these lines are a rhetorical irony, denying what they desire, the divination of a poetic survival into strength. Behind these lines are Wordsworth on the Simplon Pass ("The immeasurable height / Of woods decaying, never to be decayed") but more crucially the entire vision of an early cosmos in Keats's *Hyperion*.

I think that the five remaining verse-paragraphs of *Tithonus* will be found to reveal, in sequence, the five expected revisionary ratios, rather too neatly, but I don't think that this is merely my own compulsion or misprision-neurosis working out; rather it is another indication that *Tithonus* truly is a High Romantic crisis-poem, masking as a dramatic monologue, so that its patterning of defenses, tropes, and images closely follows the models of poems like *Tintern Abbey*, *Intimations of Immortality*, *Dejection*, the *Ode to Psyche*, and all their companions. Rather than trace the next five verse-paragraphs through my map of misreading, I will leave that operation to my readers' curiosity or skepticism. Let us assume that my apprehension of the patterns of misprision here will be confirmed. What will that tell us about the poem?

In an essay on Christopher Smart's *Rejoice in the Lamb*, Geoffrey Hartman speaks of Freud as our latest doctor of the Sublime, as a diagnostician of "the pathology of ecstasy," the true culminator of the tradition that goes from Boileau on Longinus through Vico and Edmund Burke on to Kant and Schopenhauer. Hartman's laconic point against a view of defense as a primary phenomenon, whether in the psyche or in poems, is made rather aggressively and ironically when he observes: "Defense mechanisms cannot blossom when there is nothing—no fire or flood—to defend against." Against this, I would name, for Tennyson, Keats as the fire and Wordsworth as the flood. *Tithonus*, as a poem, is at once a narcissistic apotheosis and a powerful repressive reaction against the greatest poets ever to have attempted a humanized Sublime, an attempt made by way of a humanization of the ancient poetic lust for divination. When Tithonus defensively turns against himself, he turns against the whole heroic enterprise that would single out the poet as a candidate for survival:

> Let me go: take back thy gift:
> Why should a man desire in any way
> To vary from the kindly race of men,
> Or pass beyond the goal of ordinance
> Where all should pause, as is most meet for all?

This is a dark synecdoche, reminding us that the burden of a trope is pathos, and that the ancient war between rhetoric and a more rational dialectic can never end. But though he yields to masochism as a vicissitude of instinct, we would do wrong to take *Tithonus* literally when he says "take back thy gift," since the gift of immortality in this poem is also the gift of divination, without which no one becomes, or remains, a poet. Against this momentary yielding to an instinctual vicissitude with its strong representation set against the self, Tithonus recoils with an obsessive force in a psychic defense of limitation, which in his case is a compulsive return to origins, a regression conveyed primarily by the metonymy of the Wordsworthian glimmer or gleam, but with a direct eroticism that derives from Keats:

A soft air fans the cloud apart; there comes
A glimpse of that dark world where I was born.
Once more the old mysterious glimmer steals
From thy pure brows, and from thy shoulders pure,
And bosom beating with a heart renewed.
Thy cheek begins to redden through the gloom,
Thy sweet eyes brighten slowly close to mine,
Ere yet they blind the stars, and the wild team
Which love thee, yearning for thy yoke arise,
And shake the darkness from their loosened manes,
And beat the twilight into flakes of fire.

What is palpable in this lovely passage is that the sexual warmth not only is but always *was* Aurora's, and also that the monologist, a solipsistic aesthete, now and always was no part of "the wild team / Which love thee." Even Ulysses is not so sublimely incapable as is Tithonus of apprehending anyone's emotions except his own. Thus, Aurora's tears are read by Tithonus as his own hysterical fear that his now noxious immortality cannot be withdrawn (which, on the level of Tennyson's own repressions, I would tend to interpret as his own evaded realization that he is doomed to go on seeking to be a strong poet, even though Hallam is dead). Again, in the fifth verse-paragraph, there is the extraordinary passivity of Tithonus as a lover, with its overwhelming emphasis not upon sexual pleasure or fulfillment, but upon the monologist's heightened powers of aesthetic perceptiveness while being embraced.

When, in the final verse-paragraph, we move into the area of East and West, or early and late, the *apophrades* or introjection of the past has about it the peculiar and unnerving accents of paranoia—not that of Tennyson, I hasten to say, but of the monomaniacal Tithonus. What is most striking to me, about these lines, is their cruelty as the masochistic Tithonus manifests a repressed sadism towards the bereaved and loving Aurora:

Yet hold me not for ever in thine East:
How can my nature longer mix with thine?
Coldly thy rosy shadows bathe me, cold
Are all thy lights, and cold my wrinkled feet
Upon thy glimmering thresholds, when the steam
Floats up from those dim fields about the homes
Of happy men that have the power to die,
And grassy barrows of the happier dead.
Release me, and restore me to the ground;
Thou seest all things, thou wilt see my grave:
Thou wilt renew thy beauty morn by morn;
I earth in earth forget these empty courts,
And thee returning on thy silver wheels.

Let us grant that the monologist's situation is extreme, but his presumably unconscious cruelty transcends even that extremity. Is it really necessary for him to assure her: "Thou seest all things, thou wilt see my grave"? Need he finally assure her that, when he is "earth in earth," he will forget her? I do not believe Tennyson was aware of this cruelty, and I am suggesting that even in these glorious closing lines, a profound repression is at work. To grow endlessly more agèd while remaining immortal is an oxymoronic or belated version of the divination that is crucial to strong poetry. The hidden concern of the poem *Tithonus*, as of the poem *Ulysses*, is Tennyson's own belatedness as a poet, his arrival on the scene *after the event*, after the triumph of poetry of "reflection" in Coleridge and Wordsworth, and of poetry of "sensation" in Shelley and Keats, to use a critical distinction invented by Hallam. Hallam's enormous contribution to Tennyson was to overcome the poet's diffidence, and to persuade him that he could become a third, with Shelley and Keats. Hallam dead, Tennyson knew not only the guilt of a survivor but also the obsessive poetic fear of belatedness, the fear that torments his own Sir Percivale, that every repressed voice crying from within will proclaim: "This Quest is not for thee."

With Percivale's Quest from *The Holy Grail*, I come to my final text from Tennyson, and begin by dismissing as a palpable evasion his own weak misreading of his own text, in which Percivale and all the other knights, except Galahad, represent a flawed Christianity, flawed in Percivale's case by an ascetic, otherworldly mysticism, a sort of St. John of the Cross Catholic temperament. But the Percivale we meet in the poem is hardly a mystical ascetic, but rather a highly familiar compound ghost, the High Romantic antithetical quester, whose every movement is *contra naturam*, even in spite of himself. We are back in that central current that goes from Spenser, in the *Prothalamion*, and from Spenser's Colin Clout to the *Penseroso* of Milton and the equivocal heroism of Satan questing onwards through Chaos to reach Eden, the New World. These are Percivale's ultimate ancestors, but much closer are the Solitary of Wordsworth, and the Solitary's younger brothers in Childe Harold, Endymion, and, above all others, the doomed, driven Poet of *Alastor*. Contemporary with Percivale is Browning's Roland as well as Tennyson's Ulysses, while looming up are the Oisin and Forgael of Yeats, and the Nietzschean parody of all these in Stevens's Crispin, or the antithetical quester reduced to the state of *The Comedian as the Letter C*.

I am suggesting that, in Percivale, the repressed element in Tennyson's poethood emerges fully, in a fury of questing that deforms and breaks all it encounters more devastatingly than even Childe Roland's vision wreaks upon his world. Hypnotic and incantatory as Tennyson is almost always capable of being, I know nothing in him as phantasmagoric, as Sublime, as much charged with a greatly controlled hysteria of repression as Percivale's destructive quest:

> 'And I was lifted up in heart, and thought
> Of all my late-shown prowess in the lists,
> How my strong lance had beaten down the knights,
> So many and famous names; and never yet
> Had heaven appeared so blue, nor earth so green,
> For all my blood danced in me, and I knew
> That I should light upon the Holy Grail.

> 'Thereafter, the dark warning of our King
> That most of us would follow wandering fires,
> Came like a driving gloom across my mind.
> Then every evil word I had spoken once,
> And every evil thought I had thought of old,
> And every evil deed I ever did,
> Awoke and cried, "This Quest is not for thee."
> And lifting up mine eyes, I found myself
> Alone, and in a land of sand and thorns,
> And I was thirsty even unto death;
> And I, too, cried, "This Quest is not for thee."

> 'And on I rode, and when I thought my thirst
> Would slay me, saw deep lawns, and then a brook,
> With one sharp rapid, where the crisping white
> Played ever back upon the sloping wave,
> And took both ear and eye; and o'er the brook
> Were apple-trees, and apples by the brook
> Fallen, and on the lawns. "I will rest here,"
> I said, "I am not worthy of the Quest;"
> But even while I drank the brook, and ate
> The goodly apples, all these things at once
> Fell into dust, and I was left alone,
> And thirsting, in a land of sand and thorns.

> 'And then behold a woman at a door
> Spinning; and fair the house whereby she sat,
> And kind the woman's eyes and innocent,
> And all her bearing gracious; and she rose
> Opening her arms to meet me, as who should say,
> "Rest here;" but when I touched her, lo! she, too,
> Fell into dust and nothing, and the house
> Became no better than a broken shed,
> And in it a dead babe; and also this
> Fell into dust, and I was left alone.

'And on I rode, and greater was my thirst.
Then flashed a yellow gleam across the world,
And where it smote the plowshare in the field,
The plowman left his plowing, and fell down
Before it; where it glittered on her pail,
The milkmaid left her milking, and fell down
Before it, and I know not why, but thought
"The sun is rising," though the sun had risen.
Then was I ware of one that on me moved
In golden armour with a crown of gold
About a casque all jewels; and his horse
In golden armour jewelled everywhere:
And on the splendour came, flashing me blind;
And seemed to me the Lord of all the world,
Being so huge. But when I thought he meant
To crush me, moving on me, lo! he, too,
Fell into dust, and I was left alone
And wearying in a land of sand and thorns.

'And I rode on and found a mighty hill,
And on the top, a city walled; the spires
Pricked with incredible pinnacles into heaven.
And by the gateway stirred a crowd; and these
Cried to me climbing, "Welcome, Percivale!
Thou mightiest and thou purest among men!"
And glad was I and clomb, but found at top
No man, nor any voice. And thence I past
Far through a ruinous city, and I saw
That man had once dwelt there; but there I found
Only one man of an exceeding age.
"Where is that goodly company," said I,
"That so cried out upon me?" and he had
Scarce any voice to answer, and yet gasped,
"Whence and what art thou?" and even as he spoke
Fell into dust, and disappeared, and I
Was left alone once more, and cried in grief,
"Lo, if I find the Holy Grail itself
And touch it, it will crumble into dust." '

I have quoted all of this sequence, so as not to lose any of its cumulative force. But what is this force? I think we recognize in it, all of us, one of our own nightmares, the nightmare that is centered upon our own self-destructiveness, and so upon our own murderousness also, our aggressive instinct whose aim is the destruction of the object. As the greatest of modern moralists—true successor of Pascal, Montaigne, Schopenhauer, Emerson, Nietzsche—Freud is the inevitable authority to cite in any account of the aggressive instinct or drive-towards-death, though the poetic variant, in Tennyson, will hardly be an exact equivalent of the Freudian insights. Rather, Tennyson's vision of Percivale's Quest, and Freud's vision of the death instinct (particularly in *Beyond the Pleasure Principle*) will be found to have a troublesome resemblance suggesting that both are complex misprisions of a common precursor, of a larger mental form to which Vico remains the surest guide I have been able to discover.

Though Percivale's Quest might seem to sustain the analysis of the ascetic ideal as given by Nietzsche in *Towards the Genealogy of Morals*, this apparent similarity has more to do with Tennyson's overt intention than with his actual representation of Percivale, in the poem. What we encounter in Percivale, as in the wandering Poet of Shelley's *Alastor*, is a repressed aggressive instinct, or what Freud calls the death instinct directed outwards. But clearly, Percivale's deathliness intends to be directed against his own self. What does it mean that Tennyson is compelled to make of Percivale a consuming force that devastates everything it encounters?

Freud's very problematic final theory of the instincts posits a group of drives that work towards reducing all tensions to a zero-point, so as to carry everything living back to an inorganic state. Freud's formulation is difficult, because it suggests that a self-destructive drive back towards origins is a universal phenomenon. As a theory, Freud's notion here is frankly daemonic, and related to his dark insight that all repetition phenomena may mask a regressive element in every human instinct. To account for life's ambivalence towards itself, Freud resorted to a more radical dualism than he had entertained earlier. The id became the center for representing every instinctual demand, with none assigned to the ego, which means that ultimately every desire, whether for power or for sexual fulfillment, is in some sense linked to the desire for death. Without pretending to be summarizing the full complexity of Freud's speculations, I will leave the notion of the death instincts there, except to note that Freud was compelled to adopt a new formulation in this area, the Nirvana Principle, which he took from Schopenhauer by way of a suggestion of the English psychoanalyst Barbara Low.

The Nirvana Principle, introduced in *Beyond the Pleasure Principle* (1920), is the psyche's drive to reduce all excitation within itself, whether the origin of the excitation be internal or external, to the zero-level, or as close to zero as possible. I have invoked all of this Freudian speculation in order to get us to the Nirvana Principle, for that is the actuality of Percivale's Quest, despite Percivale's apparent intention and Tennyson's stated and overt intention. Percivale believes he is questing for the Holy Grail, but in reality he quests for Schopenhauer's quasi-Buddhistic Nirvana, where desire shall vanish, the individual self fade away, and quietude replace the strong poet's search for a stance and word of his own. Percivale, I am suggesting, is as close as Tennyson can come, not to a return of the repressed, but to an absolute or total freshening of self-repression. And though *The Holy Grail* is ostensibly a critique of Percivale and an exaltation of Galahad, and even of the humane and sweet Ambrosius, what any reader is going to remember is that sublime and terrific destructive march to the zero-point that is the litany of Percivale's quest. Reflect even upon the exchange between Ambrosius and Percivale that ends the account of Percivale's ruinous march. Ambrosius cries out, in the name of common humanity:

> 'O brother, saving this Sir Galahad,
> Came ye on none but phantoms in your quest,
> No man, no woman?'

> Then Sir Percivale:
> 'All men, to one so bound by such a vow,
> And women were as phantoms ... '

How shall we read "such a vow"? Only I think, despite Tennyson's intentions, as the vow to be a strong poet, whatever the human cost. Percivale, in the deep sense, is Tennyson the poet, unable to get out of or beyond the shadow of Galahad, the quester who beholds and becomes one with a strength that resists the Nirvana Principle. I am not proposing any simple equation of Galahad = Keats, but a more complex formula in which Galahad does represent the High Romantic quest, and Percivale the belated quest of Victorian Romanticism. Tennyson was too sublimely repressed a poet to develop very overtly his ambivalence towards his prime precursors, and the death of Hallam, who was the great champion of Keats, augmented the repression. But Tennyson too was a preternaturally strong poet, and we have seen something of his strength at misprision. The shadow of Keats never did abandon him wholly, and so the stance of belatedness became a kind of second nature for him. But what he may have lacked in priority of stance, he greatly compensated for in priority of style. He prophesies his true ephebe, the late T. S. Eliot, and time, I am persuaded, will show us how much stronger a poet Tennyson was than Eliot.

A. DWIGHT CULLER

"Maud or the Madness"

What is called mania and melancholia, are for the most part effects of the same power being overactive, but overactive in different directions. If the distressing passions are overactive, we have melancholia,—if the animal propensities, we have furious mania,—and if the exhilarating passions, we have an exuberance of joyous activity.

This excitement of the depressing and exhilarating passions alternatively, is the most striking characteristic of the insane.

—DR. MATTHEW ALLEN,
Essay on the Classification of the Insane (1837)

$\mathbf{A}$ubrey de Vere, in his superficial way, observed to Tennyson that in *In Memoriam* he had written the first two-thirds of a *Divine Comedy* and "suggested that perhaps he might at some later time give to the whole work its third part, or Paradise." To which the poet replied gruffly, "I have written what I have felt and known; and I will never write anything else." Part of the reason for Tennyson's gruffness may have been that he himself felt that he had already written a kind of *Paradiso* in the Epilogue to *In Memoriam* and that what was lacking was the *Inferno*. "It's too hopeful, this poem," he said to James Knowles, "more than I am myself. I think of adding another to it, a speculative one . . . , showing that all the arguments are about as good on one side as the other, and thus throw man back more on the primitive impulses and feelings." *Maud* is, in a certain sense, that poem. Not that it is speculative, but it does throw man

---

back on the primitive impulses and feelings and show that the arguments are about as good on one side as the other. Moreover, it is curiously parallel to *In Memoriam* in form. Both are composite poems, consisting of a series of meditations or lyrics arranged in a certain order. *Maud*, according to Tennyson, is a "monodrama," whose peculiarity is that "different phases of passion in one person take the place of different characters." But *In Memoriam* is also a sort of monodrama. "The sections were written at many different places," says Tennyson, "and as the phases of our intercourse came to my memory and suggested them. . . . The different moods of sorrow as in a drama are dramatically given." *In Memoriam* is, of course, written in the first person, but Tennyson was eager to establish that " 'I' is not always the author speaking of himself, but the voice of the human race speaking thro' him." It is, he said to Knowles, "a very impersonal poem as well as personal." *Maud*, on the other hand, though written in dramatic form, is a very personal poem as well as impersonal, and readers are not easily persuaded that "I" is not often the voice of the author speaking through the hero. *Maud* deals almost exclusively with the social relations of man, whereas *In Memoriam* is concerned with the solitary individual in relation to nature and God.

To continue the contrast, *Maud* is a catastrophist poem, whereas *In Memoriam* is uniformitarian. *Maud* opens with the reported suicide of the hero's father, who has apparently killed himself when a "vast speculation had failed," and although the hero gradually recovers from this trauma through the ministrations of Maud, he is again plunged into madness through the violence of the duel with her brother and is only redeemed therefrom by the collective violence of war. Toward the end of *In Memoriam* Tennyson had qualified his faith in progress by asserting that there would be "vast eddies in the flood / Of onward time" and that these would be social in character. *Maud* deals with one of those eddies. It deals, in other words, with the cataclysm which in *In Memoriam* is subsumed under the law of progress. *Maud* and the related poems *Locksley Hall* and *Locksley Hall Sixty Years After* also ultimately assert a faith in progress, but their immediate focus is on the cataclysm, the epicycle, the social violence which interrupts it. In a certain sense they are the obverse of the English Idyls. Like the idyls they are modern in subject matter—*Maud* may be called a verse novel as the idyls are verse tales—and they generally treat situations in which young people are frustrated in their love by the barriers of social class. But whereas the English Idyls breathe a spirit of reconciliation in an effort to bring the two classes together, *Maud* and *Locksley Hall* treat these matters more angrily. Tennyson seems to be saying that just beneath the surface of English life lurks an element of violence, madness, and bestiality which hitherto has not entered very largely into his poetry. Why should it enter now?

Some have said that *Maud* is Tennyson's "spasmodic" poem and so have attributed it to literary fashion. The Spasmodics were a group of poets, never so much as a school, who flourished from about 1839 to 1854 and who represent the last galvanic twitchings of Romanticism. They derive from Byron's *Manfred* and Goethe's *Faust* and are the endeavor, without the talent necessary for the operation, to elevate the poet to the status of a prophet-hero. Their own self-appointed prophet, the critic George Gilfillan, urged them to wrestle with the great problems of the age, to be modern and relevant, to probe the deep recesses of the soul, and to give voice to the scientific-pietistic mishmash that was their philosophy. They succeeded in producing a number of very long poems that were for the most part pretentious and dull, in substituting psychological violence and dubious morality for insight and truth, and in losing all sense of what Arnold called "architectonics." They were ultimately laughed out of court by William Edmondstoune Aytoun's parody of them in *Firmilian* in 1854, and it seems odd that Tennyson would have imitated a style that was just on the point of being discredited. On the other hand, he had already begun *Maud* before *Firmilian* appeared, and he did admire the Spasmodic poets. He praised John Philip Bailey's *Festus* when he first read it in 1846, and he thought Alexander Smith, the author of *A Life Drama* (1852), "a poet of considerable promise." He pointed out the "real merits" of Sydney Dobell's *Balder* when it appeared the following year, and he was nettled by the refusal of George Gilfillan to consider him a great poet. Moreover, *Maud* does have Spasmodic characteristics—the gloomy egoistic hero, the psychological violence, the dubious morality, and the ranting tone—and the critics had no hesitation in including it among the productions of the school. They were only sorry that the laureate had succumbed to temptation.

Apart from the question of literary fashion, there is the question of the autobiographical element in *Maud*. In recent years Sir Charles Tennyson and Professor Ralph Rader have made us aware how much of morbidity and violence is to be found in Tennyson's background and how specifically *Maud* and the related poems reflect it. There are three major elements. Tennyson's father, though the eldest son, had been virtually disinherited by his father, the "old man of the wolds," in favor of a younger son, Charles, who was set up in splendor in Bayons Manor, took a coat of arms and a French name (Tennyson d'Eyncourt), and generally occupied the station in life that his more talented but less stable brother ought to have occupied. This act of injustice was bitterly resented at Somersby and, as it rankled in the mind of Dr. Tennyson, contributed, along with the pressure of poverty and an uncongenial vocation, to the alcoholism which resulted in his mental breakdown and early death. There was mental instability in several of the Tennyson children, one of whom went actually insane, and so Tennyson's youth was overshadowed by precisely the morbid resentment and fears of madness represented by the hero of *Maud*. Secondly, Tennyson as a youth had several love affairs with young ladies of the neighborhood which could not possibly have culminated in marriage, had such a thing been thought of, because of the disparity in social and economic status. The most serious of these was with Rosa Baring, the daughter and stepdaughter of a wealthy couple who in 1825 settled two miles from Somersby in Harrington Hall. In 1838, about the time *Locksley Hall* was written, she married Robert Duncombe Shafto, scion of a wealthy Durham family, and so may have been the original of Amy in that poem. Tennyson has several poems addressed to her, and roses throughout his poetry glow with the physical beauty of her presence. A second, less serious affair was with Sophy Rawnsley, daughter of the rector of Halton Holgate, a good friend of Tennyson's father, whose lighter, more intellectual nature provided Tennyson with a contrasting image. She was the original of "airy, fairy Lilian," perhaps also of Lilia in *The Princess*, and in general lilies in Tennyson's poetry often carry suggestions of Sophy.

Finally, in 1838 Tennyson became acquainted with a Dr. Matthew Allen, who ran a private lunatic establishment near High Beech, in Epping Forest, and a few years later was persuaded by Allen to invest his entire patrimony of £3,000 in a wood-carving scheme which was to make them both rich. By 1843 all was lost and Tennyson was precipitated into an intense depression. *Sea Dreams*, which reflects this episode, shows that Tennyson objected to Dr. Allen's oily religiosity as much as to his unscrupulous business methods and that he saw his own credulousness in this "get-rich-quick" scheme as the worldly equivalent of evangelical Christianity.

All these elements in Tennyson's life contributed to *Maud*, and in that sense one may say that the poem is autobiographical. Every poem is autobiographical in the sense that the poet could not have written it if he had not in some degree known and experienced the emotions with which it deals. But that does not mean, as one critic has claimed, that the writing of *Maud* was "an act of cathartic recapitulation by which [Tennyson] defined and judged his early life and attempted to put it behind him." There is no evidence that the bitterness still rankled in 1854 or that at that date the difficulties of his youth were still of moment to him. What was of moment was the purely literary question of how to express the passionate morbidity which he felt infected the land. Both on the national and the international scene there was a festering evil, the product of a peace that was no peace and a prosperity ill divided, that he felt was corrupting the national life. Thus, when in January 1854, a month before beginning the composition of *Maud*, he invited Frederick Denison Maurice to Farringford, he indicated that what they would talk about was "the Northern sin / Which made a selfish war begin" and also "How best to help the slender store, / How mend the dwellings of the poor." The Spasmodics had been right in attempting to express these "spasms" in the national life, but they had not found the proper form. The form that Tennyson found was dramatic, but because the drama with which he was concerned was an inward one, a psychomachy within the national soul, it was a monodrama, a poem in which "successive phases of passion in one person take the place of successive persons."

This form was invented by Rousseau in 1762. Rousseau at this time was deeply concerned about the problem of French opera and particularly about the inadequacy of its artificial style to express the passions. The actor was inhibited by the demands of the music from delivering his lines in a natural and expressive manner, and the singer was unable fully to exploit the power of music because of the constraints of language. Rousseau determined to separate the media one from another and use them alternately. Thus he wrote a short dramatic piece entitled *Pygmalion* in which Pygmalion, alone on the stage, speaks a few lines, which are then followed by a passage of instrumental music which underlines and interprets his mood. He speaks again, and again there is a short passage of music. This "mood music" is obviously related to melodrama, and melodrama (literally, "musical drama") did in fact grow out of this form. Rousseau's situation, however, was not melodramatic. He was interested in the exploration of the passions, and so in the twenty-six short intervals of spoken language and instrumental music which make up his piece he had Pygmalion run through the entire gamut of the passions. Beginning in lassitude and ennui, he rises through the stages of a growing love for his own statue of Galatea, horror at the thought of so unnatural a love, anger, self-reproach, ecstasy, wonder as the statue begins to move, fear that he is going mad, quietude, and death. These feelings succeed upon one another with dazzling rapidity, and Rousseau's drama perfectly fits Tennyson's definition of monodrama as a poem in which "successive phases of passion in one person take the place of successive persons."

Out of Rousseau's *Pygmalion* arose an art form which flourished for over half a century in the theaters of France, Germany, Italy, and Spain. Goethe was interested in the form and we are told that Mozart was tempted. The most famous of the European monodramas were Johann Christian Brandes's *Ariadne auf Naxos*, with music by Georg Benda, and Benda's later *Medea*. As these examples indicate, there was a tendency to take one's subjects from classical legend or history, particularly from Ovid's *Heroides*, where the laments of the abandoned heroines provided a fine display of passion. Œnone would have made a good subject for a monodrama, and indeed Tennyson's poem, though often called an epyllion, may be so considered. The form was introduced into England by William Taylor of Norwich and his friend Dr. Frank Sayers in 1792 and was quickly imitated by Southey and "Monk" Lewis. Because it did not often achieve stage representation, however, it soon lost the connection with music, and by the 1840s the term *monodrama* was commonly used of any dramatic poem placed in the mouth of a single speaker. It was used where we would use the term *dramatic monologue*. R. H. Horne, for instance, speaks of Tennyson's "powerful monodrama of 'St. Simeon Stylites,' " and a writer in the *Eclectic Review* (1849) says, "The entire sum of [Browning's] poetry may be said to be dramatic, though much of it, like so much of Tennyson's, is simply *monodrama*."

There is, nonetheless, a difference between monodrama and the dramatic monologue which it would be well to revive and retain. The latter form, which did not really become established as a genre until the late nineteenth century and then on the basis of Browning's work more than Tennyson's, emphasizes the ironic distance between the speaker's actual words and the reader's understanding of those words. The Bishop in ordering his tomb gives to us and his "nephews" a very different understanding of his character than he himself possesses. The dramatic "conflict" of such a poem, one would say, is the conflict between the conscious intention of the speaker and his unconscious self-revelation. In monodrama, however, there is no such ironic distance. We do not need either to sympathize with or to judge the speaker but only to wonder at the range, variety, and power of the passions and at the remarkable linguistic (and musical) resource with which they are displayed. The tradition here is a rhetorical tradition, deriving not only from Ovid but also from Richardson, from the great virtuoso soliloquies on the English stage, and from choral odes like *Alexander's Feast* and Collins's *Ode on the Passions*.

This is the tradition that Tennyson follows in *Maud* and *Locksley Hall*, and it would be well to illustrate its use in the shorter poem before we return to the major work. In *Locksley Hall* the immediate model which Tennyson had before him is not the European monodrama but Sir William Jones's translation of the Moâllakát, the seven Arabian poems hung up in the temple of Mecca. Remote as these poems may appear to be from so English and Victorian a work as Tennyson's, most of them do indeed follow almost exactly the pattern of *Locksley Hall*: the poet, coming upon the place where the tent of his beloved had formerly been raised but which is now desolate, dismisses his companions and alternately cries out upon her faithlessness and upon his own weakness in still being affected by her. In a wild Oriental manner he darts from subject to subject and mood to mood with an extravagance hardly equaled by Rousseau. In one instance the scene is even terminated by a thunderstorm, as it is in *Locksley Hall*. The poems are certainly the original of that poem but they are also Arabian versions of monodrama, and one notes that Jones's translation was published in 1799, just as the interest in monodrama was at its height.

It has even been suggested that Tennyson's choice of his long, loping couplets was determined by the long, rhythmical cadence of Jones's prose translation, though Tennyson himself says that he wrote the poem in this meter because "Mr. Hallam said to me that the English people liked verse in trochaics." If so, they do not like it any more, but this is probably because we do not know how to read trochaics any more. If the poem is read slowly, understressing rather than overstressing and with great attention to the pauses, then the true character of this meter comes out, which is that it can accommodate itself to any mood. It can be stately or passionate, furious or tender, angry or elegiac, and this is what it is called upon to be. For *Locksley Hall* is a true monodrama in that, like *Pygmalion*, it is an exploration of the passionate heart of man. The modern reader, approaching it as a dramatic monologue and looking for some evidence of ironic intention, finds none and so leaps to the conclusion that the poet is to be identified with the hero and is to be condemned for that character's extravagance. But the true element of complexity in the poem is not the ironic detachment of reader from speaker but the internal conflict among the speaker's various voices. "Well—'tis well that I should bluster!" "But I *know* my words are wild." There are seven or eight places where the speaker rounds sharply on himself, repudiating what he has just said and introducing a new line of meditation. The orchestration of these moods, leading from the idyllic recollections of childhood with Amy through a series of bitter outbursts which gradually are mingled with efforts toward calm, until at last the speaker's faith in progress is restored—this is the structure of *Locksley Hall*. It is a musical structure which can easily be understood in musical terms. Needless to say, there is also a narrative element, in that, by moving through these phases of feeling, the speaker recapitulates the phases of his past life. Born with a faith in the future, he has been deeply embittered by the social injustice of the age, and he now vacillates between locking himself into this bitterness and freeing himself from it so he can join in the march of mind again. The essential problem is the recovery of the visionary imagination. As a boy, "nourishing a youth sublime / With the fairy tales of science and the long result of Time," he had

> ... dipt into the future far as human eye could see;
> Saw the Vision of the world, and all the wonder that would
>   be.—

When that couplet is repeated a hundred lines later, but deepened and expanded by the vision of "the Parliament of man, the Federation of the world," the speaker can cry,

> O, I see the crescent promise of my spirit hath not set,
> Ancient founts of inspiration well through all my fancy yet.

With this perception he can put Locksley Hall behind him, knowing that his destiny lies not in brooding over the past but in working out this vision of the future.

Unfortunately, the vision did not materialize. Sixty imaginative years later (actually it was fifty) Tennyson published *Locksley Hall Sixty Years After*, in which we see all these same events from the point of view of an octogenarian living not in 1837 but in 1887. Amy's husband has now died, and we learn that she herself had died in childbirth many years before. Indeed, in all likelihood she was already dead while the youth was fulminating outside her Hall. He himself has married Edith, whom he had first seen in early childhood when she looked out of a casement window and he, fool that he was, did not have the wit to realize that she was far superior to the shallow Amy. The one son she gave him, Leonard, has died at sea, heroically trying to save the lives of others, and his grandson has now come down by rail to meet him at the funeral. He is late because some mischievous boy had put an object on the track—so it appears that "the ringing grooves of change" are subject to minor derailments. He is to be the heir of Locksley Hall, but out of delicacy they will not stay there tonight—rather in the one decent hostel the town still affords. Then tomorrow they will attend the service and after that the grandson would do well to imitate the virtues of Amy's husband, for it now appears that he was not a clown but a very worthy squire. If anyone was a clown, it was the speaker himself, who in his arrogance once refused to take his rival's proffered hand.

The grandson, who has just been jilted by his lady love, as the speaker had been sixty years before by Amy, is informed that the cases are not parallel. His passion was not the equal of the speaker's, and whereas Amy was weak, Judith is a worlding. In fact, the world in general has deteriorated, and as the speaker moves out into larger considerations, he finds more comfort in the immortality of the soul than in the cry of "Forward." That cry should be muted now, for the marvels of his day have grown stale through repetition and, in any case, there is no moral progress to keep pace with that of knowledge. Chaos alternates with Cosmos, and although the old man still retains his faith in progress, he remembers "how the course of Time will swerve, / Crook and turn upon itself in many a backward streaming curve." The present age, with its absurd doctrine of equality and the debased literary ideals of France, is certainly one of those backward curves.

T. S. Eliot has said that the creation of any new work of art alters the meaning of all previous works, and that is particularly true in the case of a sequel like *Locksley Hall Sixty Years After*. We learn from this poem that the speaker of the previous poem was simply wrong in many of his facts and judgments. Does this mean that Tennyson has written a palinode or that he has produced a bitterly sardonic account of how the youthful liberal turns into an archreactionary in old age? Probably neither one nor the other, but it is certainly true that with the accession of the second poem we cannot read the first as readers did in 1842. Each poem enters into relation with the other, so that the two together form a diptych, enclosed within a common frame. Like *L'Allegro* and *Il Penseroso*, they are a kind of Youth and Age, and this means that each ceases to some degree to be a monodrama and becomes, with respect to the other, a dramatic monologue. The irony that was lacking to the first poem is provided by the second, and although the second claims to supersede the first, it cannot supersede it in our mind or in the mind of the young grandson looking on. Thus, the two poems taken together are relativistic and historical. Tennyson dedicated the second poem to his wife because he thought that "the two 'Locksley Halls' were likely to be in the future two of the most historically interesting of his poems, as descriptive of the tone of the age at two distant periods of his life." Lord Lytton agreed. "The old lover, . . ." he says, "is exactly what the young man must have become . . . if he had grown with the growth of his age.—For that reason alone, the poem in its entirety [he is apparently regarding the two poems as one] has a peculiar historical importance as the impersonation of the emotional life of a whole generation."

Locksley Hall, however, is not a diptych but a triptych, for its large central panel, positioned in 1855, almost exactly halfway between the first poem and the second, is *Maud*. And it too was asserted by Tennyson to be historical. "I took," he wrote to Archer Gurney in December 1855, "a man constitutionally diseased and dipt him into the circumstances of the time and took him out on fire." By this he did not mean to deny that there were autobiographical elements in *Maud*. "In a certain way, no doubt, poets and novelists, however dramatic they are, give themselves in their work. The mistake that people make is that they think the poet's poems are a kind of 'catalogue raisonné' of his very own self, and of all the facts of his life, not seeing that they often only express a poetic instinct, or judgment on character real or imagined and on the facts of lives real or imagined." *Maud* contains much that is real but a great deal more that is imagined.

Yet this is what the British public was unwilling to grant. Though not all reviews were unintelligent or unfavorable, many were, and Tennyson perceived that they had not understood the form. "As it is a new form of Poem altogether," he wrote to Mr. Ticknor in October 1855, "the critic not being able to make it out, went at it: why not? he is anonymous." To Charles Weld on November 24 he wrote: "It is a poem written in an *entirely new form*, as far as I know." And a few weeks later to Archer Gurney: "The whole was intended to be a new form of dramatic composition." The name of this new form Tennyson did not publicly apply to the poem until 1875, when he added the subtitle A *Monodrama* to the edition of that year, apparently in reaction to an uncomprehending review in a Liverpool newspaper. "Thanks for your Liverpool paper," he wrote to R. C. Hall on January 17, 1873. "*Maud* is a drama—a monodrama—& what is said in it is dramatical." It has usually been assumed that Tennyson got the term from a pamphlet, *Tennyson's 'Maud' Vindicated: An Explanatory Essay,* published by Robert James Mann, a physician, in 1856. For in that pamphlet Mann gives a full explanation of the form of *Maud* and calls it a "mono-drama." We have seen, however, that the term was current in England in the 1850s and that Tennyson would not have had to learn it from a medical man. Indeed, it is all but certain that not only the name "monodrama" but also the entire substance of Mann's pamphlet derived from Tennyson. For Tennyson was a near neighbor of Mann's on the Isle of Wight, and in the spring and summer of 1855 used to walk over to his house and look at the stars through his telescope. One night they looked at Orion and Dr. Mann drew a diagram of the constellation which Tennyson sent to his wife. "Look out at Orion," he wrote, "at a faintish star under the lowest star of his belt. That is really 8 stars, all moving in connection with one another, a system by themselves, a most lovely object thro' the glass." "Orion low in his grave," in the third and final sections of *Maud* may owe something to this evening. So friendly did Tennyson become with this "clever, interesting doctor" that before he purchased Farringford he thought of living in one of the houses on the Bonchurch Terrace, near Ventnor, occupied by Dr. Mann, for then, he explained to his wife, she would have "a 'most careful' physician always at hand & ready to serve you. I think him a most excellent & pure-minded man—from whose society everyone must reap advantage."

Certainly Tennyson reaped advantage, for in October 1855, as the bad reviews came in and he became more and more exasperated at being confounded with his hero, he received a letter from Dr. Mann accompanying the loan of his valuable telescope. "Many thanks," wrote Tennyson, "but it is a loan that I shall accept with fear and trembling." And then he added, "I am curious to hear your 'plan' touching Maud." One can hardly doubt that Dr. Mann's plan was that he should put forth under his own name an explanation and vindication of *Maud* the substance of which he had undoubtedly received from Tennyson. (One may suppose that Tennyson had read the poem aloud to him, as he later did to James Knowles, with full explanation and commentary.) Mrs. Tennyson, it should be noted, was "utterly against that Defense Vindication as it was called, however kindly meant," declaring that *Maud* "must stand or fall of itself." However, Dr.

Mann went ahead, and when he finished, he sent the proofsheets to Tennyson to look over and emend. "It is very difficult to recriticize a critique on oneself," wrote Tennyson. "I don't quite like your 'word-sculpture' but if you choose let it stand. I don't quite think that the lines *jar*; they rather rush with the impetuosity of passion, jarring perhaps once or twice. However, 'recalls clearly' is wrong—the memory [presumably of the hero's betrothal in part I, section vii] is a phantasmal one, which he cannot trace to its origin." Type and style he thought did very well, but he declared, "If I were with you, we could settle it together viva voce much better than by letter."

Settle it they did, for when the pamphlet appeared, Tennyson gave it his official blessing: "No one with this Essay before him can in future pretend to misunderstand my dramatic poem, *Maud*." It is, indeed, one of the best critiques of the poem that has ever been written, and the central passage about the monodramatic form is as follows:

> *Maud* is a drama;—that is, an action. . . . The *dramatis persona* of the action,—for there is but one individual who is ever brought forward in it *in person*,—exhibits his story through the mental influences its several incidents work in himself, and this exhibition is made, not directly and connectedly, but, as it were, inferentially and interruptedly, through a series of distinct scenes, which are as varied as the circumstances involved. It is in this peculiarity of the poem,—the one person revealing to the reader his own sad and momentous history, by fits and starts, which are themselves but so many impulsive utterances naturally called forth from a mind strung to the pitch of keen poetic sensibility,—that its absolute originality and the surpassing skill of the Laureate are displayed. Nothing can be more exquisitely consonant to the proceedings of nature than that such utterances should be made in fitful and broken strains, rather than that they should march steadily on to the measure of equal lines, and regularly recurring rhymes. . . . Every utterance, whether it be of sentiment, passion, or reflection, is an impulsive outburst; but it is an outburst that involuntarily clothes itself in language of the most appropriate character and vivid power. Such, both in the matter of sense and of music, is the language of *Maud*. The syllables and lines of the several stanzas actually trip and halt with abrupt fervour, tremble with passion, swell with emotion, and dance with joy, as each separate phase of mental experience comes on the scene. The power of language to symbolize in sound mental states and perceptions, has never before been so magically proved. In the successful employment of this kind of word-music, the author of *Maud* stands entirely unrivalled, as, in its general form of severe dramatic uni-personality, the poem itself is absolutely unique.

Clearly, Dr. Mann is right in declaring that the central feature of *Maud* is the dazzling variety of mood as expressed in the varied forms of the individual lyrics. When Maud smiles upon the speaker, he is ready to fall at her feet, but when his dark imagination broods upon the significance of her smile, he is plunged into gloom. When he sees her in church, he is exalted; but when he sees her riding upon the moor with his rival, he is like a spark extinguished in the night. Even within the lyrics the mood shifts abruptly from one state of feeling to another. In part I, section ii, when the hero first sees Maud, he exclaims, "Long have I sigh'd for a calm," but then observes bitterly, "It will never be broken by Maud," whose cold and clear-cut face is "dead perfection, no more." "Nothing more," that is, "if it had not been / For..."—and he then enumerates all the interesting little beauties with which he is already half in love, until, drawing himself up short, he declares, "From which I escaped heart-free"—adding the admission, "with the least little touch of spleen." Every lyric and part of lyric can be analyzed in this way, as if spoken by the Two Voices of Tennyson's earlier poem, or by the several voices of love, resentment, jealousy, pique, moodiness, melancholy, tender longing, self-depreciation, anger, whimsy, playfulness, lyric exultation, and mad pride. The basic conflict in part I is between the hate with which the poem opens and the love in which it closes, between morbidity and health, madness and sanity, violence and calm—ultimately, between life and death—and this is its dramatic action. Though ultimately the conflict is objectified in the characters, particularly the speaker and Maud's brother, primarily the "different phases of passion in one person take the place of different characters."

Moreover, the sequence of the passions in Maud follows a common monodramatic formula. Beginning in morbidity and bitterness, it rises through the alternating moods of dark suspicion and growing love to the exaltation of the garden scene. It then plunges down through the remembered violence of the duel into the madness of part II and reemerges with the hero calm but shattered in part III. The final scene, where the hero resolves his problems by embarking for the Crimean War, has been criticized as unsatisfactory, and from a moral point of view it is. But French and German monodramas often resolved themselves in spectacle at the close, and something of that sort seems to be happening here. If the work were performed on stage, there is no doubt but that the hero's dream, in which Maud is seen to separate herself from the band of the blest and pronounce a benediction upon the war, would actually have been performed in the upper regions of the theater; and the lines in which the hero "stood on a giant deck and mix'd my breath / With a loyal people shouting a battle cry" would have been accompanied by a panorama of ships-of-the-line passing across the rear of the stage much as Tennyson saw them move down the Solent as he was writing this scene. The whole would have been accompanied by martial music, the booming of guns in the distance, fireworks, and other displays of theatrical machinery. It is, indeed, a pity that we cannot see *Maud* performed. Skeptics who heard Tennyson read the poem were normally convinced, and Hallam Tennyson's account of his father's reading emphasizes the variety of intonation. "The passion in the first Canto was given by my father in a sort of rushing recitative," but with the section "I have led her home, my love," "my father's voice would break down," and in the garden scene his eyes, "which were through the other love-passages veiled by his drooping lids, would suddenly flash as he looked up and spoke these words, the passion in his voice deepening in the last words of the stanza." From the little disc issued by the Tennyson Society, which reproduces a recording made by Tennyson on wax cylinders in 1890, one may confirm Hallam Tennyson's impression.

On the other hand, one cannot claim that *Maud* is pure monodrama, for Tennyson has created an "objective correlative" for the emotions of his hero which is far more extensive than was ordinarily the case. Ordinarily, monodrama dealt with classical figures whose character and situation were sufficiently well known that they did not need to be developed. Had Tennyson written a Hercules Furens or Orlando Furioso, he would have had a proper monodrama. But instead, he has taken a slice of modern bourgeois life and treated it realistically as in a novel, and in so doing he has created a plot which asks to be judged in accordance with the normal canons of dramatic action. The puzzling thing about this plot is that it moves through two cycles. The hero is moved from the disorder by the duel and is redeemed from that through what we can only call the holy power of war. Why this second movement? Tennyson said that *Maud* was akin to *Hamlet,* and there is an analogy with Hamlet's morbidity, occasioned by his father's death, with the possibility of redemption through Ophelia's love, and the tragic conclusion of the duel with Laertes. But Shakespeare ended the drama at that point. He did not have Hamlet recover and go to war with Fortinbras. One feels that Tennyson could also have so managed it that, although the "dreadful hollow" once again reechoed with the violence of hate, the values of the garden would have been reestablished in the poem. Tennyson also compared the work to the *Oresteia,* and although that does provide a parallel for the curse between the two houses which goes on in cycle after cycle, Aeschylus had a means of terminating the cycle in the emergence of a new conception of justice. As it stands, what Tennyson's drama seems to mean is that the evils of the age are so great that they cannot be assuaged gradually by the holy power of love but only catastrophically by the holy power of war.

This may well be what Tennyson meant, and one could argue that he was merely unlucky in his choice of war. If he had set his poem in the Middle Ages and had his hero go off on the Crusades, no one would have objected, for it has always been considered legitimate for a hero to solve his personal problems by giving himself to some larger cause. But Nolan's blunder at Balaklava, the state of the hospitals at Scutari, plus modern pacifism have effectively ruined Tennyson's symbol, and it is idle to say that anyone can now read the final scene of *Maud* and like it. Moreover, Tennyson *was* quite bellicose at this time. Ever since the coup d'état of Louis Napoleon in 1852, when Tennyson felt that the government had allowed the national defenses to deteriorate to the point where England was dangerously exposed to invasion, he had been writing violent anonymous poems for the newspapers—poems so violent that, as he humorously observed to his wife, some of them might in themselves be a cause for war. If *Maud* is a national and historical poem, as on one level it certainly is, it urges that post-Romantic English youth, who have very properly been brooding on their social wrongs, particularly upon that central evil the marriage of convenience, should not confirm themselves in morbidity but come out of their shells and give their lives for England. In *The Charge of the Light Brigade* and the slightly later poems *Havelock* and *The Defence of Lucknow*, which describe the gallant stand of a little band of Englishmen against a horde of Indian rebels, Tennyson gave models of how he expected his hero to act. It is undoubtedly true that he did not expect him to return alive.

But the great model he had already given, just a year and a half before, in the *Ode on the Death of the Duke of Wellington*. The theme of that stately utterance is that "the last great Englishman is low." Not once does Tennyson address his subject by name. With befitting generality he is the Great Duke, our chief state-oracle, the statesman-warrior, the man of amplest influence, the foremost captain of his time, the great World-victor's victor. Neither is Nelson, whose rest in the crypt of St. Paul's is broken in upon by the procession, called by name.

> Mighty Seaman, this is he
> Was great by land as thou by sea.

The poet then reviews his hero's career from the early charge at Assaye to the late defense of Lisbon, culminating in "that world-earthquake, Waterloo!" For such a man the "Civic muse," the muse of Tennyson's early political poems, preserves a broad approach of song, for, thanks to be God! "we are a people yet." The word "people" had for Tennyson a special meaning. It connoted that law consonant with liberty which was imposed upon a nation by itself. Unlike foreign nations, where "brainless mobs" and "lawless Powers" contend, the English cherish

> That sober freedom out of which there springs
> Our loyal passion for our temperate kings.

The only danger is lest the English be not vigilant to preserve freedom, for only so can mankind be preserved. To do this they must look to their seaward walls. The poem falters a little toward the close, but in its stateliness, its lofty dignity and sense of national purpose, and in the solemn rhythms and sonorous rhymes by which this is conveyed, it is one of Tennyson's great public utterances. Had he been able to strike the same note at the end of *Maud*, instead of the slightly jingoistic note he has struck, he would have ended his drama more worthily.

Still, the final scene makes it apparent that the hero rises at this point from a purely personal conflict to one in the national interest. This is betokened by the fact that the wraith, which has dogged him ever since the duel, now leaves him and is replaced by the Spirit of Maud in Heaven. In the drama itself the distinction between the wraith and the Spirit is not made entirely clear, but in the original version of "O that 'twere possible," the lyric out of which *Maud* grew, it is clear that the wraith is a purely sensuous and psychological phenomenon. It is precisely of the same character as the ghost that Tennyson says in *In Memoriam* he will *not* see because it would not be truly spiritual but a mere product of his own brain. So this shadow that flits before him is "not thou, but like to thee." As contrasted with the "happy Spirit" of the beloved in Heaven, this "dull mechanic ghost" is a mere "juggle of the brain," an obsessive, compulsive memory of the beloved, a product of the "blood" rather than the "will." It is clearly a manifestation of disease, and one gets the impression that the cause of this disease is wasting sexual desire.

Once the protagonist frees himself from his disease, then the Spirit of Maud appears in his dream and pronounces a benediction on the coming war. This scene would correspond to section xcv in *In Memoriam*, where the poet is united with the spirit of Hallam, and although in *Maud* it is merely a dream, not a true mystic trance, still the hero had to achieve wholeness for it to happen. When it does happen, the phantom flies off into the North, the devil's quarter.

The question arises, then, what is the nature of the madness of the hero in *Maud*? For it is clear that madness is central. Tennyson says that the original title of the poem was "Maud or the Madness," and there is evidence that even after publication he thought of reverting to that title. It is an odd one for several reasons. It is odd, in the first place, to call the poem after the lady rather than the protagonist and particularly odd (and inconvenient) to leave him nameless. But then it is odd to add a subtitle which stands as if in apposition to Maud but obviously is in opposition to her, and finally it is odd to use an abstract noun and definite article, as if the phrase alluded not to a person but a condition—the condition of England. It is like Camus's *The Plague* or the madness that infuses Pope's *Dunciad*. For it is not merely the protagonist who is mad but Maud's brother, the young lord, the two feuding fathers, the shopkeepers and mine operators, the baker who adulterates his bread, the lying politicians, the Quaker who does not know peace from war, the treacherous and tyrannical czar—all are mad, and there is a sense in which the protagonist, who alone seems to perceive this fact, is the only sane person among them. Certainly, when he enters the asylum, he finds it an image of the mighty world, with the lord, the statesman, and the physician performing in their usual way, only with a certain exaggerated clearness. Tennyson was very proud of his delineation of madness and quoted again and again the letter of the asylum doctor who told him it was "the most faithful representation of madness since Shakespeare." The doctor was an excellent literary critic, for Tennyson's representation of madness is not only the best since Shakespeare—it is right out of Shakespeare. It cannot really have owed very much to his visits to Dr. Allen's establishment, where his reaction, as reported to Spedding, was that he was "delighted with the mad people, whom he reports the most agreeable and the most reasonable persons he has met with." This is in line with his method—employed also by Shakespeare—of having his madman speak home truths but in a slightly crazed and translucent way. To Archer Gurney he wrote,

> I do not mean to say that my madman does not speak truths too: witness this extract from an enlightened German, quoted in one of our papers about the state of all England, and then think if he is all wrong when he calls our peace a war, and worse in some respects than an open civil war— "Every day a murder or two or three—every day a wife beaten to death by her husband—every day a father or mother starving their children, or pinching, knocking, and kicking them into a state of torture and living putrefaction." Then he asks, "Has this always been so? or is it so only of late?"
> "Is not the true war that of evil and good?"

The madness in Maud manifests itself on three levels: first, that "nature is one with rapine," secondly, that man has modeled himself upon this natural world, adding thereto his own refinements of civilized cruelty, and thirdly, that the hero, by brooding upon these evils, has created within himself a world of lust and anger, violence and hate. All this is due to the absence of God, for if In Memoriam is a poem where God is perpetually sought, Maud is a poem where he is perpetually neglected. "The drift of the Maker is dark," says the hero, "an Isis hid by the veil," but the only ones who attempt to ascertain his drift are the three sainted women, who mediate between the hero and his maker. Hence at the very end of the poem he "embrace[s] the purpose of God and the doom assigned," but previously he had employed God's name primarily as an imprecation.

The process by which the hero is gradually restored involves both a growth in self-knowledge and a more accurate knowledge of the external world. As his dark suspicions of Maud are dissipated and he comes to know her better, he discovers that a hazy, phantasmal recollection he has of two men betrothing their children over the wine was true: he and Maud had been destined for one another from the very beginning. Further, in the intervening years, when Maud's family was abroad, the mother had ever mourned the rift between the two houses and on her deathbed had expressed a wish that it might be healed. So there arose in the heart of the child, as a kind of sacred duty, the desire to fulfill this wish of her mother, and the hero was amazed to learn that, while he was raging and cursing, these silent forces for good were at work in the land. He even learned, though with some skepticism, that her brother was "rough but kind," and under this new perception of reality he began to perceive himself differently. He realized that he had a kind of self-tormenting imagination that could easily destroy him if he did not control it—that there were two men within him and the one had better die if the other was to live.

Indeed, all is deeply ambiguous in this divided soul. When he first saw Maud, her cold and clear-cut face appeared in his dreams passionless, pale, deathlike, and yet it so troubled his spirit that he arose and flung himself out into the night, finding solace in the deep, ship-wrecking roar of the tide and the scream of the maddened beach. Because of her connection with her family Maud was associated in his mind with Death, but by virtue of her own person she was the incarnation of Love. This paradox was intensified for him when he heard her singing a battle song "in the happy morning of life and of May." That Maud "in the light of her youth and her grace" should be "singing of Death, and of Honour that cannot die" was so strange that he was fain to distinguish in his mind between her and her voice, being both drawn and repelled by both one and the other. This theme of Love and Death is further emphasized in the lovers' moment of supreme felicity when they seem to sense that this felicity will be short.

> O, why should Love, like men in drinking-songs,
> Spice his fair banquet with the dust of death?

To which Maud replies,

> The dusky strand of Death inwoven here
> With dear Love's tie, makes Love himself more dear.

Death is symbolized throughout the poem by the pallor of the lily, as Love is by the ardor of the rose. But both symbols are ambiguous, for the lily also symbolizes the purity and spirituality of Maud, as the rose symbolizes the blood and passion that unsealed their love. Maud in her wholeness and balance is "Queen lily and rose in one," and the hero, after oscillating wildly between extremes, is finally brought to rest in a similar, if precarious, balance. The culmination of this movement is the beautiful lyric, "I have led her home, my love, my only friend."

In form this lyric is an epithalamion, breathing memories of Spenser's Epithalamion and the Song of Songs, and it seems likely that Tennyson intended us to understand by his use of this form that at this point their love is consummated. The brother has been away for a week, they have just enjoyed "twelve sweet hours that past in bridal white," and whether the bridal rites were actually celebrated or not, certainly the poem breathes the peace and serenity of sexual fulfillment. Vows have been exchanged, the hero has promised "to bury / All this dead body of hate," and they are in effect man and wife. By contrast the rose-garden scene, which Lewis Carroll so easily parodied in *Through the Looking-Glass*, throbs with the frenzy of sexual passion. It is early dawn, after the ball to which the hero has not been invited, and he is frustrated and impatient. These are the lines which Tennyson read, according to his son, his voice dark with passion.

> She is coming, my own, my sweet;
>   Were it ever so airy a tread,
> My heart would hear her and beat,
>   Were it earth in an earthy bed;
> My dust would hear her and beat,
>   Had I lain for a century dead;
> Would start and tremble under her feet,
>   And blossom in purple and red.

The lines are strangely prophetic in that they foreshadow the hero's own insanity when he fancies he is buried under the city street and hears the trample of feet above him, and in that they foreshadow the "blood-red blossom of war" about to burst forth in miniature in the dreadful hollow.

The brother cried, "The fault was mine!" and doubtless it was, but the hero is not willing to exonerate his own "guilty hand." Dueling was widely condemned in Victorian society, and the hero joins in that condemnation of "the Christless code, / That must have a life for a blow." He recognizes that the duel was occasioned by "wine and anger and lust," wine on the part of the brother, anger on the part of both, lust on his own part. He has exchanged vows with Maud which he has essentially broken. If she by her singing had attempted to enlist him as her knight in some great chivalrous cause, he has acted like Lancelot by not listening, not attending, by turning away. And so, instead of her song, what he now hears is a passionate cry that arises out of the darkening land, for it is not simply the cry that Maud will utter when she learns of her brother's death, and the cry that his own mother has uttered when she learned of her husband's death, but the cry that all tender, loving things utter when they suffer from violence and crime. And the ghastly Wraith that glides out of the "joyous wood"—a wood that has been made joyous by their love—is not the true Spirit of Maud (which will go to heaven) but the ghastly creature of "sunk eye" and "dreary brow" that he has created by killing their love. This creature will not leave him. It is the madness that infects him and all of his countrymen, and as he moves from the hilltop to which he had fled immediately after the duel, to Brittany, and then back to England again, it follows him. It will not leave him until he learns that "lawful and lawless war / Are scarcely even akin." One may observe that they are akin by virtue of being violent, and when Tennyson excuses himself by saying that surely the true war is the war between good and evil in the human heart, one may agree but still feel that gradualism has been put aside in this poem in favor of the old apocalyptic stance.

"And most of all," cried the hero of *Maud*, "would I flee from the cruel madness of love." "If I cannot be gay," he continued, "let a passionless peace be my lot . . . like a stoic, or like / A wiser epicurean." The story of this "wiser epicurean" is told in one of Tennyson's most successful dramatic monologues, *Lucretius*, written ten years after *Maud*, from October 1865 to January 1868. It is based on a legend told by Jerome in the Eusebian Chronicle that Lucretius "was rendered insane by a love potion and, after writing, in the intervals of insanity, some books, which Cicero afterwards emended, he killed himself by his own hand." One may fancy, after reading the description of the frenzy of love in the *De rerum natura*, that the potion was brewed in his own veins, and indeed Tennyson's statement that the wicked broth tickled "the brute brain within the man's" indicates that it merely released something that was already there. This is Lucretius's tragedy. His tragedy is the deeply ironic one of a man who has lived all his life by a philosophy which now fails him, who finds himself racked by a passion that is the very opposite of his ideal, who discovers to his horror that there is a wild, irrational element in his own nature, a driving sexual frenzy, which destroys him, with some suggestion that a more adequate, less superficial philosophy might have saved him. Lucretius's ideal has been that of the "Passionless bride, divine Tranquillity." "O ye Gods, . . ." he cries,

> I thought I lived securely as yourselves—
> No lewdness, narrowing envy, monkey-spite,
> No madness of ambition, avarice, none:
> No larger feast than under plane or pine
> With neighbours laid along the grass . . .
> Nothing to mar the sober majesties
> Of settled, sweet, Epicurean life.

Such had been his ideal.

But now it seems some unseen monster lays
His vast and filthy hands upon my will,
Wrenching it backward into his; and spoils
My bliss in being.

The process by which he has discovered this is the Freudian one of dreams. A vast storm in the night, corresponding to the turbulence in his own nature and the civil war within the state, has given him three dreams, of which only the first he recognizes. That was of atoms "ruining along the illimitable inane"—a fearsome sight, but his own conception of the universe. That dream "was mine,...I knew it— / Of and belonging to me...: but the next!" All the blood that Sulla shed came raining down on earth to produce, not the warriors he expected, but "girls, Hetairai, curious in their art, / Hired animalisms"; and then, last dream of all, from out the gloom appeared the breasts of Helen, and, hovering near, a sword pointed to pierce, which "sank down shamed / At all that beauty." Lucretius needs no analyst to explain the significance of these dreams—he is only horrified to discover them his. For though with one half of his mind he repudiates them—"twisted shapes of lust, unspeakable, / Abominable, strangers at my hearth / Not welcome"—with another he knows the mind could not clasp these idols to itself unless it loved them. And so, when the disease invades his waking life and he suddenly sees a naked Oread pursued by a satyr, he cries, "A satyr, a satyr, see...; but him I proved impossible; / Two-natured is no nature"—though his own double nature is all too apparent. Indeed, as the creatures are about to fling themselves upon him, he does not know what he wants—"do I wish— / What?—that the bush were leafless? or to whelm / All of them in one massacre?" For this mixture of sex and sadism, of love and violence, is thoroughly his own.

His effort had been to free men from fear by proving that the universe operates according to fixed laws, by showing that there is no life after death of which one need be afraid, that the gods, though they do exist, do not intervene in human affairs, and that the only thing to be concerned about is human passion, which presumably can be controlled by reason and moderation. But now he has been proved tragically wrong. He has vastly underestimated the wild, irrational element in human life, and it is clear that if he had allowed it a freer play and not tried to repress it, and if, on the other hand, he had acknowledged the immateriality of the soul and the existence of an afterlife, along with the concern of the gods for man, he might have established the spiritual values by which to control passion. As it is, when his wife, who has administered the potion, suggests that she has failed in duty to him, he can only say, "Thy duty? What is duty? Fare thee well!"

Tennyson's friend, W. Y. Sellar, noted in his *Roman Poets of the Republic* (1863) that Lucretius was a distinctly modern figure. His atomism anticipated the scientific thought of the nineteenth century, and his epicureanism was the ancient equivalent of Utilitarianism. He represented the modern rationalistic, positivistic approach to life, and if there is no single nineteenth-century figure whom he can be said to represent, it is because Tennyson has caught him in a moment of crisis. Too much Mill, Tennyson seems to be saying, has given us Swinburne. Too much reason has produced licentiousness. Too much of the spirit of 1832 has produced the spirit of 1867, for it was just at the time of the political anarchy preceding the passage of the Second Reform Bill that Tennyson was writing. Lucretius was perfectly aware that the unruly passions welling up within himself had a political dimension. They are like

> ... crowds that in an hour
> Of civic tumult jam the doors, and bear
> The keepers down, and throng, their rags and they
> The basest, far into that council-hall
> Where sit the best and stateliest of the land.

Precisely such throngs Arnold had described in *Culture and Anarchy*, and his solution was to educate the lower classes before they became our masters. Carlyle's solution in *Shooting Niagara, and After?* was to drill the raw recruits of the world in platoons. Tennyson undoubtedly thought that a more spiritual philosophy that would give man a firmer conception of duty would help. Initially, he omitted the phrase "What is duty?" from the last line of the poem "because Lucretius nowhere I think makes any mention of Duty in that sense," but he later decided that that was the very point and put it back in.

ROBERT BERNARD MARTIN

Silent Voices
1890–1892

In February 1890 Tennyson fell ill
again, this time with a combination of bronchitis and influenza. In the
confusion caused by fever he constantly returned to the past; in the initial
stages he 'talked about his firstborn, & broke down describing the fists
clenched as if in a struggle for life'. During his recovery he told stories of his
grandparents, of his own childhood and schooldays, and of his first visit to
the cataracts of the valley of Cauteretz. The national newspapers carried
grossly exaggerated accounts that were more alarming than the illness itself,
and it was some time before Hallam discovered that a beggar from Hasle-
mere, who came to the door for scraps of food each day, was being paid by
newsmen to bring them kitchen gossip. Tennyson's recovery was slower
than it would have been a few years earlier, but it was still amazingly fast. By
the end of April he was entertaining large tea-parties nearly every day in the
ballroom at Farringford, from which a few privileged guests were allowed
into the drawing-room to talk to Emily on her sofa. He was able to get up
twenty times in succession from a low chair without using his hands, and he
took to waltzing again. When Mrs Brookfield came to Farringford, he
suddenly turned to her and said, 'Jane, let us dance.' On her refusal to join
him, protesting that they were both too old for such nonsense, he 'pro-
ceeded with deliberation and stateliness, to pirouette by himself all down
the room'. He regularly walked a mile or two, accompanied by his nurse and
the dogs, usually up the steep hill to the Beacon on the cliffs, and he could

From *Tennyson: The Unquiet Heart*. Copyright © 1980 by Robert Bernard Martin. Oxford
University Press, 1980.

still climb a difficult gate or run down the hill on the way home.

Thomas Edison's representatives came to Farringford in May to record Tennyson's readings of his own poetry, and for several days he shouted into a tube: 'Blow, bugle, blow', 'The Charge of the Light Brigade', 'Come into the garden, Maud', 'Ask me no more', and other extracts and short poems. For many years the original wax cylinders leaned against a radiator in Farringford, their continued existence proving, as his grandson said, something of the efficiency of the heating in the house. In recent years they have been transferred to discs. The fidelity of the recording was primitive, so that only a ghost of his powerful voice emerges from the mechanical scratching, but it is still possible to fall under the hypnotic quality of his reading. Either because of the quality of the recording and the conditions under which the cylinders were kept or because of his advanced age, his voice is curiously high, almost contralto in quality (he said it sounded like the squeak of a dying mouse), but it does not obscure the magnificent control of breathing and the length of his phrasing. It is old-fashioned recitation, with heavy stress on the rhythm in poetry that already seems to have sufficient of that, and with what sounds like deliberate neglect of the prose meaning. When Edmund Gosse heard him read 'Boädicea', he said that 'He hangs sleepily over the syllables, in a rough monotonous murmur, sacrificing everything to quantity. Had I not known the poem well beforehand it would have been entirely unintelligible.' It is difficult, however, to understand Gosse's judgement that 'His reading is worse than anyone's I ever heard', for it conveys a startlingly vivid impression of how Tennyson wanted his works read aloud. Today the record gives the listener a *frisson* to be in such intimate contact with the greatest Victorian poet, a man born in 1809.

Before leaving Farringford for the summer Tennyson sat for two portraits by Watts, rather under protest, although he seemed perfectly happy once the sittings had begun.... During the winter he had been amusing himself by painting in water-colours; 'Add a daub every day', Watts told him, and he 'would then soon have a picture'.

In late June he went to London to be examined by Sir Andrew Clark, who said his general condition was better than it had been for years, although it was obvious to his friends that his ill-used, once magnificent body was running down. He was told that his eyes and ears were in surprisingly good shape for his age, but since he always brushed aside any qualifications in statements about his health, he then claimed that he was going totally blind but that his hearing was perfect. Visitors had noticed, however, that Emily carefully arranged the seating so that he could be near enough to his guests to hear what they said.

While Tennyson and Hallam were in London they stayed with

Knowles. Shortly before their arrival Knowles had met Gladstone in the street, and Gladstone had said he would like to see Tennyson when next he was in town. Since his review of 'Locksley Hall Sixty Years After' he and Tennyson had exchanged several letters that were sufficiently affectionate in tone, but the memory of his rap over the knuckles still rankled with Tennyson. He also violently disapproved of Gladstone's campaign for the Home Rule Bill, and when he heard that his old acquaintance was coming for dinner he was so annoyed that he refused to sit down at the table with him, saying that he would instead have his meal in his room, quite unrepentant that one of the busiest men in the kingdom was making time to come to see him.

When the Gladstones and the other guests arrived, Knowles invented an imaginary illness to explain Tennyson's absence during the meal. After the ladies had left the dining-room. Knowles turned to Gladstone and said, 'Lord Tennyson may be much better now; don't you think you could go up and persuade him to come down?' He accompanied Gladstone to the door of Tennyson's room, then left him. Ten minutes later the two old men came shuffling down the stairs, arm in arm. They sat together on a sofa, so that they could hear each other well, discussing Homer, Browning, and finally even Home Rule. They were both aware of their advanced age and of the fact that they were bound together by memories that were more important than the differences that separated them. As Gladstone wrote after Tennyson's death, 'He and I had both lived with great loneliness after beginning in the midst of large bands of friends.' Gladstone was at his most charming and Tennyson seemed gradually to forget his disapproval. Their unspoken reconciliation was appropriate, for it was apparently the last time they ever saw one another. When the guests were gone, Tennyson turned to Knowles and his wife as he took his candle to go to bed and said with embarrassment, 'I'm sorry I said all those hard things of that old man.' Even more grudgingly he admitted of Home Rule: 'He has quite converted me. I see it all; it is the best thing if one looks at it from all sides.'

At breakfast the next morning Tennyson was gloomy as he talked over the previous evening: 'It is all right; he spellbound me for the time and I could not help agreeing with him, it was the extraordinary way in which he put it all; his logic is immense, but I have gone back to my own views. It is all wrong, this Home Rule, and I am going to write and tell him so.' He thought it over, then with a clatter he threw down his knife and fork: 'I never said anything half bad enough of that damned old rascal.'

Some time after this when he was reading the 'Ode on the Death of the Duke of Wellington' to the Duke of Argyll at Farringford, he suddenly stopped at the words:

> Who never sold the truth to serve the hour,
> Nor paltered with Eternal God for power...

'As I am afraid Gladstone is doing now,' he added.

During his London visit in 1890 Tennyson also had his last glimpse of the Queen, who bowed to him when driving in Hyde Park; although she invited him to come to see her again, he was never able to do so.

The Royal Family had by no means forgotten the old man. Princess Mary, Duchess of Teck, asked to see him, but he claimed to be too afraid of newspaper reporters to be seen going to her; instead, she good-naturedly came to Knowles's house, where he read parts of *Maud* to her. When he was back in Aldworth, the Duchess of Albany came to luncheon with him on his birthday, and he read to her, as he had done two years earlier for Princess Beatrice and Prince Henry of Battenberg when they called. Other visitors noticed his alternation between gaiety and the lethargy of old age. Occasionally his old sense of fun would flash out as it did when a guest said of the tangles of wild roses, 'What beautiful hips!' to which Tennyson demurely replied, 'I'm so glad you admire 'em, ma'am.'

His good health and spirits continued into 1891. In February, when Princess Louise visited him at Farringford, he walked with her to the top of the down and raced her to the Beacon. He still liked having the house full of guests, although their presence soon tired him. In the summer he went by yacht to Devon, where he and Hallam went up the river Exe by rail. As he had always done on such trips, he asked to be left alone to smoke at the places where the scenery made poetry spring to his mind.

In June he wrote for Emily, in honour of their forty-first wedding anniversary, the gentle little poem called 'June Heather and Bracken' that stood as the dedicatory poem for his last volume of poetry:

> There on the top of the down,
> The wild heather round me and over me June's high blue,
> When I looked at the bracken so bright and the heather so brown,
> I thought to myself I would offer this book to you,
> This, and my love together,
> To you that are seventy-seven,
> With a faith as clear as the heights of the June-blue heaven,
> And a fancy as summer-new
> As the green of the bracken amid the gloom of the heather.

It is a poem that more adequately states the quality of his love for her than any other that he ever wrote.

When the composer Hubert Parry stayed at Farringford in January

1892 he found Tennyson much exercised about eternal punishment, which, as other visitors had noticed, seemed to frighten him. Tennyson told Parry that he had been discussing the subject with a bishop (probably Boyd Carpenter of Ripon) and had asserted that he simply did not believe in hell, 'whereon the Bishop replied in a whisper that he didn't either'. But his feelings of the imminence of death had not made Tennyson conventional, for he told racy anecdotes, said he preferred 'bloody' to 'awfully', drank from two bottles of brandy placed before him at dinner, read 'The Lotos-Eaters' aloud while holding a candle by his nose, repeated his wonder at the lack of music in Browning's poetry, and kept Parry up late listening to his conversation. On such occasions the old man of eighty-two could rouse himself to behave as if he were fifty.

In spite of his age he was still interested in the work of younger poets and wrote to congratulate Kipling on his 'English Flag'. Kipling replied in suitably military language: 'When the commander in chief notices a private of the line the man does not say "thank you", but he never forgets the honour and it makes him fight better.'

A natural reluctance to leave familiar surroundings was overtaking Tennyson, and he seemed more than ever disinclined to quit Farringford that spring, as if knowing that he would not return. It was unusually sunny, and he sat in the summer-house talking to friends, pointing out the fruit blossoms, or walking with them to the kitchen garden to see the fig tree, which he still contentedly described as 'like a breaking wave'. There had always been something otherworldly about the seclusion of Farringford, and now it had become almost ghostly, with the remote stillness of its gardens, the outmoded furniture and faded wallpaper of its rooms, and the dim candle lamps in the passages that made Parry think it 'the most old-fashioned house I ever saw'.

In part the strange tranquillity of the house was due to the increased gentleness of its owner, who was remarked by his guests to have lost much of the awkwardness and truculence that had so often marked his behaviour in the past. He was simpler, more like a boy, tender in his consideration of others. There were, however, still outbursts of the old Tennyson, as is indicated by a letter written on the eve of the general election to an unknown correspondent. It reads in its entirety:

Sir,
    I love Mr Gladstone but hate his present Irish policy.
        I am yours faithfully,
        Tennyson.

In June Tennyson and Hallam went by borrowed yacht to the Channel Islands, where Tennyson climbed like a young man on the rocks of

Sark. In Jersey he visited his brother Frederick for the last time, renewing all the old ties of love in the knowledge that they would never see one another again, and trying unsuccessfully to get Frederick to come back on the yacht with them to Farringford.

On his last day at Farringford Tennyson took solemn farewell of it by having the Rector of Freshwater, Dr Merriman, come to administer Holy Communion to the family in his study. Tennyson, who had never been a regular church-goer, was determined that there would be no High-Church practices in his house, and before taking the sacrament he stoutly quoted Cranmer's Protestant assertion in *Queen Mary*:

> It is but a communion, not a mass,
> No sacrifice, but a life-giving feast.

On the first day of June the annual removal to Aldworth was made, and Tennyson went from there for his final visit to London, where he was characteristically occupied with two of his strongest interests: science and money. Sir William Flower, director of the Natural History Museum, escorted him around the new building, where he was most interested by the ichthyosaurus and the display of birds' nests. At Macmillan's he spent some time with G. L. Craik, arranging for a new volume of poetry and discussing arrangements for payment; as it turned out, the volume was not published until some three weeks after Tennyson's death. Craik was able to tell him that he had earned more than £10,000 that year, which was one of the most successful financially of his entire career. (After a lifetime of worry about money, he left an estate of more than £57,000 at his death.) In London Tennyson also heard that after its success on the New York stage, *The Foresters* had been published, and that Irving was once more making plans to produce *Becket*. Other indications of his popularity, if he had needed them, were the honorary degrees offered to him by Cambridge, for the fourth time, and by Trinity College, Dublin. He declined both.

At Aldworth he was happy to receive visitors, but he could seldom take his usual long walks with them. Instead, he would sit in the shelter of the hedges on the lawn or in his large study overlooking it, his head protected from draughts by a velvet skull-cap like that worn by one of Rembrandt's models. When he was talking to friends, he would sometimes seem to absent himself from the conversation, and without the stimulation of direct response to others, his watery old eyes would recede beneath the heavy bony brow, and his face, framed by straggly hair and unkempt beard, would settle into the elongated wrinkles of old age.

At the end of July, just before his eighty-third birthday, Tennyson came down with 'a slight cold which has affected the right side of his face & throat', as Hallam informed Sir Andrew Clark. He had 'a good deal of neuralgic pain', which was ascribed to a 'horrible & perpetual North Easter', and he could eat but little. The neuralgia soon resolved itself into Tennyson's old enemy, gout, and though he had periods of relative freedom from pain, he was never well again. Tennyson realized that the end could not be far off, but he was chiefly concerned to keep the news of his condition from being made public, knowing that the last days of famous men are often made more terrible by the curiosity engendered in others, and that there may be a scarcely concealed anticipation of their death. With the onset of his final illness began the well-meant persecution by his friends, of whom even the closest seem to have been divided in motive between genuine sympathy and the wish to be among the last to have seen him alive. For a fortnight they streamed to Aldworth, then Hallam, who was making a brief trip to Somersby to see the old Rectory before it was sold, put a strict ban on visitors during his absence. When he returned, the visitors began again, and they could not be turned away for fear of alarming Tennyson unduly about his own condition. During the late summer Dakyns was there, bringing with him John Addington Symonds, accompanied by his Venetian gondolier, who hid in the bushes outside the house. Bram Stoker came to discuss Irving's plans for *Becket*; Craik brought proofs of the new volume with him; Jowett came to suggest loyally but unrealistically that Tennyson should continue writing daily. Tennyson's weakness is shown by his unwillingness to continue his years-old debate with Jowett; he begged him 'not to consult with him or argue with him, as was his wont, on points of philosophy and religious doubt'. The fragility of his religious position flickers through 'The Silent Voices', presumably composed in the last two or three months of his life:

> When the dumb Hour, clothed in black,
> Brings the Dreams about my bed,
> Call me not so often back,
> Silent Voices of the dead,
> Toward the lowland ways behind me,
> And the sunlight that is gone!
> Call me rather, silent voices,
> Forward to the starry track
> Glimmering up the heights beyond me
> On, and always on!

As his remark to Jowett suggests, there were moments of utter desolation when eternity seemed as uncertain as it ever had; once he told Wilfrid Ward that when he tried to pray in his illness, he felt as if God did not hear him. When Allingham's widow came to see him and said rather tentatively that she trusted he would soon be in better health, he said with a flash of his old irritability, 'Aren't we both being rather hypocritical?'

On 29 September Tennyson took his last drive in the carriage. After eating, he was so nauseated that Hallam summoned the doctor from Petworth, then sent for both Sir Andrew Clark and Dr Dabbs of Freshwater, who had tended the family for years. Tennyson lay dying for a week in a ritualized hush that seems more like an elaborate death-bed scene from a Victorian novel than the end of an actual man's life. According to the doctors he was suffering from a combination of influenza and gout. No visitors were allowed, Hallam's children were sent away, and Tennyson had the constant attendance of the three physicians, several nurses, and the faithful Hallam, who scarcely slept for a week. Emily Tennyson was too feeble to help with her husband, but she was brought into his bedroom and put on a couch at his feet. Apparently Audrey was not thought to have much ability as a nurse, but she was detailed to keep a record in a notebook of every symptom, every conversation, in preparation, it seems, for Hallam's account of the death-bed in his biography of his father.

Part of Hallam Tennyson's deep love of his father was his total adoration of everything that Tennyson represented for his countrymen, so it is perhaps churlish to feel that he occasionally lost sight of a worn-out old man dying in a draughty bedroom on a Sussex hillside and saw instead the apotheosis of Victorian poetry. More of the sense of the end of Alfred Tennyson comes from Audrey's patient, factual record of his physical functions than from the elaborate hagiography of her husband, which was only the obverse of the morbid interest that Tennyson feared from the press.

At 8 a.m. on 3 October Tennyson asked for the volume of the Steevens edition of Shakespeare that contained *Cymbeline*, but when he had it in his hands he could read only a word or two before putting it down on the bed and saying to Dr Dabbs that now he was convinced of his approaching death. That night at midnight he woke, found Hallam at his bedside, and asked with concern why he was not asleep. 'I make a slave of you,' he said in remorse for the life that his son had given to him.

The following morning he called out fretfully, 'Where's my Shakespeare, I must have my Shakespeare', but his reaction to the book the day before had frightened the family, and he was told he must not read. He was at first pleased to hear that the Queen had sent a telegram of concern, then he muttered, 'O, that Press will get hold of me now!' Early in the evening he awoke from a vivid dream and asked, 'Have I not been walking with Gladstone in the garden this morning and shewing him my trees?' That night he was once more disturbed until he had the Shakespeare beside him on the bed.

The next day, 5 October, he found that the volume had again been removed, and when it was returned at his insistence he fumbled with it, then put it face down with his hand laid heavily on it, cracking the spine, so that today it still falls open to the speech of Posthumus to Imogen: 'Hang there like fruit, my soul,/Till the tree die', a passage that had always moved him to tears. He tried again that afternoon to read but could not, although he handled the book and said something that sounded like '. . . opened it'. As Hallam told the Duke of Argyll, Tennyson then spoke his last words, calling out, 'Hallam, Hallam', and whispering indistinctly to Emily, 'God bless you, my joy.' Audrey's more unimpassioned version was that 'it was almost impossible to make out more than a word here and there of what he said owing greatly I think to his having no teeth in'. When he had spoken to the family, he lapsed into unconsciousness from which he never recovered.

The family sat waiting for the end, with only the glow of the fire in the unlit room, like a group in a Victorian narrative painting. The account by Dr Dabbs shows the visual terms in which they comprehended Tennyson's death: 'On the bed a figure of breathing marble, flooded and bathed in the light of the full moon streaming through the oriel window; his hand clasping the Shakespeare which he had asked for but recently, and which he kept by him to the end; the moonlight, the majestic figure as he lay there, "drawing thicker breath," irresistibly brought to our minds his own "Passing of Arthur".' At 1.35 a.m., 6 October, after a few spasms that Dr Dabbs had calmed with chloroform, he died peacefully.

The coffin in which he lay remained open until 10 October. On his head was a wreath of laurel from Virgil's tomb, gathered specifically for the purpose eleven years before by Alfred Austin, who hoped to succeed him as Poet Laureate. On his chest lay a bunch of roses from Emily, and in one hand was a copy of *Cymbeline*: it was not, however, that which had been in his hands during his illness but a volume taken from Audrey's edition of Shakespeare.

Emily Tennyson sent a wire to the Dean of Westminster after her husband's death: 'Decide as you think best. If it is thought better, let him have the flag of England on his coffin, and rest in the churchyard of the dear place where his happiest days have been passed. Only, let the flag represent the feeling of the beloved Queen, and the nation, and the empire he loved so dearly.' But there was no real question in her mind of where he should be buried, and Dean Bradley of course chose the Abbey. Emily Tennyson was too weak to attend the service on 12 October.

The Abbey was filled for the funeral, the nave was lined by men of the Balaclava Light Brigade, the London Rifle Volunteers, and boys of the Gordon Boys' Home, and there were huge crowds standing outside, but the service turned out to be disappointingly impersonal and conventional. The procession was long, swollen by what Edmund Gosse called a stream of nonentities. Among the twelve pallbearers were one duke, two marquises, two earls, a baron, and the American minister, but there was not a poet among them, not a Lincolnshire man, not an Apostle, and of the twelve Jowett was probably the only one who had ever called Tennyson by his Christian name. There was no lyricism, no beauty, no passion, no spontaneity: it was hardly to be distinguished from the funeral of any eminent public servant or military hero. Nearly every poet in the country who could lay claim to a modest reputation was there, and all of those who were hoping to succeed to the Laureate's bays, but Swinburne, who was acknowledged as the greatest poet after Tennyson, refused to attend. The Queen sent two wreaths, but there was no member of the Royal Family present. As Gladstone explained, he had 'been kindly invited to be a pall-bearer at the funeral: but unhappily his occupations of the moment are so heavy, that he could not spare the two days it would have required'. Nor, apparently, could he spare the two hours it would have required to attend the funeral.

Henry James, who had once worried that the Laureate was not sufficiently Tennysonian, wrote that it was 'a lovely day, the Abbey looked beautiful, everyone was there, but something—I don't know what—of real impressiveness—was wanting'. There seemed to be 'too many masters of Balliol, too many Deans and Alfred Austins'.

But it was Burne-Jones who best expressed both his own disappointment and a sense of how Tennyson should have been remembered: 'O but yesterday was so flat and flattening. I'll never forgive the Queen for not coming up to it, and I wish Gladstone had. And there should have been street music, some soldiers and some trumpets, and bells muffled all over London, and rumbling drums. I did hate it so heartily, but as he sleeps by Chaucer I daresay they woke and had nice talks in the night, and I have spent much of the early dark morning making up talks for them; I suppose he'll be hurrying off to Virgil soon. I wish I hadn't gone.'

Within a fortnight Hallam Tennyson was hard at work on his biography, soliciting the return of letters that Tennyson had written, asking for contributions from all of his respectable friends. Palgrave and Henry Sidgwick helped him to read and sort out some 40,000 letters, then to destroy three-quarters of them, including practically all of Tennyson's letters to Emily before their marriage and those he had received from Arthur Hallam, as well as anything else that Hallam and Emily Tennyson had decided was unworthy of the tame, saintly character whose image they wanted to perpetuate. The process of making Tennyson's memory respectable was well in hand, and it was so successful that it took another half-century before the world began to suspect that behind the bland features of the Watts portraits and Hallam Tennyson's biography was the complicated mind and awkward personality of one of England's greatest poets.

In spite of the bad health from which she had suffered for sixty years, Emily Tennyson survived her husband by four years, and he continued to occupy her thoughts until the end. When Hallam assumed his inherited title, she asked not to be addressed as the Dowager Lady Tennyson but as Emily Lady Tennyson: 'A small matter but there seems to be in it a feeling that one is still his wife as one feels that one is.' Suitably, she died shortly after the completion of *Alfred Lord Tennyson: A Memoir*, on which she had given her son so much help. The great task of her life was complete.

Chronology

1809	Born August 6 at Somersby, Lincolnshire, fourth son of the Rev. George Clayton Tennyson and Elizabeth Fytche Tennyson.
1815	Enters Louth Grammar School.
1820	Leaves school and subsequently is taught at home.
1827	Publication in April of *Poems by Two Brothers*, actually containing poems by Alfred and his brothers Charles and Frederick. Enters Trinity College, Cambridge, in November.
1829	Friendship with Arthur Henry Hallam commences. Is elected to Cambridge "Apostles" society. Wins University Medal for poem *Timbuctoo*.
1830	Publication of *Poems, Chiefly Lyrical*. Summer tour of Pyrenees with Hallam.
1831	Death of father, compelling Tennyson to leave Cambridge for home without his degree.
1832	Publication of *Poems*.
1833	Death of Hallam in Vienna, September 18.
1837	Moves with family to High Beech, Epping.
1838	Announces engagement to Emily Sellwood.
1840	Engagement is broken.
1842	Publication of *Poems*, in two volumes.
1847	Publication of *The Princess*.
1850	Publication (anonymous) of *In Memoriam* in May. Marries Emily Sellwood in June. Appointed as Poet Laureate in November.
1852	*Wellington Ode*.
1855	*Maud and Other Poems*.
1859	Four *Idylls of the King*.
1864	*Enoch Arden*.
1865	*Selected Poems* published.
1869	*The Holy Grail and Other Poems*.
1880	*Ballads and Other Poems*.
1883	Accepts baronetcy.

1885   *Tiresias and Other Poems.*

1886   Death of son, Lionel.

1889   *Demater and Other Poems.*

1892   Death on October 6. The *Death of Oenone* published posthumously.

Contributors

HAROLD BLOOM, Sterling Professor of the Humanities at Yale University, is the author of *The Anxiety of Influence, Poetry and Repression* and many other volumes of literary criticism. His forthcoming study, *Freud: Transference and Authority*, attempts a full-scale reading of all of Freud's major writings. He is the general editor of *The Chelsea House Library of Literary Criticism*.

T. S. ELIOT received the Nobel Prize for Literature in 1948. His major achievements are gathered together in his *Collected Poems, 1909-1962* and his *Selected Essays, 1917-1932*.

G. M. YOUNG was a civil servant and independent scholar, and one of the foremost British historians of this century. His books include *Early Victorian England: The Portrait of an Age, Victorian Essays* (edited by W. D. Handcock) and *Last Essays*.

CLEANTH BROOKS is Gray Professor of Rhetoric Emeritus at Yale. He is widely known as the dean of the New Criticism. His books include *The Well Wrought Urn* and two studies of Faulkner.

MARSHALL McLUHAN achieved fame for his pioneering studies, *The Gutenberg Galaxy* and *Understanding Media*. Originally a Professor of English at the University of Toronto, he became perhaps the first academic specialist in media studies.

ROBERT LANGBAUM is James Branch Cabell Professor of English at the University of Virginia. His books include *The Poetry of Experience, The Mysteries of Identity* and *The Modern Spirit*.

CHRISTOPHER RICKS is Professor of English at Cambridge University. His books include studies of Milton and of Keats. He is the editor of the now standard edition of *The Poems of Tennyson* (London: Longman, 1969).

JOHN ROSENBERG is Professor of English at Columbia University. His books include *The Fall of Camelot, The Darkening Glass* and *The Genius of John Ruskin: Selections*.

JOHN HOLLANDER is Professor of English at Yale University. His poetry includes *Spectral Emanations: New and Selected Poems*. His critical work includes *Vision and Resonance* and *The Figure of Echo*.

ARTHUR DWIGHT CULLER is Emily Sanford Professor of English at Yale. His books include *The Imperial Intellect* (a study of John Henry Cardinal Newman), *Imaginative Reason* (on Arnold's poetry) and *The Poetry of Tennyson*.

ROBERT BERNARD MARTIN is Professor Emeritus of English at Princeton University. His books include studies of Charlotte Brontë and of Charles Kingsley, as well as *Tennyson: The Unquiet Heart*.

Bibliography

Brashear, William R. *The Living Will: A Study of Tennyson and Nineteenth Century Subjectivism.* The Hague: Mouton, 1969.

Buckley, Jerome Hamilton. *Tennyson: The Growth of a Poet.* Boston: Houghton Mifflin, 1965.

Colley, Ann C. *Tennyson and Madness.* Athens: University of Georgia Press, 1983.

Eggers, Philip J. *King Arthur's Laureate: A Study of Tennyson's "Idylls."* New York: New York University Press, 1971.

Gerhard, Joseph. *Tennysonian Love: The Strange Diagonal.* Minneapolis: University of Minnesota Press, 1969.

Hellstrom, Ward. *On the Poems of Tennyson.* Gainesville: University of Florida Press, 1972.

Jump, John D., ed. *Tennyson: The Critical Heritage.* New York: Barnes and Noble, 1967.

Killham, John. *Tennyson and the Princess: Reflections of an Age.* London: University of London, Athlone Press, 1958.

————. *Critical Essays on the Poetry of Tennyson.* New York: Barnes and Noble, 1960.

Kincaid, James R. *Tennyson's Major Poems: The Comic and Ironic Patterns.* New Haven: Yale University Press, 1975.

Kozicki, Henry. *Tennyson and Clio: History in the Major Poems.* Baltimore: Johns Hopkins University Press, 1979.

Martin, Robert Bernard. *Tennyson: The Unquiet Heart.* New York: Oxford University Press, 1980.

Mattes, Eleanor Bustin. *In Memoriam.* New York: Exposition Press, 1951.

Nicolson, Harold George, II. *Tennyson: Aspects of His Life.* Boston: Houghton Mifflin, 1925.

Paden, William Doremus. *Tennyson in Egypt: A Study of the Imagery in His Earlier Work.* Lawrence: University of Kansas Press, 1942.

Palmer, David John, ed. *Writers and Their Background: Tennyson.* Athens: Ohio University Press, 1973.

Pattison, Robert. *Tennyson and Tradition.* Cambridge: Harvard University Press, 1979.

Priestly, F. E. L. *Language and Structure in Tennyson's Poetry.* London: Deutsch, 1973.

Reed, John R. *Perception and Design in Tennyson's "Idylls of the King."* Athens: Ohio University Press, 1969.

Richardson, Joanna. *Tennyson: The Pre-Eminent Victorian.* London: Jonathan Cape, 1962.

Ricks, Christopher. *Masters of World Literature: Tennyson.* New York: Macmillan, 1972.

Rosenberg, John D. *The Fall of Camelot: A Study of Tennyson's "Idylls of the King."* Cambridge, Mass.: Belknap Press, 1973.

Ross, Robert H., ed. *In Memoriam: An Authoritative Text, Background and Criticism.* New York: Norton, 1973.

Ryals, Clyde de L. *Theme and Symbols in Tennyson's Poems to 1850.* Philadelphia: University of Pennsylvania Press, 1964.

Shatto, Susan, and Shaw, Marion, eds. *In Memoriam: Text and Criticism.* New York: Oxford University Press, 1982.

Shaw, William David. *Tennyson's Style.* Ithaca: Cornell University Press, 1976.

Smith, Elton Edward. *The Two Voices: A Tennyson Study.* Lincoln: University of Nebraska Press, 1964.

Steane, John Barry. *Tennyson.* New York: Arco, 1969.

Tennyson, Alfred Lord. *Idylls of the King.* Edited by J. M. Gray. New Haven: Yale University Press, 1983.

———. *In Memoriam: An Authoritative Text, Background and Criticism.* Edited by Robert H. Ross. New York: Norton, 1973.

———. *In Memoriam: Text and Criticism.* Edited by Susan Shatto and Marion Shaw. New York: Oxford University Press, 1982.

———. *Poems.* Edited by Mildred M. Bozman. New York: Dutton, 1965.

———. *Selected Poems from the Poetry of Alfred, Lord Tennyson.* Edited by W. H. Auden. Garden City, N.Y.: Doubleday, Doran and Co., 1944.

———. *Selected Poetry.* Edited by Douglas Bush. New York: Modern Library, 1951.

———. *Tennyson: Poems Selected by Kingsley Amis.* Harmondsworth: Penguin, 1973.

———. *Works, Annotated by Alfred, Lord Tennyson.* Edited by Hallam, Lord Tennyson. London: Macmillan, 1907–08.

Acknowledgments

"Introduction" by Harold Bloom from *The Ringers in the Tower* by Harold Bloom, copyright © 1971 by The University of Chicago Press. Reprinted by permission.

"*In Memoriam*" by T. S. Eliot from *Essays Ancient and Modern* by T. S. Eliot, copyright © 1950 by Harcourt Brace Jovanovich; renewed 1978 by Esme Valerie Eliot. Reprinted by permission of Harcourt Brace Jovanovich and Faber & Faber Ltd.

"The Age of Tennyson" by G. M. Young from *Proceedings of the British Academy*, vol. 25 (1939), copyright © 1939 by G. M. Young. Reprinted by permission of the British Academy.

"The Motivation of Tennyson's Weeper" by Cleanth Brooks from *The Well Wrought Urn* by Cleanth Brooks, copyright © 1947, 1975 by Harcourt Brace Jovanovich. Reprinted by permission of the publisher.

"Tennyson and Picturesque Poetry" by H. M. McLuhan from *Critical Essays on the Poetry of Tennyson*, edited by John Killham, copyright © 1960 by John Killham. Reprinted by permission of Barnes and Noble Books.

"The Dynamic Unity of *In Memoriam*" by Robert Langbaum from *The Modern Spirit: Essays on the Continuity of Nineteenth and Twentieth Century Literature* by Robert Langbaum, copyright © 1970 by Robert Langbaum. Reprinted by permission.

"The Days That Are No More" by Christopher Ricks from *Tennyson* by Christopher Ricks, copyright © 1972 by The Macmillan Publishing Company. Reprinted by permission of the MacMillan Publishing Company, London and New York.

"*Idylls of the King*: Evolving the Form" by John Rosenberg from *The Fall of Camelot* by John Rosenberg, copyright © 1973 by the President and Fellows of Harvard College. Reprinted by permission of Harvard University Press.

"Tennyson's Melody" by John Hollander from *The Georgia Review* 3, vol. 29 (Fall 1975), copyright © 1975 by the University of Georgia. Reprinted by permission of *The Georgia Review* and John Hollander.

Index

Modern Critical Views